SANDRA GUSTAFSON'S

CHEAP
EATS IN
LONDON

FOURTH EDITION

**A Traveler's Guide to the
Best-Kept Secrets**

CHRONICLE BOOKS
SAN FRANCISCO

Printed in the United States of America

FOURTH EDITION

ISSN: 1074-5041
ISBN: 0-8118-1833-0

Book design: Words & Deeds
Author photograph: Marv Summers

Distributed in Canada by
Raincoast Books
8680 Cambie Street
Vancouver, B.C. V6P 6M9

10 9 8 7 6 5 4 3 2 1

Chronicle Books
85 Second Street
San Francisco, CA 94105

www.chroniclebooks.com

In memory of Virginia Smith . . .
a very special person in my life.

Contents

To the Reader

London—a nation, not a city ...
—Benjamin Disraeli

Cheap Eaters in London can forget all those horror stories about menus featuring only gluey meat pies, bangers and mash, and soggy puddings. London's reputation as a first-rate city with second-rate dining can be laid to rest. Food has become fashionably correct and as the range and quality of eateries continue to grow, British cooking has become gourmet; restaurateurs have become tycoons operating giant, innovative food shrines that feed up to two thousand grazers each day; and the media and dining public avidly follow and promote their favorite chefs. Today, in addition to new interpretations of all the old English staples, you can sample superb Indian, Southeast Asian, and Italian cuisine. In vogue, too, are minimalist settings and humble foods that challenge creative chefs to make something out of very little. Liver and tripe are enjoying a revival; mackerel and anchovies have replaced partridge, lobster, and prawns. Vegetarian cuisine has grown in popularity, and vegetarians can look forward to hearty meals as opposed to a diet of cabbage and Marmite on toast. Today, dining in London can vary as much as your taste allows, and it's possible to travel gastronomically around the world without going beyond the Circle Line of the London tube.

Leave it to the British to maintain a stiff upper lip in every crisis. In these financially hard times, Londoners are putting a bright face on their sagging economy by making stinting stylish. For them, no-nonsense quality dining is in, and unchecked extravagance is out! You won't find London's smart diners in high-priced restaurants eating and drinking recklessly. You will find them eating out, however, especially during lunchtime or after the theater, when they take advantage of the amazing set-price meals offered for a fraction of the price of an à la carte meal.

But *Cheap Eats in London* is not concerned solely with finding the cheapest food in London. If all you want to do is eat as cheaply as possible, regardless of quality, stop reading this book right now. *Cheap Eats in London* is for those who want to obtain top dollar for their dining pound without sacrificing taste in the bargain. I list over two hundred of the best eateries in London, providing a comprehensive sampling of cuisines and restaurant types, all the while balancing the considerations of budget and palate alike. When selecting places to include, I limited my choices to eating establishments located within the Circle Line on the London tube. Like many travelers, when I'm in a city for a short while, I don't want to spend my time and energy traveling to a restaurant on the outskirts of the city when I can eat just as well for the same price several bus or tube stops away from my hotel or particular focus of interest.

Cheap Eats in London tells you not only what restaurants to go to, but what to order once you arrive. You will find a wide variety of ethnic cuisines, cheap and cheerful snack bars, historic pubs, cozy tearooms, fish-and-chips joints, sophisticated wine bars, and Big Splurges for those special occasions. The book also answers the important dining questions most London visitors have, such as, What is a "service charge"? Are you expected to tip, too? Is there a children's menu, a nonsmoking section, a special meal deal, a dress code? Which is the best table?

Cheap Eats in London is straight-from-the-hip, no-nonsense information you can use and depend on. Because I have personally been to every address in this book, I am able to write with firsthand knowledge. So that I receive the same service you can expect, I always dine anonymously and pay my own way. I never rely on advance-screening teams, hearsay, printed forms filled out by the restaurant, or local gofors. If I like a place, I consider it. If I'm rudely treated, or the food is poorly prepared and/or served, or if the kitchen is dirty and the rest rooms terrible, then the restaurant is out, no matter how cheap or popular it may be. I wish I could include an entire section of some of the famous restaurants I think are rip-offs and tourist traps, but unfortunately, too many people would sue my publisher and me.

Cheap Eats in London is organized by postal code to help you find the restaurants closest to your hotel or to whatever tourist attraction you are visiting. You will find several indexes in the back of the book listing all the restaurants alphabetically as well as by the type of food served. There are lists of Big Splurges (for those with more flexible budgets), nonsmoking restaurants, and a glossary of English food and restaurant terms. Finally, there is a page for your comments. I cannot overemphasize how valuable your comments are to me. They help me reconsider, investigate, question, and discover new places. If you agree with me, please let me know that, too. I have done my best to be accurate, but eateries change faster than I can write. Therefore, I'm eager to hear any news you have about changes you find, or ideas you may have for future editions.

Dining out is meant to be pleasurable, but it does cost money. Of course, no one takes a trip to London in order to save money, but you don't want to waste it either. Revising this edition of *Cheap Eats in London* reinforced my view that there is plenty of good food in London at affordable prices. I hope using *Cheap Eats in London* guides you toward memorable dining experiences, saves you money, and inspires you to return soon. Have a marvelous trip, eat well . . . and don't forget to write.

Tips on How to Enjoy Cheap Eats in London

1. If a restaurant is empty at a peak mealtime, ask yourself why.

2. Always read the menu posted outside before going in. This avoids you being seated and finding you don't like anything on the menu, or worse yet, that the prices are too high. If the menu is not posted (which by law it should be), ask to see one before deciding to stay. All menus must clearly state the prices, including the VAT (value-added tax is the British equivalent of sales tax); whether a service charge is included and if so, how much; the cover charge; and the minimum if there is one.

3. Watch the fine print. A cover charge is per person; a minimum charge is also per person. A steep cover charge along with a hefty 12½ percent service charge on top of a three-course meal with wine, dessert, and coffee could be hard to swallow.

4. The service charge, whether discretionary or added automatically, is the tip. You are not expected to pay a single extra pence, unless the service has been out of this world. Beware of the double service-charge trick. See "Paying the Bill," page 13.

5. While the set-price two- or three-course meal may have limited choices, it represents the best value for your money on the menu.

6. If you like haute cuisine without haute prices, consider making lunch your main meal of the day. Usually, restaurants offer a set-price menu that often includes dessert, wine, coffee, and the service charge. Many of the more expensive restaurants in London have not only delicious and cheap set-price lunch meals, but different à la carte lunch and dinner menus. The lunch prices on these menus are always significantly less than the exact same meal would be at dinner.

7. Two other great Cheap Eats for lunch are a pub or a picnic. At the pub, go early for the best and freshest selection and try to stick with the daily specials for the best results. For a picnic, shop the local markets and then take your feast to a park bench and watch the world wander by.

8. Another Cheap Eat is to order something from a sandwich shop or a takeaway restaurant. Besides being cheap, ordering your food to go can save you service charges and may land you a 10 percent discount on top of that.

9. If reservations are recommended, take this advice seriously and make them. Remember, it costs nothing to reserve a table, and you will generally get a better table than the walk-in diner. Many restaurants overbook, so it is imperative that you arrive on time or risk losing your reservation. If you find you will not be able to go, please call and cancel so the restaurant can rebook your table.

10. Always order a restaurant's specialty. If you are in a fish-and-chips takeaway, opt for the deep-fried fish and save the hamburger for another time. Carefully consider the daily and house specials because these will be fresh and represent the best efforts of the kitchen.

11. *Someone* has to sit in "Siberia" and be waited on by the new trainee, but it doesn't necessarily have to be you. Whenever you dine out, make sure you get what you are paying for. You should always treat the restaurant staff with the same courtesy you expect to receive from them. When you have a problem, however, it pays to complain quickly, although it seldom pays to be rude. Give the restaurant a chance to correct the situation for you and prevent it from happening to someone else.

12. You have nothing to lose and only good value to gain by asking questions. Don't be shy about this.
    - If you are dining with children, ask if the restaurant has a children's menu or reduced prices for them (some restaurants offer up to half off a regular meal). This won't work for a sixteen-year-old halfback, but for the little ones, it is a Cheap Eating money-saving strategy.
    - When reserving a table, it is perfectly acceptable to ask about the average cost of a three-course meal with wine and service.
    - If you are a vegetarian or have dietary restrictions, ask what the chef can prepare for you. For the best results, do this when you are making your reservation.
    - If your waiter asks, "Would you like vegetables or a salad with your meal?" ask if they are included with the main course. If they cost extra, watch out: A round or two of vegetables and a side salad at £2 to £4 extra per person can add up in a hurry and turn a once-reasonable meal into a budget disaster.
    - Finally, when the bill arrives, tally it up yourself and protest if it doesn't add up according to your calculations. Mistakes unfortunately happen quite frequently.

13. Afternoon tea can be a meal in itself, and it's a lovely experience that I encourage everyone to have at least once in London. If you are going to the theater, or want an early evening meal, afternoon tea is a lifesaver. With a proper tea, you will enjoy dainty finger

sandwiches, scones with clotted cream and jam, and rich tea cakes and tarts.

14. If the waiter spills something on your clothing, the restaurant should offer to pay your cleaning bill.

15. Never tip the bar staff in a pub. You can offer to buy them a drink, but never, never offer money (see "Pub Etiquette and Survival Techniques," page 23).

16. Dress for success. If you are going to a nice restaurant, leave the jogging shoes and running outfits where they belong . . . in the hotel closet. Nothing brands you as a tourist more quickly and results in poor service faster than improper attire.

17. "Please" and "thank you" still go a long way toward getting good treatment and service. In London, this is especially true.

18. Be patient. Relax. You are on vacation, remember? Even though you are in London and speak the same language (more or less), you are in a foreign city with its own unique culture and customs. Let your hosts do it their way—it's all part of the experience of traveling. If you insist on having things the same as they are at home, you may as well not even leave home in the first place.

How to Use Cheap Eats in London

Each listing in *Cheap Eats in London* includes the following information: name and address, telephone number, general area or neighborhood, postal code, tube stop, days and hours of operation, whether reservations are needed, which credit cards are accepted, the average price for an à la carte and a set-price meal, whether service is included or not, how much you should tip if the tip isn't included, and any special details about each establishment. A dollar sign ($) indicates a Big Splurge restaurant. In the listings, the map key number appears in parentheses to the right of each restaurant name; an entry without a number means it is located beyond the parameters of the map. Finally, there is the Readers' Comments page, which gives an address where you can send me your suggestions or share your experiences with *Cheap Eats in London*.

These abbreviations indicate which credit cards are accepted:

American Express	AE
Diners Club	DC
MasterCard or Access	MC
Visa	V

BYOB indicates that you can bring your own liquor to an unlicensed restaurant.

BIG SPLURGES

Restaurants that fall under the Big Splurge category are for those with more flexible budgets or for special occasion dining to celebrate a birthday, anniversary, or just being in London. In the text, Big Splurges are marked with a dollar sign ($). Please refer to the index for a complete listing of all the Big Splurge restaurants in London.

HOLIDAYS

More restaurants in London are staying open on holidays, especially bank holidays (legal holidays) other than Christmas, New Year's Day, and Easter. However, this policy varies. To avoid disappointment, please call ahead to verify if a particular restaurant is open and what its holiday hours are. When December 25 and 26 fall on a weekend, extra holidays are given on the preceding Friday or following Monday. If New Year's Day falls on a weekend, the first Monday in January is a public holiday. Major holidays include the following:

New Year's Day	January 1
Good Friday	Friday before Easter
Easter Sunday	Varies, late March or April

Easter Monday	Monday after Easter
May Day	First week of May
Spring Bank Holiday	Last week of May
Summer Bank Holiday	Last week of August
Christmas Day	December 25
Boxing Day	December 26

HOURS

Mealtimes in London are similar to those in the United States: Breakfast is served between 7 and 9 A.M., lunch is served between noon and 2:30 P.M., and dinner is served anytime from 6 until 11 P.M. If the last time given for a meal is 11 P.M., it means you will not be able to order after that time, but should be able to continue eating without feeling hurried. Between lunch and dinner, most restaurant managers want to let the waitstaff go home one hour after the last order has been taken. Restaurants with continuous food service usually like to stop serving about a half hour before closing.

LICENSED AND UNLICENSED RESTAURANTS

A surprising number of restaurants in London do not have liquor licenses. In many cases you can bring your own bottle (this is noted in the listings with the abbreviation BYOB), but you may be charged a corkage fee by the restaurant for them to pour your wine or beer. The corkage fee is usually nominal, and if you buy your liquor in an off-license shop (such as a retail liquor store), it will cost you less than you would pay to buy the same bottle in a restaurant. In a few cases, alcohol is prohibited altogether. If a restaurant is unlicensed, that should be clearly noted on the menu, along with any corkage fee. If nothing is said about licensing, that indicates that the restaurant is licensed and bringing your own liquor is not acceptable.

MAPS

All of the London postal codes covered in *Cheaps Eats in London* have an accompanying map and restaurant key, and in the text, these map key numbers appear in parentheses to the right of the restaurant's name. If a restaurant does not have a number, it is located beyond the boundaries of the map.

Please note that the maps in *Cheap Eats in London* are designed to help the reader locate the restaurant listings; they are not meant to replace fully detailed street maps. If you plan on being in London for any length of time, even a day, I strongly suggest you buy the *Inner London A-Z* street map, which comes in a handy booklet form or in a super-scale foldout model. This street map is a *must,* showing you everything you could ever want or need to know about the nooks and crannies of London. The maps you pick up at your hotel or at a tourist shop are virtually useless when it comes to finding anything more complicated than Buckingham Palace and Piccadilly Circus.

NONSMOKING RESTAURANTS

Nonsmokers will quickly realize that there is no British surgeon general or multimillion-dollar ad campaign extolling the virtues of a smoke-free environment in eating establishments in London. However, more restaurants today are assigning small areas as smoke-free zones. During busy times in pubs, which are the last refuge of tobacco addicts, the gray haze can get as thick as London fog. In the restaurant write-ups, *Cheap Eats in London* notes those restaurants where smoking is prohibited or that contain a special nonsmoking section. Please see the index for a complete list of nonsmoking restaurants (page 253).

PAYING THE BILL

I am so far beyond my income that we could be said to be living apart.
—*e. e. cummings*

The bill can be confusing, even traumatic, for U.S. visitors to London because there are so many things on it that differ from U.S. billing practices. Armed with the following knowledge, you should be able to avoid the common traps and keep from being overcharged or confused when the bill arrives. It is important to go over the bill carefully before paying it. Unfortunately, mistakes are rampant and rarely favor the diner. If in doubt, always question.

Prices

There are two prices given in the restaurant listings in *Cheap Eats in London*: the *set-price* menu and the *à la carte* menu. If a set-price menu is available, the listing will state what is served for this fixed amount of money. You can expect to pay extra for the cover charge, wine, coffee, and service if they are not specifically included in the set-price. The à la carte menu prices represent the average cost of a three-course meal that includes a starter, a main course, and a dessert. Drinks, the service charge, and the cover charge, if there is one, will be extra. In determining the average prices of the restaurants in this book, I have avoided the cheapest and most expensive items on the menu, as well as the cost of beverages. Therefore, you could spend more or less depending on what you order and how much you drink. All prices quoted are in British pounds and were correct at press time. You should expect a certain margin of error in the prices due to inflation, the passage of time, and the whims of owners and chefs.

Cover Charge

The *cover charge* is not to be confused with the *service charge*. The cover charge is a great moneymaker. It's ostensibly charged to pay for the bread and butter (unless you do not intend to touch it, in which case you should have it removed from your table), any flowers on the table, the tablecloth and napkins, and who knows what else. All menus must state clearly the amount of the cover charge, and it usually appears in microscopic print at the bottom of the menu. If none is mentioned, none is imposed. The cover charge is *per person,* and is listed separately on your bill, but it's added to the total to hike the amount of service you will pay. Thankfully, more and more restaurants are dropping this rip-off, but many Italian places are tenaciously hanging on, and even raising them. Pubs, takeaways, cafés, and less expensive restaurants never impose a cover charge.

Minimum Charge

Minimum charges are given in the text when applicable and are *per person,* not per couple, table, or group. These charges may be enforced during peak periods or in fancier eateries to discourage people from coming in only for a salad, thus occupying time and space that could be devoted to higher-paying customers. If the restaurant does not state a minimum charge, you are expected to order enough to add up to at least a main course. However, in cafés, pubs, tearooms, wine bars, sandwich shops, fish-and-chips shops, and takeaways, it doesn't matter how much you spend.

Service Charge

The service charge is the tip. You are not required or expected to leave one ha'penny more. That being said, trying to find out if the service is included on the bill is one of London's great after-dinner games. *Cheap Eats in London* clearly states what you can expect in every listing.

No service charged or expected This means none has been charged and you are not expected to pay any at all. You will find this in all pubs (but not in a sit-down restaurant in a pub that has a waitstaff), in takeaways where you do not consume your food on the premises, and in casual cafés.

XX percent service charge This means the restaurant will add a service charge, usually 10 to 15 percent, to the total of your bill as the tip.

Service discretionary This means the restaurant will not automatically add it, but hopes you will, or they will add it themselves . . . softening the blow by saying it is discretionary on your part to leave it (although at that point it is only technically up to you, since removing or reducing it might require explanation). If none has been added, you should leave at least 10 percent, or even better, 12½ percent. If the evening has been extraordinary and you are feeling flush, give 15 percent. Anything more is excessive.

If the service or food is poor, the law says you do not have to leave any service charge, even if it is included and added onto your final bill. You must, however, make your complaint to the management and explain why you are deducting the service charge.

Service included This means that the service charge has been included in the price of the meal, and no other tip need be left. The service charge percentage may or may not be noted on the menu or on the bill—watch out for the service charge scam (noted below) if it's not.

Important! Beware of the service charge/credit card scam. This is a gouging of the customer in no uncertain terms. If the restaurant has imposed a service charge and added it to your bill, but left the space on your credit card signature slip for the "tip/gratuity" blank, they are trying to get you to pay twice. Often this happens in restaurants that say "service included" on the menu, but then make no other note of the service charge on your bill, hoping you'll forget and leave another tip. Watch out for this because it happens with increasing regularity. If this happens to you, you should definitely deduct at least a portion (if not all) of the original service charge to discourage such underhanded tactics. To avoid the double charge, draw a line through the space marked "tip/ gratuity."

Remember: Only when *no* service charge has been added to your final bill (and you are not in a place where none is expected), and if the food and service have been satisfactory, are you expected to leave a tip at all.

VAT

The value-added tax is the British equivalent of a sales tax, and is always silently included in the price of any meal, no matter how big or small, simple or fancy. Some restaurants may note the VAT percentage on the menu or bill, but it is not an extra; at press time the VAT was 17 percent.

RESERVATIONS

When making a reservation you are, in fact, making a contract with the restaurant. Your part is that you will arrive at the right time, order a meal, and pay for it. The restaurant's part of the bargain is that it will have a table for you at the agreed time and serve you food that has been prepared with reasonable skill and care. If you are told when booking that the table will be needed by a certain time, then that is also part of the contract. If you do not think you will have long enough to eat your meal, then go someplace else, because when your allotted time is up, you will have to vacate your table.

TAKEAWAY SERVICE

Many restaurants in London prepare food to go, which is called "takeaway service." Takeaway is also a money-saver for the Cheap Eater because there is never a service charge on any food not consumed on the premises. For those of you with children or who need a fast bite on the go, this is a great convenience. If you don't want to queue for your food and are placing an order for more than one sandwich, it often pays to telephone ahead with your order. Takeaway service is also important to keep in mind if you are going on a train trip anywhere in Britain. The food on British Rail varies from downright terrible to simply inedible. Do yourself a favor . . . take your own.

TRANSPORTATION

Each listing in this book gives the closest tube stop (London underground railway). However, *close* is a relative term, because in all honesty, some of the walks are very long. Often you can do better by bus, or by combining the tube and the bus, and arrive almost at a restaurant's doorstep. With a few exceptions, bus routes are not given because they change frequently and do not always run every day or at night. My best advice is to purchase *The Guide to London by Bus and Tube*—and use it! It is available at most London news kiosks and bookstores, and it will save you not only time and energy but money. You will see much more from the top deck of a London bus than you will by wearing yourself out walking miles to get to a restaurant—or taking a long and expensive cab ride—and then having to face the same trip back after eating.

WHERE TO SIT

"Do you mind sitting upstairs, or downstairs in the basement?" Be wary if you're asked this. It invariably means being shunted to a large, unfriendly, and often deserted room that is used for catered groups or for seating unwary tourists. Unfortunately, these are often the nonsmoking sections of restaurants. But when they don't refer to nonsmoking sections, "up or downstairs" can mean windowless rooms that get hot and unbearably smoky after one or two diners light up. If you are stuck in this Siberia, no matter how wonderful the food and service may be, you will lose something in the experience and probably won't enjoy your meal. That is why I have mentioned the most desirable places to sit in restaurants when it makes a difference.

Eating Establishments in London

Nearly everyone wants at least one outstanding meal a day.
—*Duncan Hines,* Adventures in Good
Eating, *1936*

TYPES OF RESTAURANTS

The following section covers the types of restaurants and major cuisines you'll find in *Cheap Eats in London.*

American

Dining American-style in London may lose something in crossing the Atlantic, but for many homesick souls, a taste of home now and then feels mighty good, even if it isn't perfect in every respect. A number of American-themed restaurants have popped up that are a combination of amusement park, diner, souvenir stand, and museum. They lend themselves to family eating and are good places to stuff yourself on pancakes and waffles, burgers, slabs of ribs, Southwestern food, chili, apple pie, banana splits, and cheesecake. Menus are laminated and full of jokes and puns; there are things for the children to do and menus to color; and the decor is usually heavy on nostalgia—with ceiling fans, old advertisements, Western kitsch, and film posters of seasoned glamour-pusses and male heartthrobs from the thirties and forties.

British

Traditional British food can be as good as it is heavy and filling—and can contribute to your girth in record time if you aren't careful. For the best of Britain, start your day with a full English breakfast of bacon and/or sausage, eggs, beans, broiled mushrooms and tomato, fried bread, and tea or coffee. There are those hearty souls who feel that the best cure for any hangover is a large plate of grease-infused food, taken internally by way of a fried breakfast. If you agree, then a full English breakfast offers all the "healthy" eating you'll be able to stand in a twenty-four-hour time period. At lunchtime, pop into a pub for a hefty portion of steak and kidney pie or stop by a salt-beef bar (corned beef) and have a freshly sliced sandwich on rye that will put those made in most New York delis to shame. If you're in a hurry, join the queue at a busy fish-and-chips shop and munch your fish from a paper cone like the locals. In the midafternoon, stop for tea. The British love their tea, usually accompanied by an assortment of finger sandwiches and delectable pastries. If you are still hungry at dinnertime, dig into a succulent roast beef served with

Yorkshire pudding and assorted vegetables and potatoes. Finish the feast with a warm treacle tart surrounded by soft custard. Who said British food wasn't filling . . . and good?

Modern British

The British have only three vegetables, and two of them are cabbage.
—*U.S. ambassador to London in the thirties*

The land of fish-and-chips and roast beef with Yorkshire pudding now boasts more Michelin-starred restaurants than any city outside France. For the first time ever, the London Tourist Board has polished a campaign promoting the city as a dining destination. This growing interest in food can be attributed to the easing of the recession and the emergence of two-income families with disposable money and a lifestyle that lends itself to eating out on a regular basis. These Londoners have also adopted a somewhat healthier and lighter approach to eating, but it is nowhere close to the almost obsessive militancy witnessed in the States over fat grams and sodium counts. This does not mean that bubble and squeak has given way to nouvelle anything. On the contrary, Britain has rediscovered its culinary past, favoring new twists on the hearty pies, stews, and puddings we all love. Even offal dishes have won new favor, and you will see liver (of calves, lamb, beef, pork, and ox), kidneys, and brains being ordered with enthusiasm.

British chefs are reinventing themselves and their food, becoming high-paid media darlings, courted by competing restaurants and promoted aggressively by the media. Huge two- and four-hundred-seat "gastro-domes" have emerged that are geared toward stimulating every sensory nerve ending, sometimes including the palate. Between low-octane drinks and high-calorie desserts, diners can ogle one another behind designer sunglasses and banter with the tanned and toned waitstaff, who are often better dressed than the diners, but may or may not speak English. There is a financial catch to all this new glamour and glitz, of course, and unless you go for lunch or opt for a set-price meal, you may feel more like a payer than a player in the modern British game of gourmet.

Central and Eastern European

These restaurants remain unconcerned with the current desire for lighter and healthier eating and are refreshingly oblivious to the current craze for minimalist decor. Most Central and Eastern European restaurants keep their food traditions alive in cozy settings geared toward making everyone feel at home. Long live borscht, dumplings, roast pork and sauerkraut, strudels, pierogi, potato pancakes, dark grainy bread, slivovitz, and vodka! It is doubtful, however, that most patrons of these restaurants come just to eat their sturdy national food ladled out in huge portions. In fact, many of the best of these restaurants are filled with old-timers reminiscing about their beloved homelands and the life and times they have left behind.

Chinese

The ruling idea in a Chinese meal is the duality of yin and yang. This means a balance between a poached, a steamed, and a pickled dish along with a stir-fried one.

Chinese restaurants in London continue to change for the better. The interiors are brighter, the service is slightly more polite, and the quality of the ingredients and the cooking has improved. Many will argue that the best Chinese food is found in Chinatown, a maze of streets behind Leicester Square, where local Chinese live and gather to eat. Their demands for authenticity keep the quality good and the prices reasonable. The advantages to eating in Chinese restaurants, aside from the Cheap Eater-pleasing prices for most meals, are that they tend to remain open very late and all day on Sunday. Children are always welcome, and you are encouraged to share dishes, which is a boon for lighter eaters.

The best Chinese food is cooked quickly and simply to enhance natural flavors. Most of London's Chinese restaurants are Cantonese, which is considered China's gourmet cuisine, since delicacy and texture are prized over pungency. While it is the type of food with which we are most familiar, it is also the one most likely to suffer in the translation, winding up as a gooey mess. The Cantonese are known for quick-boiling a variety of vegetables, lightly steaming fish, and stir-frying chicken with cashews. They are also experts in making dim sum. Years of experience and hours of skill go into the preparation of these Cantonese snacks, yet they sell for £1.75 to £3. Most come in portions of three or four; seven sets should be large enough for two for lunch. The only drawback to dim sum is that most restaurants stop serving it around 5 P.M.

French

French restaurants in London can be haute, haughty, and high priced . . . much more so than for the same quality and service in Paris. If you do decide you want a French meal in London, and if price is a consideration, go for lunch when the set-price meals are usually available. Even if there is no set-price menu at lunch, the food will cost less than if the same meal is served for dinner. As in Paris, nouvelle anything is *out* and homey bourgeois cooking is *in*.

Greek

London's Greek community is largely made up of Greek Cypriots who immigrated after World War II, again in the early sixties, and after the Turkish invasion in the midseventies, when thirty thousand people arrived at London's doorstep. Largely unskilled, they found jobs in the garment industry and in restaurants in Soho and Camden. Over time they opened kebab joints and cafés that served as social gathering places where they could meet, eat, gossip, read, and speak their own language.

Greek food can be traced back to the second century. It has evolved through many influences and now has a newfound popularity, as the Mediterranean diet is a simple, healthy way of eating that emphasizes fruit and vegetables, pure spices and herbs, olive oil, grains, fish, and little meat. The *meze,* made up of cold and hot starters and a series of main dishes, is a good way to sample a variety of their most popular cuisine.

Indian

A fellow colleague, Richard McIntyre, gave me the benefit of his wide knowledge and appreciation of Indian food in Britain. He pointed out that while one can enjoy Chinese and Italian cuisine in almost any city in the world, Indian cuisine is not so readily available. When in Britain, therefore, visitors should take advantage, especially in London, where there seems to be more Indian restaurants displaying Raj pomp than in India itself. For most Americans, Indian food is exotic and different, but not for the Brits, who governed the subcontinent for hundreds of years. Having tandoori chicken for dinner is as normal for them as going out for pizza is for us. In London, Indian cuisine is becoming more sophisticated. Mouth-searing hot dishes have been replaced by those with subtle seasonings. Regional Indian dishes are becoming popular, proving that there is more to Indian food than curry. The downside is that there are still too many Indian restaurants that do not adhere to the same health and cleanliness standards that we do in the States.

Richard issued a word of warning about *balti,* which is an individual Indian dish cooked in a mini-wok that is currently all the rage because it is lighter and cooked to order. "Any decent Indian restaurant will cook an individual dish from scratch, so who needs a balti," he said. "Forget them. They are a gimmick." He had one final piece of advice concerning Indian food in pubs: "Never touch it."

Indian restaurants have much to offer the Cheap Eaters in London. They are open late, and the servings are plentiful for the money. Service is generally polite, and the waitstaff is used to explaining various dishes to novices. With two or more in a group, it is best to order several dishes and share, as you would in a Chinese restaurant. Always try the bread and ask for yogurt to help put out the fire if you get something too hot. And remember, beer goes better with Indian food than wine.

Italian

Italian cuisine remains the first choice of most Londoners and one of the most fashionable. With the current emphasis on a high-carbohydrate diet, pasta has become a healthy alternative. In addition to pasta and pizza in every size, shape, flavor, and variety imaginable, you will find risotto, gnocchi, thick bean soup, fish, tender veal, and often wild game in season. New-wave Italian cooking is making quite a splash with its focus on regional dishes.

Japanese

Bowls of Japanese noodles continue to be the food that has London talking and slurping. These one-bowl meals are easy to make and can be topped with a variety of ingredients, from a single pork slice to a jumbo prawn. At the other end of the scale are the restaurants catering to Japanese business and corporate people. These cost a fortune and are best left alone, unless someone else is paying the bill.

According to a Japanese proverb, "If you eat something you have never tasted before, your life will be lengthened by seventy-five days." The Japanese restaurants listed in *Cheap Eats in London* offer suggestions for good-value lunches and dinners, and you are bound to find something you have never tasted before.

Southeast Asian

Authentic Southeast Asian food need not be expensive. It is an interesting dining experience because it offers well-flavored dishes using ingredients and spices most of us don't eat on a regular basis. As in Chinese restaurants, dishes are served all at once, thus it's customary for everyone at the table to share. If you order two or three starters and main courses with rice or noodles, you won't go away hungry. As with most Asian food, beer is a better accompaniment than wine.

Malaysian, Indonesian, and Singaporean food are closely related and often appear side by side on the menu. Ethnic Malaysians are Muslim, so pork is not served. Bali is Hindu, so beef is out. The principal flavorings are chili, coriander, lemongrass, coconut, tamarind, and fermented dried-shrimp paste. The simpler dishes and salads are often dressed with peanut sauce. While restaurants serving this food are not as widely recognized as Thai or Chinese, the cooking is good and the prices are much more reasonable.

Thai cuisine is tremendously popular in London, probably because so many people spend their holidays on package trips to Bangkok and at the beaches up-country. The nice thing about a Thai meal is that it isn't always a multicourse affair. Many Thai restaurants offer single-dish meals that can be eaten there or taken out. The food has a reputation for being fiery hot, so if you cannot handle lots of heat, ask to have the chili content reduced.

Vietnamese cooking has come into its own in London. Not too long ago, there was only one small noodle shop selling *pho,* the traditional Vietnamese breakfast of noodles and beef in broth. Now many more restaurants offer delicate dishes that in many cases are much more interesting than Chinese or Thai food. If you're not used to Vietnamese cuisine, go very easily on the pungent fish sauce, *nuoc mam,* which is served on the side with almost everything. With most Western palates, it is an acquired taste that may take a long while to develop.

Vegetarian

Vegetarians in London are no longer reduced to eating in dull restaurants that serve brown rice, lentils, and insipid veggies to a group of righteous, whacked-out health hippies grooving on an alternative lifestyle. Vegetarianism is now part of the mainstream, and it attracts a cross section of diners interested in a diet that is both delicious and healthy. Today, vegetarians, vegans, and even macrobiotics fare very well in London, and in a variety of price ranges. Almost every restaurant has a vegetarian dish, including pubs, and if one is not on the menu, ask and chances are good that something can be made up for you. When reserving in a nonvegetarian restaurant, it is smart to mention how many in your party are vegetarians, thus alerting the chef ahead of time to make special preparations if necessary. Ethnic cuisines also lean heavily toward a vegetarian diet, notably Italian, Indian, and Malaysian.

PUBS

No greater institution has ever been developed to further human happiness than that of a good public house.
—*Dr. Samuel Johnson*

What do you mean get rid of the pinball machines? They earn between £200 and £300 per week for the pub.
—*London publican*

Every traveler going to London considers a visit to a pub to be as important as seeing the changing of the guard at Buckingham Palace and the Crown Jewels at the Tower of London. As a visitor you can rely on being made welcome and enjoying yourself in a pub. In some, the welcome after a few pints will be more enthusiastic, and in only a few will you be politely ignored.

The word "pub" comes from "public house," and in that phrase lies the essential character of this British institution. The British pub, licensed by the government, is a place where people can come together and talk freely. Pubs date back to Roman times, when they began as taverns offering overnight accommodations and entertainment for travelers. In the thousand or so years since they were first introduced in Britain, people have talked about them, written about them, laughed and played in them, and relied on them for food, drink, and companionship. Pubs have been the haunt of highway robbers and smugglers, artists and writers, criminals and comics, and above all, ordinary people. Nowhere else in England can you find such a diversity of pubs as in London. Around almost every corner will be the welcoming door of a pub, and they include many of the most ancient and historic buildings in the capital city. In fact, there are over five thousand in greater London, and more per square yard in the City than in any other part of England.

Until the early twentieth century, pubs set aside different sections for different groups of customers. The tradesmen drank in the public bar and were shielded from the gentry, who drank in the lounge behind etched-glass "snob screens." Until 1970, few pubs were open to a woman alone, and those that were, were unsavory to say the least. Today, pubs still have a strong aura of masculinity, but a woman alone in a pub is no longer looked at in an unflattering light.

The Slug and Lettuce, Spotted Dog, Widow's Son, Dog & Duck, the Sugar Loaf, the Rose and Crown, the Three Stags—what is it with names? It was the Roman invaders who first required innkeepers to display signs outside their premises to guide the illiterate masses. In 1393, Richard II introduced legislation that every inn should be clearly signed so travelers might swiftly find shelter from the robbers and murderers who stalked them. By pub signs you can identify loyalties and great events that date back to these early times. The Crown, for example, originated in the Middle Ages, when innkeepers felt it necessary to display their loyalty to the monarchy. The Rose and Crown commemo-rated the end of the conflict between the red rose of Lancaster and the white rose of York. The Stag was an early religious symbol, and the Sugar Loaf recalls the way sugar was sold many years ago.

English pubs are national institutions similar to cafés in Paris and coffeehouses in Vienna. For millions of Londoners, their local pub is a home away from home, where they gather at the same time every day to meet their friends, catch up on local gossip, argue over politics, discuss the dreary weather, cheer their favorite sports team, and unfortunately for many a visitor, get boisterous around the pinball machines.

It isn't just the beer that defines a pub. A pub takes on the flavor of its neighborhood and location, and in many busy metropolitan pubs, the clientele changes almost hourly. Many regulars meet for lunch. Others get together in the afternoon for a game of cards or darts. In the evening, they stop by on their way home after work for a relaxing pint or two, and after dinner they come back to watch a sporting even on the "telly." The clientele in a pub represents a cross section of society, from the blue-collar workers in the East End to the aristocrats in Belgravia and Mayfair. In the City, expect to see lawyers in pinstriped suits discussing their cases. In Bloomsbury, known as literary London, you can mix with students and tweedy professors. The Hooray Henries (British yuppies) crowd the Chelsea pubs, and farther west along the banks of the Thames, writers, actors, and artists fill their favorites.

Pub Etiquette and Survival Techniques

1. There is no service charged or expected in pubs. If, however, you eat in a pub that has a restaurant with table service, there will be some sort of service charge either levied or suggested as "discretionary."

2. You can offer to buy the bartender a drink, but never tip him or her or anyone else working behind the bar.

3. Be prepared for no-nonsense service. You order your food from the food area and drinks from the bar. You pay for each separately at the time of service. In busy pubs you are often given a number when you place your food order, and when it is called, you return to the food service area to get your plate. Otherwise you will be served cafeteria-style from a small food display area or have your food brought to your table.

4. You must be eighteen years old to drink in a pub. Children under fourteen are not allowed in at all, but they may go into a pub restaurant.

5. In a pub, stick to beer; avoid wine or fancy mixed drinks.

6. If the Englishperson next to you offers to buy you a drink, it is OK to accept, but you should offer to buy the next round.

7. Conversation is part of the reason people go to pubs. Barside chats are quick and easy ways to meet people, but don't expect an invitation to that person's home. The easiest way to start a conversation is to talk about the beer served in that particular pub. Then fall back on the weather and the latest sports scores before getting into heavier topics of the Crown and taxes.

8. The best pub food is usually in a pub that also has its own restaurant. The bar food will be less expensive than the restaurant, even if some of the dishes are identical and come out of the same kitchen.

9. When pub food, or "pub grub," as it is called, is described in *Cheap Eats in London* as "good," that means good by general pub standards. With only a very few exceptions, the quality of pub food, which is often frozen and microwaved to order, must never be compared to that of restaurants because it is aimed at clientele who want a quick, filling bite to go with their beer.

10. If you are ordering a hot dish, stay with the daily specials listed on the chalkboard, and ask if it is made from scratch in this pub. If you want a sandwich, ask for one "freshly cut," which means it will be made to order for you. A "ready made" one was probably made way ahead of time and its freshness might be questionable.

11. Most pub desserts are terrible. Forget them.

12. If you want to relax in a pub in the afternoon and be assured of getting a good place to sit, arrive after 2 P.M. or before 6 P.M., but be aware that the hot meals may no longer be available, even though cold sandwiches and snacks will. Pubs will be least smoky at these times, as well. The flood of office workers who arrive

around noon and after work prevents visitors from seating themselves or breathing any fresh, smoke-free air.

13. If you want to experience pub life at its fullest, go for lunch or around 6 P.M., when everyone stops by for a pint or two on their way home for the day. At lunch, don't expect to always get a seat. More often than not, your English neighbor will stand with a pint in one hand and a plate of food in the other and somehow manage to finish both without spilling either.

14. Pub hours are governed by Parliament. They are Monday to Saturday 11 A.M. to 11 P.M., and Sunday noon until 10:30 P.M. Depending on the pub, its location, and types of trade, there are certain variations.

15. Ten minutes before closing time you will hear the closing bell, which signals that you have ten minutes to finish your drink before the pub closes and you are asked to leave.

Pub Food

If you want to eat without punishing your pocketbook, where do you go? To a pub, of course. For Cheap Eaters in London, pub food is a godsend because it is so filling, so cheap, and so British. But you must be forewarned. At lunch most pubs are wall-to-wall people, and getting a seat requires either arriving early or a stroke of good luck. Also, the food is filling and fattening: don't even think of counting calories or of monitoring your fat or cholesterol intake on your pub outings.

Even though pub food all tends to look, smell, and taste the same after a while, it is the soul and comfort food most British grew up on. Several standbys you will find in most pubs are meat pies, the ploughman's lunch, and a roast joint served for Sunday lunch. The pies are usually steak and kidney or shepherd's, and they consist of diced meat and vegetables covered with gravy, topped with mashed potatoes, and baked in a casserole. The ploughman's lunch is a piece of crusty bread served with a large chunk of cheddar or Stilton cheese with chutney and a pickle on the side, and it's a good accompaniment to a pint of English bitter. On Sunday, you can expect to have some sort of roast served with potatoes, vegetables, and the appropriate trimmings. Beyond these staples, pub food varies from wrapped sandwiches of undetermined age to hot and cold buffet spreads, lasagna, salads, and in some instances, unimpressive attempts at dessert.

Despite its general mediocrity, food is considered a moneymaker in most pubs. In order to squeeze profits to the limit, many breweries now mass-produce their food in central kitchens, resulting in dull preparations with zero imagination. The food is then frozen and delivered to the pubs, which in turn cook it as needed. If you see a pub touting its food as "home cooked," that will usually mean made elsewhere, cooked here. If you see it advertised as "home made," someone in the pub kitchen is cooking over a hot stove and not just zapping your lasagna in the microwave. There is hope, however, thanks to an increasing number of independently owned pubs run by people who are more attuned to the restaurant business. In these pubs, you can still enjoy the pub atmosphere and drink to your heart's content, but you will also have the food quality of a restaurant, even if the same restaurant standards of service are not always present.

English Beer

A large majority of pubs are "tied" to a particular brewery and sell only that brewery's ales. Free houses are not "tied" and can sell a wider range of brands. This doesn't really help visitors to England, who are often bewildered by the number of brews available in most pubs. In some, there are as many as two dozen ales alone. Every pub will always have at least one bitter, plus stout, lager, and a range of bottled beers. One of the major attractions of English beer is its wide variety. No two are alike and the taste of each depends on the techniques used by the brewery for that particular type of brew.

Asking for a "beer" will get you nowhere. You must specify not only the type and the brand but the amount you want: a pint or half-pint. For the novice, the best thing to do is tell the bartender the type of beer you like: light, dark, heavy, loaded with the flavor of hops, low alcohol, and so on, and let him or her suggest something. Part of the fun is experimenting—try three or four before you settle on a favorite. Note that U.S. brands of beer are expensive in England, so "when in Rome . . . "—drink English beer in London, if only to save money. But if you don't want to drink beer in a pub, there are alternatives: soft drinks, hard liquor, wine, and cider, which is a potent alcoholic apple drink that's not for the kiddies.

While it is beyond the scope of *Cheap Eats in London* to present an in-depth discussion of English beer, the following glossary should shed some light on this confusing subject for beginners.

A Beer Glossary

ABV Alcohol by volume. An ABV of 6 percent means that 6 percent of the beer is alcoholic.

ALE Ale is weaker and a little sweeter than bitter, though it is still much more robust than a typical American beer. Light or pale ale is bottled and served at room temperature.

BITTER If you want to drink what the locals do, order a pint of bitter, a clear yellowish beer with a strong hops taste. This traditional British beer is the most popular, but it is hard for many Americans to get used to because it is never chilled—that would ruin the taste. The best bitter is real ale. Because of the real ale movement, most pubs serve brews that are still fermenting when they are delivered. Real ale is alive, and continues to mature in the cask, and it has to be pumped to the bar using a hand pump, and served immediately. The taste of real ale is best at 56°F. It comes in two grades: ordinary and best or special, which is stronger.

BOTTLE-CONDITIONED A beer that continues to ferment in the bottle, causing a slight amount of sedimentation.

CASK-CONDITIONED Draught beer that leaves the brewery still fermenting in its cask.

EXPORT ALE Stronger than ale, and it is also bottled.

KEG BEER As processed as you can get. All the yeast is killed off, and the brew is pasteurized, filtered, and heaven forbid, chilled. Most of the big American beers are made this way.

LAGER If you want to drink what most Americans call beer, ask for a cold lager and stress the word *cold*. This brew is served in bottles or on draught, and there are over twenty-five varieties.

SHANDY An equal mixture of bitter and lemonade or ginger beer. Definitely an acquired taste.

STOUT Strong, dark, rich, creamy brew with the foam lasting from the first sip to the last. This is actually a very dark version of an ale, and it is always served at room temperature. Guinness is the most popular. If you want to go slowly with your first stout experience, order a "black and tan," which is half stout and half lager.

Pub Crawls

Guided pub walks, or pub crawls, meet in the early evening near tube stations, tour a neighborhood, and visit several typical pubs along the way. It is a good way to become better acquainted with London and have a party while doing it. Check with your hotel or the London Tourist Authority for brochures on guided walking tours of London. There are several operating, and they generally seem about the same. The outings last two or three hours, are worth the nominal fee, and go rain or shine, even if you are the only one going. Call 020-8883-2656 for tour itineraries.

TEAROOMS AND PÂTISSERIES

Everything stops for tea.
—*Popular English saying*

Name one other drink which cools, which warms, which calms, and which cheers all at once. There aren't many drinks like tea.
—*Anonymous*

For three hundred years, tea has been part of every level of British society. In the seventeenth century, it was so expensive that tea caddies had locks on them. Now it is the cheapest drink after tap water.

Teatime conjures up so many images, all very comforting and all very British. Whether served in plastic foam cups or in fine, translucent bone china, tea is serious business in England, which is just as it should be for the nation's favorite drink. According to the British Tea Council, more than 171 million cups are consumed daily in Britain.

If tragedy should happen, the ultimate English cure is a cup of tea. It doesn't matter if you get hit by a truck or lose all of your money, a "cuppa" will make things right again and cure the ills of the world as well.

English tea was served during the Regency days by the Duchess of Bedford to fill the gap between lunch and dinner. Victorian ladies drank tea in the drawing room while nannies passed the scones and tarts to the nursery set. A century ago, tearooms were about the only public place a lady could venture unchaperoned and yet maintain her good reputation. The first recorded English tearoom was a woman's idea. In 1864, the manager of a bread shop near the London Bridge started serving tea to her favorite customers, and before long everyone wanted some. She then asked the bakery if she could sell pots of tea with scones. The result was a huge success. Tea shops became a part of the nation's heritage and part of every Englishperson's childhood memories.

A proper English tea in a lovely setting is a pleasant and filling alternative to a big lunch or dinner. It is also theater at its best, complete with lovely tea dishes, special silverware, trays, and hovering waitstaff in fancy dress. Many London tourists associate sipping in high style at teatime with the elaborate offerings at Brown's Hotel or the Ritz. However, the only people who take afternoon tea in hotels seem to be tourists. Tea at the Ritz Hotel on Piccadilly is as famous as dinner at Maxim's in Paris—it's only slightly less expensive and almost as difficult to get a table. Men must wear ties, ladies should arrive in pretty dresses. A *proper* tea should not be confused with a *high* tea, which is a light supper with a hot dish followed by dessert and tea. High teas are more common in Scotland and Northern England.

Few Londoners dress to kill and pay in excess of £25 to sip tea at a fancy address. Instead, they go to a neighborhood tearoom. These informal tea places usually serve light lunches, followed by tea and fancy cakes and pastries until 6 or 7 P.M. These tearooms offer good value and a nice atmosphere in which you can have a pot of tea and a little sandwich or a sinfully rich treat that will keep you going until dinner, or in many cases until after the final curtain call at the theater.

Note: For something interesting and out of the ordinary, treat yourself to a visit to the Bramah Tea & Coffee Museum on Butler's Wharf near the Tower Bridge. The museum tells the 350-year history of coffee and tea, two of the world's most important commodities, in a fabulous collection of ceramics, silver, and prints. The collection includes a thousand coffeemakers and teapots, including the world's largest teapot. The shop sells ground coffee and a range of Brach teas (but no tea bags), as well as tea caddies, strainers, tea towels, and coffeemakers. They also serve coffee and tea.

The Bramah Tea & Coffee Museum is on Butler's Wharf near Tower Bridge, in the Clove Building at 1 Maguire Street, SE1 (tel: 020-7378-0222). It's open daily from 10 A.M. to 6 P.M. and closed on holidays.

WINE BARS

Wine, the plasma of life.

—Mary Gregg Misch

Wine bars offer new dimensions to dining out in London. In order to survive the competition, wine bars have been forced to serve better food as well as a wider variety of wines. In many wine bars, you can order anything from a smoked salmon salad to a three-course meal at lower prices than you would pay for the equivalent in a nice restaurant.

For many people, wine bars have become attractive alternatives to pubs. Not only is the food better, but there is usually a place to sit and the pinstripe/black pump crowd is quieter and more upmarket. Wine bars are also less crowded and smoky, and they seldom have blasting juke-boxes, loud videos, or pinball nuts drowning out conversation. They are busy during lunch and after work, but if you avoid these peak hours, you should find a relaxing setting in which you can go and drink a variety of wines and sample a selection of foods especially chosen to go with the vintages being served. Most of the staff in wine bars are well-versed on their bar's particular wines and are willing to spend time helping you decide what to taste.

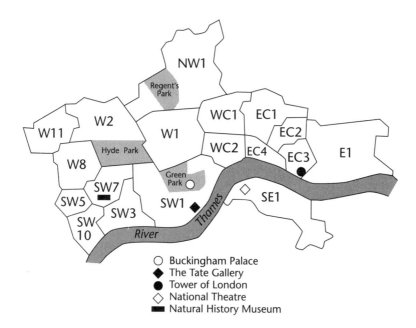

NW1

Regent's
Park

W11   W2   W1   WC1   EC1
                              EC2
            Hyde Park   WC2   EC4   EC3   E1
      W8
                  Green   ●
SW7   Park   ○
SW5   ▬   SW1   ◆   ◇   SE1
      SW3   River Thames
SW
10   River

○ Buckingham Palace
◆ The Tate Gallery
● Tower of London
◇ National Theatre
▬ Natural History Museum

Restaurants in London by Postal Code

London is chaos incorporated.
—*George Mikes,* Down with Everybody, *1951*

Greater London has a population of more than nine million people and covers an area of over six hundred square acres. Despite these statistics, it is one of the world's easiest cities to get around in, if you know what to do. First, arm yourself with a good map that shows all the streets and tube stops. The best is the *London A–Z* street map, available at most news kiosks and large bookstores. I prefer the foldout version to the book format because it gives me a better perspective about where I am and where I am going.

Just as Paris is divided into arrondissements, London is divided into postal districts. The postal code prefixes (made up of letters and a number) appear on London street signs and in every street address. The letters stand for compass directions in reference to the central district, and the numbers increase the farther you get from the center. If you are in London W1, you are in the middle of things, probably standing in Piccadilly Circus, dining in Soho, or shopping along Oxford or Regent Streets. If you are in London SW3, you are in Chelsea, and in London WC1, you are in the Bloomsbury area, wandering through the British Museum. A London address followed by NW8 means it's far from the action.

W1

The West End: Mayfair, Piccadilly, Soho, Marylebone, and Marble Arch

Marble Arch was modeled after the Arch of Constantine in Rome, and it originally stood in front of Buckingham Palace. It was moved to its present site in 1851 and is now marooned on a traffic island, hardly noticed by frazzled motorists and inaccessible to pedestrians. Today, only royalty and the King's Troop Royal Horse Artillery may pass through its central gates.

Marylebone (pronounced MAR–lee–bun) is a rather dull stretch between Regent's Park and Oxford Street. Britain's finest doctors have their offices on Harley Street.

The upmarket area known as Mayfair is between Piccadilly, Regent Street, and Oxford Street. This includes New and Old Bond Streets and South Moulton Street, all of which are lined with designer boutiques, prestigious jewelry stores, art galleries, Sotheby's, and elegant shops with a quiet assuredness only old money can buy. Some of the most expensive real estate in London is here: Grosvenor Square, the American Embassy, and the famed Savile Row, where the man in your life can order his excessively priced bespoke (custom) tailored wardrobe. Mayfair's posh residential neighborhoods are filled with beautiful eighteenth-century apartments. The Rolls Royces and Jaguars quietly parked by the curb remind you that unless you have just won the lottery, or inherited a vast sum of money, the lifestyle of the rich and famous may not yet be yours.

Both sides of Oxford Street have a dizzying variety of shops, department stores, and impossible crowds, especially on Saturday. Large department stores—Marks and Spencer, Selfridges—are worth visits if you like mass merchandising. The smaller stores are generally full of the fashion fads of the moment, and while fun to browse if you are a size two, or under thirty, they are hardly the choice for discriminating shoppers. Intersecting the middle of Oxford Circus is Regent Street, home to many quality stores—Jaegar, Liberty, Aquascutum, and the fabulous toy store Hamleys.

Piccadilly Circus is alive day and night with crazy traffic, waves of tourists, neon lights, and the largest Tower Records store on the planet. Across from the statue of Eros is Rock Circus and Trocadero, considered one of the largest indoor theme parks in Europe. Piccadilly Street runs from the Circus to Hyde Park Corner and is home to the Royal Academy of Arts, Fortnum and Mason, the Ritz Hotel, and the edge of Green Park.

Soho has a cosmopolitan atmosphere with crowded streets full of bistros, cafés, avant-garde shops, galleries, first-run cinemas, and famous theaters in buildings that once housed massage parlors, porn shops, and shady hotels. In the 1950s, Soho was a beatnik stomping ground and the home of London jazz. In the 1960s, the Rolling Stones and the Who headlined its clubs. In the 1970s, punk moved to King's Road, and Soho became commercialized and fashionable. Soho is also the home of many Italian restaurants on Old Compton Street, and it's a major gathering center for the gay community. On Berwick Street, look for the lively street market selling the season's best produce.

Gerrard Street is the main street of Chinatown. It is a pedestrian walkway framed by massive, scrolled dragon gates. The area is loaded with restaurants and Asian markets selling everything imaginable.

RESTAURANTS in W1

Amalfi Ristorante	37
Café Flo	37
Canadian Muffin Company	38
Chez Gérard	39
Chuen Cheng Ku Restaurant	40
Condotti	41
Country Life	42
Cranks Restaurants	42
Da Corradi	43
De Gustibus	44
Dumpling Inn	45
Ed's Easy Diner	45
Far East Chinese Restaurant	46
Govinda's	47
Granary	47
Ikkyu	48
Indian YMCA Cafeteria	48
Justin de Blank Bar and Restaurant	49
La Spighetta	49
L'Odéon ($)	50
Malaysian Dining Hall	51
Marino's Restaurant and Sandwich Bar	51
Melati	52
Mildred's	53
New Piccadilly Cafe Restaurant	53
The Original Carvery Restaurant at the Cumberland Hotel	54
Paul Rothe & Son	55
Pescatori Fish and Seafood Ristorante ($)	55
Pollo	57
Raw Deal	57
Sofra Bistro–Mayfair	58
Sofra Café	59

W1

RESTAURANTS in W1 (continued)

PUBS

TEAROOMS/PÂTISSERIES

WINE BARS

($) indicates a Big Splurge

Restaurants

AMALFI RISTORANTE (47)
29–31 Old Compton Street, Soho, W1

Amalfi has been an upscale Cheap Eat on the Soho dining scene for more than three decades. The manager, Mr. Ramos, who has been there almost that long, shows no sign of slowing down and neither does his Italian-speaking waitstaff. Clad in bright red shirts, they laugh, joke, and kibitz with the regulars, who vie for seats in the upstairs dining room, which has a ceiling brightly painted with clouds and tiled tabletops hand-painted with scenes from the Amalfi coast. Just off the entrance is a pâtisserie and a takeaway counter. Downstairs are four arched grottoes that can seat a combined total of 140 people. One of the grottoes is papered with photos of well-known Italian stage and screen stars; another is romantically candlelit with Chianti bottles hung above.

The best meal deal, upstairs or down, is the £6–8 pasta plate. For this Cheap Eater price you have a choice of six types of pasta topped with any of their thirteen homemade sauces accompanied by their house salad. Or, you can enjoy cannelloni, lasagna, tortellini, or risotto with mushrooms. All of these dishes also come with a tossed green salad. Every January they feature special set-price menus and wines from various regions of Italy. Priced at under £14, they offer very good value and plenty of delicious food. Amalfi also offers pizza, some wonderful veal and chicken dishes, and a small selection of fresh fish. All desserts are homemade and are seductively displayed in the window by the takeaway counter. Try to save room for dessert. You won't be sorry when you taste your first bite of a cream-filled cake or the rich tiramisu.

TELEPHONE
020-7437-7284

TUBE
Piccadilly Circus, Leicester Square, Tottenham Court Road

OPEN
Daily

CLOSED
2 days at Christmas

HOURS
Mon–Sat noon–11:15 P.M., Sun noon–10 P.M., continuous service

RESERVATIONS
Advised

CREDIT CARDS
AE, DC, MC, V

PRICES
À la carte, £7–18; set-price, £6–8 for pasta and a salad; January regional menus from £13.50, 2 courses, dessert, and coffee

SERVICE
£1 cover charge, 12½ percent service charge

MISCELLANEOUS
Takeaway available

CAFÉ FLO (11)
13–14 Thayer Street (off Marylebone High Street), W1

Café Flo has a sleek new look defined by the use of chrome, wood, and multicolored china. The menu varies slightly with each location, but changes seasonally and offers all the recognizable French dishes: *soupe de poisson* (traditional fish soup topped with *rouille,* croutons, and Gruyère cheese); *fromage de chèvre* on a bed of rocket (arugula) and roasted tomatoes, *confit de canard avec pommes*

TELEPHONE
020-7935-5023

TUBE
Bond Street

OPEN
Daily

CLOSED
Christmas Day

HOURS
Mon–Fri 11 A.M.–11:30 P.M.,
Sat noon–11:30 P.M., Sun
noon–10:30 P.M., continuous
service

RESERVATIONS
Not necessary

CREDIT CARDS
AE, MC, V

PRICES
À la carte, £12–20;
set-price, £9

SERVICE
12½ percent service charge

MISCELLANEOUS
Nonsmoking section

sautés (duck leg with roasted potatoes, garlic, and red wine sauce), *moules marinières* (mussels, white wine, garlic, shallots, and parsley), *cassoulet* (broad beans, Toulouse sausage, bacon, duck confit, and smoked garlic sausage), and of course, *steak frites*. For dessert, order a rich crème brûlée, or a fresh fruit tart. On Saturday and Sunday, brunch is served at all three Café Flos, but here, you can have *le petit déjeuner* (coffee and croissants) from 9 A.M. until noon if you are looking for a light way to start the day.

NOTE: There are other locations in Covent Garden (see page 127) and Notting Hill (see page 91).

CAFÉ FLO–WARDOUR STREET (39)
103 Wardour Street, W1

See Café Flo above for full description. All other information is the same.

TELEPHONE: 020-7734-0581
TUBE: Piccadilly Circus
OPEN: Daily
HOURS: 10 A.M.–midnight, continuous service

CANADIAN MUFFIN COMPANY (60)
9 Brewer Street, Soho, W1

TELEPHONE
020-7287-3555

TUBE
Piccadilly Circus

OPEN
Daily

CLOSED
Christmas Day

HOURS
Mon–Fri 8 A.M.–9 P.M.,
Sat 9 A.M.–10 P.M.,
Sun 10 A.M.–9 P.M.

RESERVATIONS
Not accepted

CREDIT CARDS
None

PRICES
À la carte, £1.20–4, early-bird
specials until 11 A.M. £2–2.50,
cappuccino and muffin;
soup, sandwiches, filled
potatoes £2–4

No smoking allowed; low-fat, low-sugar, and fat-free muffins; good coffees made with skim milk if need be; fat-free frozen yogurt for the virtuous; and a friendly staff to serve you or pack your goodies to go. Are we still in London? You bet, and at one of the Canadian Muffin Company's locations, where each day more than eighty varieties of vegetarian, sweet, or savory oat bran muffins are baked on the premises.

Recipes combine organic flour, buttermilk, fresh fruits, nuts, and vegetables to create a delicious high-fiber, low-fat, low-sugar treat. All the orthodox flavors are here—banana, bran, blueberry, apple-cinnamon—and some far-out choices. Try garlic; olive, feta, and sun-dried tomato; pizza; or spinach, corn, and cheese. For a sweeter bite, nibble on peanut butter and chocolate; rhubarb, apple, and ginger; piña colada; dark chocolate and orange; or white chocolate and raisins. Special offers that invite Cheap Eats include the baker's half dozen (buy six and get one free) and the early-bird morning specials until 11 A.M. Monday through Friday, and the souper specials: a bowl of homemade soup and a muffin.

NOTE: In addition to the one below, there are two other locations, one in WC2, page 130, and one in SW10, page 204.

SERVICE
No service charged or expected

MISCELLANEOUS
No smoking allowed

CANADIAN MUFFIN COMPANY (10)
10 New Cavendish Street, Soho, W1

See Canadian Muffin Company above for full description. All other information is the same.

TELEPHONE: 020-7486-0707

TUBE: Bond Street

OPEN: Daily

CLOSED: Christmas Day

HOURS: Mon–Fri 7:30 A.M.–6 P.M., Sat 9 A.M.–6 P.M., Sun and holidays 10 A.M.–4 P.M.

CHEZ GÉRARD (5)
8 Charlotte Street, Soho, W1

For a decade, the Chez Gérard restaurants have been little corners of London that forever signified France. Francophiles, off-duty French chefs, and red-blooded carnivores have been drawn to the group's restaurants to revel in an atmosphere straight from Boulevard St-Germain and savor the best *steak frites* this side of the Channel. Today the *steak frites* are as good as ever, but diners whose idea of heaven is not a juicy steak will appreciate the lighter touch of some of the menu selections. Grilled fresh salmon, a plate of roasted vegetables drizzled with fine olive oil and garnished with roasted garlic and *pistou* (a sauce of basil, garlic, cheese, and olive oil), or a simple fish or roast chicken will please. To start, there are always escargots baked with garlic butter, onion soup gratinéed with croutons and Gruyère cheese, and the plats du jour, featuring French faves such as *boeuf bourguignon* and *filet de sole farci*. The set-price menu offers top-notch value when you consider that it is available Monday to Saturday evenings and weekend lunches, and that it offers choices from four starters, four main courses (including a vegetarian option), and whatever dessert you want from the menu. An optional fourth course, featuring a selection of French cheeses, is available for a little extra.

TELEPHONE
020-7636-4975

TUBE
Goodge Street

OPEN
Mon–Fri, Sun; Sat dinner only

CLOSED
Sat lunch, holidays

HOURS
Lunch noon–3 P.M., dinner Mon–Sat 6–11:30 P.M., Sun 6–10:30 P.M.

RESERVATIONS
Essential

CREDIT CARDS
AE, DC, MC, V

PRICES
À la carte, £20–26; set-price, Mon–Sat dinner and weekend lunches, £16, 3 courses, £4 extra for 4 courses

SERVICE
£1 cover charge includes freshly baked French bread and butter, anchovy butter, marinated olives, and toasted salted nuts; 12½ percent service charge

MISCELLANEOUS
Nonsmoking upstairs at this
particular location, varies with
the others

The Charlotte Street location features an authentic Parisian zinc bar and chrome railway carriage luggage racks for coats and bags in a light room with scrubbed tile floors. Upstairs, where smoking is prohibited, the atmosphere is almost antiseptic, with white walls and a marble bar separating a dozen or so tables from a line of banquettes.

NOTE: In addition to the one below, there are five other Chez Gérards: two in WC2 (see page 130), one in EC1 (see page 219), one in EC2 (see page 228), and one in SW3 (see page 171).

CHEZ GÉRARD (65)
31 Dover Street, Mayfair, W1

See Chez Gérard above for full description. All other information is the same.

TELEPHONE: 020-7499-8171
TUBE: Green Park
OPEN: Mon–Sat; Sun dinner only
CLOSED: Sun lunch, holidays
HOURS: Lunch noon–3 P.M., dinner Mon–Sat 6–11 P.M., Sun 6–10:30 P.M.
MISCELLANEOUS: Nonsmoking section

CHUEN CHENG KU RESTAURANT (31)
17 Wardour Street, Chinatown, W1

TELEPHONE
020-7734-3281

TUBE
Oxford Circus, Tottenham
Court Road

OPEN
Daily

CLOSED
Christmas Day

HOURS
11 A.M.–11:45 P.M., continuous
service

RESERVATIONS
Suggested, especially for
Sunday lunch

CREDIT CARDS
AE, DC, MC, V

PRICES
À la carte, £10–18; set-price,
£11–26, 2-person minimum

The functionally impersonal Chuen Cheng Ku in London's Chinatown is the place to have dim sum, the Asian treat of bite-size appetizers. This meal provides one of the best opportunities to sample a wide range of tastes, but the experience of choosing here can be frustrating. Hard-working waitresses wheel dim sum carts around the tables, chanting the names of their offerings in Chinese. Diners then take their pick of the exotic mouthfuls wrapped in leaves or delicately arranged in willow baskets. Since most of the waitresses only know the Chinese names of the dishes, your only help deciding is the picture menu on each table. Actually though, it is much more fun and adventurous to just point as the cart passes and enjoy the surprise. This is, of course, if you wouldn't balk at a chicken foot doused in black bean sauce.

In addition to dim sum, the long menu lists almost every other Cantonese dish you have ever heard of, and some you probably wish you hadn't. The best advice, however, is to stick with the dim sum, which is served daily until 6 P.M. The most interesting time to go is for Sunday lunch, when you can observe extended Chinese families happily indulging in their favorite dim sum delicacies.

NOTE: There is a second address at 20 Rupert Street, W1; tel: 020-7734-3281. The same hours, food, and prices apply.

SERVICE
10 percent service charge

MISCELLANEOUS
Takeaway available

CONDOTTI (52)
4 Mill Street (off Conduit Street), Mayfair, W1

Delicious pizza served in upscale surroundings is exactly what you can expect at the classy Condotti, just off Regent Street. It looks and feels expensive, with a good-looking crowd sitting around well-spaced tables with starched linens and fresh flowers. The walls are hung with an interesting collection of the owner's contemporary art, and the service is polite and professional. But is pizza all that they serve? That's right, along with starters, assorted salads, desserts, and Italian wines.

All the pizzas come with a mozzarella and tomato sauce base. Extra toppings are available, and the chefs use only free-range eggs. Favorites include the Pizza Veneziana with onions, capers, olives, pine nuts, and sultanas. The Venice in Peril fund gets 40 pence for every Pizza Veneziana sold. The total amount paid to the fund from the sales of Pizza Veneziana through June 1998 was £794,943.36 (almost a half million dollars). I like the simple Pizza Condotti, topped with ricotta and Gorgonzola cheeses, and the La Reine with ham, olives, and mushrooms. Dessert decisions are never easy, but I am always partial to the dense chocolate fudge cake. A light Italian wine or a bottle of Peroni beer makes a perfect accompaniment to the meal, and a bracing espresso is the best ending.

TELEPHONE
020-7499-1308

TUBE
Oxford Circus

OPEN
Mon–Sat

CLOSED
Sun, holidays

HOURS
11:30 A.M.–midnight, continuous service

RESERVATIONS
Suggested for lunch

CREDIT CARDS
AE, DC, MC, V

PRICES
À la carte, £11–20

SERVICE
Service discretionary, 12½ percent service charge for 6 or more

COUNTRY LIFE (59)
3–4 Warwick Street, Piccadilly Circus, W1

TELEPHONE
020-7434-2922

TUBE
Piccadilly Circus

OPEN
Mon-Thur, Sun; Fri lunch only

CLOSED
Sat, Fri dinner, holidays

HOURS
Restaurant: lunch 11:30 A.M.–
3 P.M., afternoon tea 3–5:30 P.M.,
dinner 5:30–9 P.M.; natural
food shop: Mon–Wed 9 A.M.–
6 P.M., Thur 9 A.M.–7:30 P.M.,
Fri 9 A.M.–6 P.M. (till 3 P.M. in
winter), Sun 11:30 A.M.–3 P.M.

RESERVATIONS
Not necessary

CREDIT CARDS
None

PRICES
À la carte, £12–18; set-price,
lunch at one pence per gram—
cannot exceed £6; £8.95, one
course, £9.95, 2 courses,
£11.95, 3 courses

SERVICE
12½ percent service charge

MISCELLANEOUS
No smoking or alcohol allowed

For a healthy vegetarian Cheap Eat in London, Country Life will fill your plate starting at the philanthropically low price of £3 for a bowl of soup and a roll, and charging a mere one pence per gram for lunch. Average cost: £5, and there is a ceiling price of £6 on this meal. Country Life is run by the Seventh-Day Adventist church, whose members are eager to convert wayward sinners, so you can expect to see their brochures and magazines prominently displayed. Monday to Friday, lunch is serve yourself cafeteria-style with a featured soup, main course, vegetable, and side dish. You pay by the gram for everything you select. No time to sit down and eat? Then they will pack it for takeaway. In the evening, cloths cover the tables, waiters replace the cafeteria chow line, and everything is à la carte, with symbols on the dishes indicating the type of food in each dish: gluten-free, yeast-free, or honey-free. In addition to the restaurant, Country Life operates a health food shop, which doesn't begin to compare with those we have in the States, but for London, it passes. They also have cooking classes, and medical, nutrition, and dietary experts to help and give advice on a variety of topics.

CRANKS RESTAURANT (37)
8 Marshall Street, Soho, W1

TELEPHONE
020-7437-9431

TUBE
Oxford Circus

OPEN
Mon–Sat

CLOSED
Sun, holidays

HOURS
Mon–Fri 8 A.M.–9 P.M.,
Sat 10 A.M.–9 P.M., continuous
service, hours vary slightly with
each location

RESERVATIONS
Not necessary

CREDIT CARDS
AE, MC, V

PRICES
À la carte, £3.50–10

SERVICE
Service discretionary

Cranks boldly claims to have the best food for vitality and health. Given their new menus and determination to prepare fat-free dishes, it isn't too far from the truth. For a quick, nutritious, and (almost) fat-free vegetarian meal (almost) any time of day, Cranks is a name to remember. This chain of inexpensive vegetarian restaurants was one of the first on the London natural-food scene, introducing whole grains, free-range eggs, and vegetable casseroles as healthy alternatives to the British staples of sausage, beans, fried eggs, and creamy snacks. The food caters to all types of vegetarians, including vegans, with only a slight nod given toward macrobiotic diners. Everything on the menu is made from natural ingredients, and that means that every dish is free of artificial additives and preservatives. I think some of the dishes are a little old hat, considering the innovations in vegetarian cuisine over the past few years, but one cannot fault their wholesomeness. All Cranks restaurants list the ingredients and fat grams for their weekly menus, which are basically the same at each location. The food is attractively displayed cafeteria-style, allowing diners to choose from a daily selection of hot and cold dishes, salads, soups, sweets, and hot and cold drinks including fruit and vegetable juices. Light breakfasts featuring their bakery products are also served.

NOTE: In addition to the two below, there are two other Cranks Restaurants in WC2 (see page 131).

(see page 131)

CRANKS–ST. CHRISTOPHER'S PLACE (28)
23 Barrett Street, Mayfair, W1

See Cranks above for full description. All other information is the same.

TELEPHONE: 020-7495-1340
TUBE: Bond Street
OPEN: Mon–Sat
CLOSED: Sun, holidays
HOURS: Mon–Fri 8 A.M.–7:30 P.M., Sat 9 A.M.–7 P.M., continuous service
MISCELLANEOUS: Patio seating on warm days on the charming St. Christopher's Place

CRANKS–TOTTENHAM STREET (7)
9–11 Tottenham Street, Bloomsbury, W1

This location is unlicensed and does not accept credit cards. See Cranks above for full description. All other information is the same.

TELEPHONE: 020-7631-3912
TUBE: Goodge Street
OPEN: Mon–Sat
CLOSED: Sun, holidays
HOURS: Mon–Fri 7:30 A.M.–7:30 P.M., Sat 10 A.M.–6 P.M., continuous service

DA CORRADI (68)
20–22 Shepherd Market, Mayfair, W1

Da Corradi is a regular lunchtime hangout for local Mayfair office workers who enjoy the low-key atmosphere and good, affordable Italian cooking in this rustic, two-floor Shepherd Market choice. A line often forms in front around noon, when the aroma of the lusty sauces flows to the sidewalk. The freshly prepared food is worth the brief wait, especially the daily specials of homemade soup, lasagna, tortellini, or the chef's weekly creations.

MISCELLANEOUS
Takeaway available, most are air-conditioned

TELEPHONE
020-7499-1742
TUBE
Green Park
OPEN
Restaurant: Mon–Fri, Sat breakfast and dinner only; sandwich bar: Mon–Fri

CLOSED
Sun, holidays

HOURS
Restaurant: 7–11:30 A.M.,
noon–10 P.M., continuous
service; sandwich bar: 7 A.M.–
5 P.M.

RESERVATIONS
Advised during peak hours

CREDIT CARDS
AE, DC, MC, V

PRICES
Restaurant: à la carte, £10–16;
sandwich shop: £3.50–6

SERVICE
10 percent service charge

MISCELLANEOUS
Takeaway available

All the pastas and sauces are made here by owner Guiseppe Corradi and his family. They even go so far as to pick their own mushrooms for the wild mushroom pasta sauce. When I asked him where he picked the mushrooms, he told me it was a secret location even the pope couldn't squeeze out of him.

If you aren't in the area for lunch, stop by for a morning cappuccino and a bowl of real porridge—the kind that is slow-cooked with milk and served with brown sugar, not zapped in the microwave. This is also a handy spot if you want an early dinner before the theater, or if you don't want to be fashionably correct and eat after 8 or 9 P.M. However, if you just want a sandwich on the run, stop in at Da Corradi's sandwich bar next door and order a Hot Italian Job . . . toasted ciabatta or focaccia bread piled with mozzarella, ham, avocado, tomato, and basil.

DE GUSTIBUS (12)
53 Blandford Street, Marylebone, W1

TELEPHONE
020-7486-6608

TUBE
Baker Street, Marble Arch

OPEN
Mon–Fri

CLOSED
Sat–Sun, holidays

HOURS
7 A.M.–4:30 P.M., continuous
service

RESERVATIONS
Not accepted

CREDIT CARDS
None

PRICES
À la carte, £3–7

SERVICE
Service discretionary

MISCELLANEOUS
No smoking allowed

"No sandwich is ever complete unless it is made with De Gustibus bread." Quite a claim, and true when you consider that De Gustibus was voted the independent baker of the year for two years in a row, and received the best bread in Britain award. All of their robust sandwiches can be made on a variety of freshly baked breads, and all come with a small salad. Every combination you can imagine is available: from a traditional English cheddar to smoked salmon or turkey, Mexican tuna, and six oversize triple-deckers. Things get going at 7 A.M. when local office workers pop in for slices of toast spread with homemade jam, a freshly baked danish or croissant, and cups of steaming lattes or cappuccinos. By 11 A.M., the painted wicker backless stools and green metal garden chairs at the window counter are full of happy munchers, and by noon, the place is chockablock full with regulars ordering a takeaway sandwich and one of the restaurant's brownies or a slice of chocolate raisin and crunch cake, which is so rich it could qualify as a candy bar. If you don't want a sandwich (which I cannot imagine if you are here), there are a dozen or more daily hot specials, salads, pizzas, quiches, and homemade soups served with a basket of bread.

DUMPLING INN (55)
2 Macclesfield Street (at the corner of 15a Gerrard Street), Chinatown, W1

A reader wrote to me about the crispy duck, eggplant in garlic sauce, and all-day dim sum served at the Dumpling Inn. The number of Chinese restaurants in this neighborhood is daunting, and I was indeed wary of another run-of-the-mill Chinese meal served by a careless, bored waitstaff. I am happy to tell you that the Dumpling Inn rises a notch or two above its competitors on several levels. First, it is quiet and offers pleasant window seating with views onto the busy pedestrian streets around it. The staff is shyly professional, properly dressed, and above all . . . civil. As for the food, I think the dim sum is one of the better choices, certainly if you want a fast bite before or after the theater or a movie around Leicester Square.

TELEPHONE
020-7734-5161, 020-7437-2567

TUBE
Piccadilly Circus

OPEN
Daily

CLOSED
2 days at Christmas

HOURS
Noon–midnight, continuous service

RESERVATIONS
Not necessary

CREDIT CARDS
AE, MC, V

PRICES
À la carte, £10–20; set-price, £12; 9-course fish meal, £25

SERVICE
10 percent service charge

ED'S EASY DINER (42)
12 Moor Street, Soho, W1

"If you can find a better diner, eat there!" says one of the many signs in Ed's American-style diners in London's Soho and Chelsea (see also page 172). This is the original one, and now there are five others where the eating is as good as the people-watching, which provides an up-close look at the latest fads for teenyboppers and fashion groupies. Seating is on stools around a circular counter, from which you watch the cooks prepare mainstream American fast food that will take you back to the days when expanding waistlines, high cholesterol, and fat levels were not on the top of our worry lists. Even the menu warns: "Healthnicks . . . Eat your heart out. Don't blame us we're only doing our job."

All the favorites are here: one-third-pound pure beef burgers served with five types of fries and three kinds of big onion rings; kosher hot dogs smothered in cheddar cheese; tuna melts; grilled cheese sandwiches with bacon or tomato; chicken served four ways; and five salads, from Caesar to tuna. Wash it all down with a thick malted milkshake, a Pepsi, or a bottle of beer (no wine is served at Ed's). On Saturday and Sunday the King's Road branch is open for breakfast. If you're in the neighborhood and starving, stop by and order the the Lumberjack: hash browns, two eggs any style, bacon, sausage,

TELEPHONE
0170-439-1955

TUBE
Leicester Square, Tottenham Court Road

OPEN
Daily

CLOSED
Christmas Day

HOURS
Mon–Thur, Sun 11:30 A.M.–11:30 P.M. (till midnight in summer), Fri–Sat till 1 A.M.; deliveries: Mon–Fri 11:30 A.M.–9 P.M., Sat noon–6 P.M.

RESERVATIONS
Not accepted

CREDIT CARDS
AE, MC, V; minimum charge: £10

PRICES
À la carte, £4–8; minimum charge at peak times: £4

SERVICE
Service discretionary

MISCELLANEOUS
Takeaway available

tomato, toast, butter, and jelly. More delicate appetites will like the French toast with maple syrup or a Belgian waffle with a side of fruit, syrup, or chocolate sauce. In the mood for sinful sweets? Consider Ed's Oreo Delight sundae, a mix of vanilla ice cream topped with chocolate fudge, butterscotch sauce, crushed Oreos, and smothered in whipped cream. Or, try the Rolo Beethoven sundae, which entices you with more vanilla ice cream, Rolo's candy, butterscotch, bananas, and piles of whipped cream. And don't forget the Cracker Jack, Atomic Fire Balls, and Reese's Pieces: Ed sells them all. The gum-chewing staff is friendly, and the original Seeburg Jukebox (circa 1948) plays popular fifties and sixties tunes. It all adds up to a wonderfully nostalgic experience.

NOTE: If you can't get to Ed's in person but are inside his two delivery areas, call his Diner Line, place your order, and sit tight until one of his Waiters on Wheels brings your meal to your door. There is also an Ed's Easy Diner in Chelsea (see page 172).

ED'S EASY DINER (62)
Pepsi Trocadero, Shaftesbury Avenue at Piccadilly Circus, W1

This is a second address in W1. See Ed's Easy Diner above for full description. All other information is the same.

TELEPHONE: 020-7287-1951
TUBE: Piccadilly Circus

FAR EAST CHINESE RESTAURANT (56)
13 Gerrard Street, Chinatown, W1

TELEPHONE
020-7437-6148

TUBE
Leicester Square

OPEN
Daily

CLOSED
4 days mid-January

HOURS
Bakery: 10:30 A.M.–7 P.M.;
restaurant: 7 P.M.–1 A.M.

RESERVATIONS
Not accepted

CREDIT CARDS
MC, V

PRICES
À la carte, £.90–1.60

The Wu family runs this friendly hole-in-the-wall restaurant, tearoom, and bakery in the heart of Chinatown. A few years ago, you would see the senior Mr. Wu holding court daily at the table in the back, chatting with his friends, reading the paper, and generally keeping an eye on things. When I asked about him recently, his son Richard told me he now reads his paper at home. It is clear, however, that he still has a firm grip on things, because Richard's modern ideas—expanding the menu, redecorating and modernizing the interior— have been met with his father's continuing disapproval. Yet the food remains as it was over thirty-five years ago: delicious Chinese cakes and pastries, including sticky glazed *char-siu* buns, lotus-seed moon cakes with egg yolk, curry beef puffs, and coconut butter buns. These delicacies don't keep particularly well, so plan to eat your booty within a few hours if you buy takeaway.

From 7 P.M. to 1 A.M. daily the Wus convert their bakery into a restaurant; that is, they add a few tables. Frankly I wasn't impressed with the restaurant side of this operation and recommend that you stick with the bakery items.

GOVINDA'S (32)
9 Soho Street, Soho, W1

Govinda's is a cafeteria-style restaurant where there is no smoking, no booze, no service charged or expected, and no meat, fish, or eggs served. What you will find at this Hare Krishna–run buffet mecca for vegan and vegetarian Cheap Eaters is all the food you can eat for under £6, served on an oval metal platter. The especially hungry will appreciate the huge casseroles or the veggie burger with cheese served with a side salad. Also watch for pizza, lasagna, jacket potatoes with all sorts of toppings, and some run-of-the-mill desserts. Cheap Eaters with only a few pence in their pockets can show up between 7 and 8 P.M. to take advantage of what's left of the buffet for only £3.

On Sunday, the restaurant is closed, but at 4:30 P.M. a "love feast" is held in the temple next door. Everyone is welcome and the food is free, but you are expected to leave a donation.

GRANARY (64)
39 Albemarle Street, Mayfair, W1

Now celebrating a half century in the business, John Shah told me, "After this time, we should get it right. We don't sell *posey* food, nothing is frozen, everything is made here, and compromises are not part of the kitchen's mandate." His Granary is an all-day lunch buffet in which there are always eight hot dishes, six salads, and ten luscious desserts available. The nice part is that you can arrive any time, be assured of a full lineup of food, and order as much or as little as you want. The inside is attractive with green plants, and the food is appealingly arranged along the glassed-in buffet line. There is room for a hundred, and every seat is occupied during the lunch crunch from 1 to 2 P.M. If you aren't counting fat grams or calories, fill up on the roast loin of pork or

SERVICE
No service charged or expected

TELEPHONE
020-7437-4928

TUBE
Tottenham Court Road

OPEN
Mon–Sat; Sun dinner only

CLOSED
Never

HOURS
12:30–8 P.M., continuous service; love feast Sun 4:30 P.M.

RESERVATIONS
Not accepted

CREDIT CARDS
None

PRICES
À la carte, £3–9; love feast by donation

SERVICE
No service charged or expected

MISCELLANEOUS
No smoking or alcohol allowed, unlicensed

TELEPHONE
020-7493-2978

TUBE
Green Park

OPEN
Mon–Fri; Sat–Sun lunch only

CLOSED
Holidays

HOURS
Mon–Fri 11:30 A.M.–7:30 P.M., Sat–Sun noon–4 P.M., continuous service

RESERVATIONS
Not accepted

CREDIT CARDS
None

chicken potpie. Virtuous diners will be happy with the vegetable-stuffed eggplant, lemon chicken, or an assortment of the salads. All hot main courses are garnished with potatoes-of-the-day or rice. Portions are large so you shouldn't fear hunger pangs later on in the afternoon. I always save room for the dessert specialty—banana layer cake—or a slice of the chocolate mousse cake. Never mind the calories . . . every single one is worth it.

IKKYU (6)
67a Tottenham Court Road (in the basement), Bloomsbury, W1

Ikkyu, located in an unpretentious, rather shabby basement on Tottenham Court Road, is run by Mr. Kawaguchi and his sister, Ms. Komori. Newcomers to Japanese food preparation may want to sit at the low wooden counter, where they can watch the action. The grilled fish set-price lunch—a steal at under £7.50—comes with rice, pickles, and miso soup, and it offers your choice of sardines, mackerel, pike, or salmon. Other set-price lunch meals feature sushi, sashimi, chicken *katsu,* and tempura, and all include rice and miso soup. The atmosphere is both hectic and friendly, and for Japanese food, it is a great Cheap Eat in London.

INDIAN YMCA CAFETERIA (1)
41 Fitzroy Square, Regent's Park, W1

For the nearest thing to Indian home cooking, eat at the Indian YMCA Cafeteria, where you will rub elbows with students at breakfast and dinner and with budget-conscious office workers and neighborhood Indians at lunch. While certainly not the place to entertain your boss, it is one place to keep in mind if you like very simple Indian food.

The philanthropically priced meals are geared toward Indian students and other guests who stay at this YMCA while studying in London. Naturally, any attempt at decor is out, and the choices for each meal are limited. The breakfasts are usually English style, but several

---

PRICES
À la carte, £6–10

SERVICE
No service charged or expected

TELEPHONE
020-7636-9280

TUBE
Goodge Street

OPEN
Mon–Fri; Sun dinner only

CLOSED
Sat, Sun lunch, holidays

HOURS
Lunch noon–2:30 P.M., dinner 6–10:30 P.M.

RESERVATIONS
Not necessary

CREDIT CARDS
AE, DC, MC, V

PRICES
À la carte, £6–12; set-price, £7–9

SERVICE
Service discretionary at lunch, 10 percent service charge at dinner

MISCELLANEOUS
Takeaway available

TELEPHONE
020-7387-0411

TUBE
Warren Street

OPEN
Daily

CLOSED
Some holidays (call to check)

HOURS
Breakfast Mon–Fri 8–9:15 A.M., Sat–Sun, holidays 8:30–9:30 A.M.; lunch Mon–Fri 12:15–1:45 P.M., Sat–Sun, holidays 12:30–1:30 P.M.; dinner daily 7–8 P.M.

---

times a week an Indian dish is added. One of the most popular Indian breakfast dishes is *upma,* a southern Indian dish made from cereal and vegetables. It is nice once in a while, but something I do not yearn for often. At lunch three meals are offered: a vegetarian, meat, and fish curry. Each is served with rice or chapati. Dal and condiments are on the shared tables. The dinner selections vary among tandoori chicken, mutton stew, and spicy prawns as well as a vegetarian selection. Desserts are absolutely forgettable, mostly canned fruit or ice cream. Tea, coffee, and fruit juice are included with breakfast and lunch; coffee is included with dinner.

RESERVATIONS
Not accepted

CREDIT CARDS
None

PRICES
À la carte, £4–5

SERVICE
No service charged or expected

MISCELLANEOUS
No smoking or alcohol allowed, unlicensed

JUSTIN DE BLANK BAR AND RESTAURANT (16)
120–122 Marylebone Lane, Marylebone, W1

The clientele at Justin de Blank Bar and Restaurant are as bright and breezy as the atmosphere inside. The big, brightly colored dining space features an open kitchen in back, set off by a curved bar and a spiral staircase leading to a downstairs dining area that everyone avoids. The upscale, modern British food features all the faves prepared with new twists. The usual bangers and mash or calves' liver become sausages or grilled calves' liver cooked in red wine and served with onions and mushroom mash, or a sage and onion mash with a side of French beans. The tagliatelle with saffron cream sauce, oyster mushrooms, and Parmesan cheese was delicious, but I would have preferred it without the peas. Desserts don't go too far overboard with the calorie intake, unless you order the chocolate cherry mud cake served with fresh cream. The wine list is above average with many choices available by a small or large glass or a full bottle.

TELEPHONE
020-7486-5250

TUBE
Bond Street

OPEN
Mon–Sat

CLOSED
Sun, holidays

HOURS
Bar: 11 A.M.–11 P.M.; food service: lunch noon–3 P.M., dinner 6–10:30 P.M.

RESERVATIONS
Advised for lunch

CREDIT CARDS
AE, MC, V

PRICES
À la carte, £20–25; set-price, £10, lunch only, 2 courses

SERVICE
Service discretionary

LA SPIGHETTA (13)
43 Blandford Street, Marylebone, W1

La Spighetta is a spin-off from Giorgio Locatelli's acclaimed Zafferano (see page 159). This should be all the recommendation you need if pizza is on your menu for the day. For the best results, reserve a banquette in the nonsmoking section and plan to arrive around 1 P.M. for lunch or 8:30 P.M. in the evening. The downstairs dining room—sleek, stylish, oh-so-fashionable—is filled with savvy diners who know that the pizzas, not the pastas, are the order of the day. Start with either the buffalo mozzarella and beetroot salad, the sweet-and-sour aubergines (eggplant), or the lighter, fresh artichoke and

TELEPHONE
020-7486-7340

TUBE
Baker Street, Marble Arch

OPEN
Daily

CLOSED
2 days at Christmas

HOURS
Lunch noon–2:30 P.M., dinner 6:30–10:30 P.M.

RESERVATIONS
Essential

CREDIT CARDS
AE, MC, V
PRICES
À la carte, £18–20
SERVICE
12½ percent service charge
MISCELLANEOUS
Nonsmoking section

designer-greens salad. La Spighetta offers ten crisp pizzas, each one wonderful and just the right size for one person. One of my favorites is the Pizza Bufala, with fresh tomatoes and mozzarella cheese scattered on a tomato base crust drizzled with olive oil. Another winner is the Pizza Bresaola, which is topped with tomato, rocket (arugula), cured beef, and a goat cheese dressing. For dessert, order the three scoops of ice cream served with a cookie and ignore the leaden apple tart.

L'ODÉON (63, $)
65 Regent Street, Piccadilly Circus, W1

TELEPHONE
020-7287-1400
TUBE
Piccadilly Circus
OPEN
Mon–Sat
CLOSED
Sun, some holidays
(call to check)
HOURS
Lunch noon–2:45 P.M., dinner
5:30–11:30 P.M., pre-theater
dinner menu served until 7 P.M.
RESERVATIONS
Essential, request a window seat
CREDIT CARDS
AE, DC, MC, V
PRICES
À la carte, £30–35; set-price,
lunch and pre-theater menu
£17, 2 courses, £20, 3 courses
SERVICE
Service discretionary, £1.50
cover charge, 12½ percent
service charge for 6 or more

In the last few years, there has been a rash of ultra-trendy restaurants opening that offer a see-and-be-seen atmosphere in which dressing to the nines and eating out is more about posing than dining. Some of these gastronomic palaces work, offering a culinary energy matched by few. Others provide more style than substance and are wildly expensive, quite beyond the spirit of *Cheap Eats in London*. But there are some notable exceptions, and L'Odéon is one. At L'Odéon the food is superb and the setting is a knockout. The 280-seat restaurant occupies a dazzling space with half-moon windows overlooking Piccadilly Circus and Regent Street. Despite its size and minimal interior, there is an intimate feel, largely achieved by the blue banquette seating that ebbs and flows throughout the room. A piano player in the evening adds just the right touch of romance to it all.

The international menu is innovative and seasonally inspired. The only difficult thing about it is trying to decide what to order. The selections change frequently, but if the *cèpe* (mushroom) and white truffle oil *velouté* (white cream sauce) with scallops and a chestnut confit is available, please consider this special winter starter. Another winner in the spring is the simply grilled asparagus topped with a soft-boiled egg sauce and fresh Parmesan. For the main course, the poached Dover sole served with sautéed potatoes or the braised lobster served with gnocchi, artichokes, and baby leeks will appeal to many. The rabbit leg braised in coconut milk and served with a crisp lemon noodle cake allows diners to branch out to an East/West treatment of this reliable favorite. Italian squab, rare-grilled tuna, lobster tortellini in a summer truffle broth, roast duck breast with a beetroot and rhubarb marmalade . . . you can quickly see what I mean by imaginative and unusual.

For dessert, I love the steamed ginger pudding with a rich custard sauce or the chocolate fondant with Grand Marnier ice cream. If these seem too formidable, then try either an assortment of ice creams, especially the mascarpone (Italian cream cheese) and basil with prune sauce, or a selection of sorbets for just the right light finish. Throughout the meal, the service is exceptional. The bargains at L'Odéon are hard to beat for the set-price lunch and pre-theater dinner, both of which are served until 7 P.M.

MALAYSIAN DINING HALL (15)
44 Bryanston Square (in the basement), Marylebone, W1

When was the last time you had rice slowly simmered in coconut milk and topped with anchovies and chili peppers for breakfast? Or how about fish head curry, *mee bandung* (spicy soup with noodles), or fried *kway teow* (a mix of seafood, eggs, and noodles)? All this plus a daily vegetarian dish, a fish plate, and one or two curries (registering mild, medium, and searing) are yours for the taking at the Malaysian Dining Hall, a little-known student canteen subsidized and overseen by the Malaysian government. Open for breakfast, lunch, and dinner every day except Christmas and two Muslim holidays, this haven for Malaysians far from home serves some of the most authentic Malay and Indonesian food in London. If you ordered everything in sight, you still would have trouble spending more than £5. The menu changes daily, the standards are high, the food is fresh, and the cafeteria—filled with students, elegant diplomats, extended families, and Cheap Eaters in the know—has a friendly, yet well-worn, atmosphere. For an unusual and mighty inexpensive dining experience, this one is hard to top.

TELEPHONE
020-7723-9484

TUBE
Marble Arch

OPEN
Daily

CLOSED
Christmas Day, 2 Muslim holidays that vary each year

HOURS
Breakfast 8:30–10:30 A.M., lunch noon–3 P.M., dinner 5–8:30 P.M.

RESERVATIONS
Not accepted

CREDIT CARDS
None

PRICES
À la carte, £3.50–5; set-price, £3

SERVICE
No service charged or expected

MISCELLANEOUS
Nonsmoking section, no alcohol allowed, unlicensed

MARINO'S RESTAURANT AND SANDWICH BAR (18)
31 Rathbone Place, Bloomsbury, W1

I would use the term "restaurant" in Marino's case rather loosely. This sandwich pit stop looks like almost every other quickie takeaway shop in London: The front counter is manned by two or three fast-working sandwich makers and in the back are a few tables on which

TELEPHONE
020-7636-8965

TUBE
Tottenham Court Road

OPEN
Mon–Sat

CLOSED
Sun, holidays

HOURS
Mon–Fri 7 A.M.–7 P.M., Sat
7 A.M.–4 P.M., continuous service

RESERVATIONS
Not accepted

CREDIT CARDS
None

PRICES
À la carte, £5–8

SERVICE
No service charged or expected

MISCELLANEOUS
Takeaway available

blue-plate specials fill the nutritionally naive during lunch. Cappuccino and cake eaters hang out here later in the afternoon, early birds tuck into a full English breakfast in the morning. The difference at Marino's is not necessarily the sandwich fillings themselves, which are good, but the bread they are on. Warm, crusty freshly baked baguettes hold tuna, bacon, turkey, egg salad, and more, lifting otherwise ordinary sandwiches way out of the doldrums. I was told they sell over five hundred sandwiches daily. Keep it up, Marino, you have a good thing going.

MELATI (49)
31 Peter Street, W1

TELEPHONE
020-7437-2011, 020-7734-1996

TUBE
Piccadilly Circus

OPEN
Mon–Sat

CLOSED
Sun, Christmas Day

HOURS
Lunch noon–2:45 P.M., dinner 6–11:30 P.M.

RESERVATIONS
Advised on weekends

CREDIT CARDS
MC, V

PRICES
À la carte, £12–17; set-price, lunch only: one noodle or rice plate, or fresh Chinese greens £5.50–6.50; lunch and dinner, 2-person minimum, £16.50, 8 courses served and coffee, £13.50 vegetarian

SERVICE
Service discretionary, 10 percent service charge for 5 or more

MISCELLANEOUS
Takeaway available

The delicious food served at Melati has been inspired by the Chinese, Indians, and Dutch who settled in Indonesia, Singapore, and along the Malay Peninsula. These dishes will provide unusual, exciting eating for those willing to experiment; and bear in mind that most hot dishes can be tailored to individual tastes. The menu is long and the choices could quickly bewilder the novice. When in doubt, ask your waiter to help you put together a typical meal. Do consider the lemon chicken, the *tahu telor* (a bean curd omelette with gravy), or the deep-fried garlic chicken with chili—an absolute must-have for any garlic lover. Beef, fish, seafood, and vegetables all figure prominently on the menu. For dessert there is a pancake stuffed with coconut and surrounded by coconut milk, *rambutans* (Malaysian fruits similar to litchi), or a banana fritter dusted with sugar. Having lived in the Far East, I have sampled many a meal there, and I can say that the food at Melati is as good as anything I had in Kuala Lumpur or Jakarta.

MILDRED'S (40)
58 Greek Street, Soho, W1

If you don't already believe it, a meal at Mildred's will convince you that well-conceived vegetarian food is a dining experience to savor and repeat. The owners, Jane Muir and Diane Thomas, became friends while working together in various restaurants in London. During that time they decided that they could run a better restaurant. The result is Mildred's, where the usually friendly service can get harried during the lunch rush, and seating on the hard seats can be slightly uncomfortable. I also wish the waitstaff would wear more than a tank top, which allows a full display of their tattoos and body piercing. Those quibbles aside, the nourishing, daily-changing menu offers a variety of vegetarian and vegan specials, soups, salads, casseroles, and homemade desserts. The portions are enormous and basically guilt-free, unless you succumb to the white chocolate and poached pear bread and butter pudding, or a slice of *banoffee* (banana and toffee) pie.

TELEPHONE
020-7494-1634

TUBE
Tottenham Court Road

OPEN
Daily

CLOSED
Holidays

HOURS
Mon–Sat noon–11 P.M., Sun noon–5 P.M., continuous service

RESERVATIONS
Not accepted

CREDIT CARDS
None

PRICES
À la carte, £6–10

SERVICE
Service discretionary, 10 percent service charge for 6 or more

MISCELLANEOUS
Takeaway available, no smoking allowed

NEW PICCADILLY CAFE RESTAURANT (61)
8 Denman Street, Piccadilly Circus, W1

As you walk down short Denman Street only a block from Piccadilly Circus, you can't possibly miss this budget diner's dream: It is the only one with the big red neon sign flashing the word "EATS" in the front window. There is nothing even remotely interesting about the restaurant's interior. In places the floors are worn through to the bare boards, and the aging booths with their yellow Formica tables have obviously held many a hungry soul. There is a wall lined with postcards sent by longtime customers to owner Lorenzo Marioni and his sister Rosita, who has held court at the cash register since her father opened the restaurant in 1951. In the evening, Dina, the other sister, is in charge. Service by waiters wearing starched white jackets can be good or downright rude. If you get one with a flippant attitude, complain to one of the bosses, since they want to know which waiters need a crash course at Dale Carnegie. Despite this service drawback, do not pass up this oasis of economy, which is filled throughout the day with locals, fringe showbiz people, and thrift-minded tourists

TELEPHONE
020-7437-8530

TUBE
Piccadilly Circus

OPEN
Daily

CLOSED
Several days at Christmas, Easter Sunday

HOURS
Noon–9 P.M., continuous service

RESERVATIONS
Not accepted

CREDIT CARDS
None

PRICES
À la carte, £5–9

SERVICE
Service discretionary

MISCELLANEOUS
Takeaway available, BYOB, no corkage fee, unlicensed

who stoke up on the heaping portions of chicken, steak, veal, spinach and ricotta cannelloni, omelettes, salads, and desserts. Definitely try their homemade apple pie with custard sauce.

THE ORIGINAL CARVERY RESTAURANT AT THE CUMBERLAND HOTEL (26)
Marble Arch, W1

TELEPHONE
020-7262-1234

TUBE
Marble Arch

OPEN
Daily

CLOSED
Never

HOURS
Lunch Mon–Sat noon–2:30 P.M., Sun noon–3 P.M.; dinner Mon–Sat 5–10 P.M., Sun 6–10 P.M.

RESERVATIONS
Suggested for Sunday lunch

CREDIT CARDS
AE, DC, MC, V

PRICES
Set-price: lunch £17, Sun lunch, £18, dinner £19, 3 courses, all you can eat

SERVICE
Service discretionary

MISCELLANEOUS
Children under 5 free, children up to 16 half price

"Help yourself" is the motto at all the Carvery restaurants, where traditional English food can be had for a modest financial investment. This is genuine value for the money, especially when you consider that you are encouraged to eat as much as you can. Children under five are free and you pay only half price for those between five and sixteen. Plan to arrive with a giant-size appetite to properly tackle the dazzling buffet tables laden with hors d'oeuvres, salads, and succulent roasts of beef, lamb, pork, turkey, and ham with all the trimmings, along with a wide selection of vegetables and potatoes. Vegetarians are not ignored; there are always two or three hot dishes without meat available. To round it all off, the dessert trolley has fruit, pastries, cakes, trifle, hot puddings, ice cream and sorbets, and a selection of English cheeses. Seconds and thirds are allowed. Carvery restaurants are big and bright in the best hotel-style with large, well-placed tables properly set. Sunday lunch seems to be the busiest time, so book ahead on that day. Also, watch for seasonal promotions, early-bird specials, and two-for-one vouchers.

The first original Carvery opened at the Regent Palace Hotel in 1959, but unfortunately, the space was sold and is now the mega-restaurant Titanic. The Carvery idea was introduced by Mr. Christopher Salmon after a stay in a small farmhouse hotel where guests served themselves. The original Carvery was open from Monday to Saturday for lunch only, and the price of the meal was ten shillings and sixpence. The first menu had a choice of four starters, three roasts, and five desserts. Guests were allowed to carve their own meat, and a chef was on hand to teach them how. A bottle of claret to accompany the meal was an extra twelve shillings. Times and prices have certainly changed.

PAUL ROTHE & SON (17)
35 Marylebone Lane, Bond Street, W1

Paul Rothe & Son specializes in sandwiches—and oh, what sandwiches they are!

For over ninety-seven years, nothing much has changed in this grocery-lined deli within a short walk of the Wallace Collection and shopping on New Bond Street. The Rothe family is on hand every day, making all of the sandwich spreads, roasting the beef, ham, and turkey, and then using the bones for some of the best soup you've ever had from a Styrofoam cup. As you can tell, formality is out, but good lunchtime food is in at this citadel of Cheap Eating, where the queue begins around noon. The homemade potato salad or a side of coleslaw goes well with any sandwich order. Pass on the desserts, unless you like fruitcake or jam tarts. Prepare to take your order to go unless you get a seat at one of their few tables or at one of the three seats at the bar.

TELEPHONE
020-7935-6783

TUBE
Bond Street

OPEN
Mon–Fri, sometimes Sat (call to check)

CLOSED
Most Sat; Sun, holidays

HOURS
8 A.M.–6 P.M., continuous service

RESERVATIONS
Not accepted

CREDIT CARDS
None

PRICES
À la carte, £3–6

SERVICE
No service charged or expected

MISCELLANEOUS
No alcohol allowed, call in orders by 11 A.M. for noon pickup, unlicensed

PESCATORI FISH AND SEAFOOD RISTORANTE (8, $)
57 Charlotte Street, Fitzrovia, W1

Since it first opened in 1961, Pescatori (Italian for fisherman) has been known for the excellence of its cuisine, its friendly Italian welcome, and its impeccable service. Marinated, chargrilled, barbecued, and roasted fish was a culture shock to many British diners when this style of cooking became popular, since it was so different from the usually overcooked, richly sauced British approach to fish. With the gradual emergence of a healthier diet, now termed "the Mediterranean diet," fish is heralded as one of the best foods around, and as a result, fish restaurants such as Pescatori have come into their own.

The menu at Pescatori offers an unusual and delicious range of fresh fish dishes cooked the Italian way. These include regional specialties such as seared swordfish with pesto-grilled radicchio, flash-grilled tuna on a bed of crushed sweet potatoes with artichoke, black olives, a red onion, and tomato salsa, and their famous *Grigliata Mista di Crostacei*—a platter of well-seasoned shellfish grilled with olive oil, garlic, and herbs. Pescatori is also famous for its *cacciucco,* the Italian version of bouillabaisse. Eating *cacciucco* (with five Cs in its name to match

TELEPHONE
020-7580-3289

TUBE
Goodge Street

OPEN
Mon–Fri; Sat dinner only

CLOSED
Sun, Sat lunch, holidays

HOURS
Lunch noon–3 P.M., dinner Mon–Tues 6–11 P.M., Wed–Sat 6–11:30 P.M.

RESERVATIONS
Advised

CREDIT CARDS
AE, DC, MC, V

PRICES
À la carte, £25–35; set-price, lunch, starter and daily special £20, £30 includes a dessert, glass of wine, half-bottle of mineral water, and coffee; spring seafood festival £30, 3 courses, wine and coffee

the standard five types of fish and shellfish in it: scallops, prawns, mussels, clams, and salmon, plus monk fish, red snapper, and whatever else may be in season) is more of a ritual than just sitting down to a plate of food. You need to take your time, use your hands if necessary, and ask for plenty of napkins and finger bowls.

Pescatori features seafood festivals in the spring. These are of special interest to Cheap Eaters in London because the set-price menus include a glass of *prosecco* with *crostini* (croutons), a selection of bread, olive oil, and butter, three courses, and coffee. These are available Monday to Saturday evenings and usually feature a menu based around oysters, shellfish, or lobster depending on the particular festival being held. Please call the restaurant to check on dates and the menu being offered.

It is important to note that non-fish eaters can be assured of a delicious meal at Pescatori. While the selection is admittedly limited, there are always three or four starters, a veal or beef entrée, and a pasta dish.

The restaurant includes three dining areas: a main section, a bar for more casual, light dining, and a private room for parties. The eclectic feel is imparted by a collection of traditional and aquatic antiques, hanging fishnets, a suspended skiff overhead, whitewashed walls, strongly accented colors, natural stonework, and metal art. The overall look is airy and comfortable. Because a meal at Pescatori can be over some people's budgets, it is smart to save this as a Big Splurge dining destination.

NOTE: There are two other locations: one at 11 Dover Street in Mayfair (see below), and one in the heart of theaterland at 66 Haymarket Street, SW1 (see page 156). The same menu is served at all three locations.

PESCATORI FISH AND SEAFOOD RISTORANTE (66, $)
11 Dover Street, W1

See Pescatori Fish and Seafood Ristorante above for full description. All other information is the same.
TELEPHONE: 020-7493-2652
TUBE: Green Park

POLLO (44)
20 Old Compton Street, Soho, W1

Prices are low and portions more than satisfying at Pollo, a Cheap Eat hot spot near Leicester Square in Soho. The specialties of the house are chicken fixed a half dozen ways and the eighty-plus pastas, over forty of which are geared toward vegetarians, and all are priced to sell at under £4. It is a virtual mob scene at lunchtime, with the famished regulars occupying every red Naugahyde seat and booth on both floors. Service can get rushed and pushy if you linger at all. Aside from the chicken and pastas, the menu covers all the bases, from meat and fish to omelettes, salads, and even a banana split. There is also a page of daily dishes that deserves careful attention. The only dessert made here is the tiramisu.

TELEPHONE
020-7734-5917

TUBE
Leicester Square

OPEN
Daily

CLOSED
Christmas Day, Easter Sunday

HOURS
Noon–midnight, continuous service

RESERVATIONS
Not accepted

CREDIT CARDS
None

PRICES
À la carte, £4–8

SERVICE
Service discretionary

RAW DEAL (2)
65 York Street (off Baker Street), Marylebone, W1

Cozy, clean, cheap, and above all, good for you! This is the unbeatable combination awaiting you at Raw Deal, a vegetarian restaurant that has thrived in this location for more than a quarter century. Every day, bountiful salads, unusual soups, hot and savory main dishes, and seasonal specials are dished out to the health-conscious regulars who are served cafeteria-style for lunch and waited on in the evening. Desserts that tempt even the most rigorous dieter include fruit crumbles and several great cakes—carrot, coffee, pecan, chocolate, and apple. I like to arrive just ahead of the lunch rush, order a half portion of the daily special main course, which comes with a selection of two or three salads, and then splurge on a dessert.

The light green interior walls combine with lush hanging plants and big picture windows to create an open and welcoming atmosphere. In the evening, candles add a nice touch, and on sunny days, two tables on the sidewalk offer ringside seats for the passing parade.

TELEPHONE
020-7262-4841

TUBE
Baker Street

OPEN
Mon–Sat

CLOSED
Sun, holidays

HOURS
8 A.M.–10 P.M., continuous service

RESERVATIONS
Suggested for lunch

CREDIT CARDS
None

PRICES
À la carte, £7–12; set-price, lunch £10, 2 courses and coffee; minimum charge at peak times: £2

SERVICE
Service discretionary, 10 percent service charge for 5 or more

MISCELLANEOUS
No smoking allowed

SOFRA BISTRO–MAYFAIR (70)
18 Shepherd Market, Mayfair, W1

TELEPHONE
020-7493-3320, 020-7499-0399

TUBE
Green Park

OPEN
Daily

CLOSED
Never

HOURS
Noon–midnight, continuous service

RESERVATIONS
Suggested for lunch

CREDIT CARDS
AE, DC, MC, V

PRICES
À la carte, £20–25; set-price lunch or dinner, £9, 2 courses, £11, 3 courses; lunch 11-dish hot and cold *mezes* for 2 people, £9 per person, dinner £10 per person

SERVICE
£1.50 cover charge, 12½ percent service charge

MISCELLANEOUS
Takeaway available, visit their Web page for their menus at www.sofra.co.uk

For high-quality Turkish food served in stylish, pleasant surroundings, you won't find anything better than the Sofra restaurants, bistros, and cafés dotted around London. Currently there are more than a dozen in operation, with more openings planned every year (see below for other locations in this book). Affable owner Hüseyin Ozer offers continuous service 365 days a year in all locations. His philosophy is simple and to the point: "If you are not entirely happy with your choice, we shall immediately replace it with another dish without hesitation. We guarantee that you will leave your table completely satisfied." Can't beat that.

The original Sofra Bistro is at 18 Shepherd Market in Mayfair. It is a two-story corner location at which you have a choice of thirty starters and almost as many main courses, which are divided into grills, casseroles, and vegetarian items. The Sofra Cafés offer snacks and small meals throughout the day at very reasonable prices. At all the Sofra outlets, bargain set-price lunches, dinners, and hot and cold *mezes* pull in an attractive crowd, eager to sample food. It is easy to see why Sofra was voted the best ethnic restaurant of 1994, and why it continues to be one of London's favorite Cheap Eats when you can dine on such mouthwatering specialties as *midye tava* (fried mussels served with walnut sauce), *hellim* (white sheep and goat cheese served hot from the grill), homemade dolmas (grape leaves stuffed with rice, onions, pine nuts, and herbs), *humuz kavurma* (diced lamb with pine kernels and hummus), or *ispanakli eriste* (homemade pasta with lamb, spinach, and yogurt). The healthiness of the food is another selling point: It's high in fiber, with fresh vegetables, herbs, olive oil, and yogurt, and low in greasy meats and saturated fats.

NOTE: Sofra Restaurants outside of W1 are in Covent Garden (see page 129) and Charing Cross (see page 140). Please consult the London telephone directory for other locations, which are too numerous to list here.

SOFRA CAFÉ (69)
10 Shepherd Market, Mayfair, W1

The Sofra Cafés, offering the most informal dining in the Sofra empire, serve sandwiches, single-dish main courses, *mezes* (assorted appetizers), pastas, pastries, Turkish sweets, and a raft of cold drinks. See Sofra Bistro–Mayfair above for full description. All other information is the same.

TELEPHONE: 020-7495-3434
TUBE: Green Park
OPEN: Daily
CLOSED: Never
HOURS: 8 A.M.–9 P.M., continuous service
RESERVATIONS: Not necessary
CREDIT CARDS: None
PRICES: À la carte, £4–10
SERVICE: Service discretionary
MISCELLANEOUS: Takeaway available

SOFRA CAFÉ (48)
33 Old Compton Street, Soho, W1

See Sofra Café above for full description. All other information is the same.

TELEPHONE: 020-7494-0222
TUBE: Leicester Square, Piccadilly Circus

SOFRA CAFÉ (19)
63 Wigmore Street, Marylebone, W1

See Sofra Café above for full description. All other information is the same.

TELEPHONE: 020-7486-7788
TUBE: Bond Street

SOFRA RESTAURANT–ST. CHRISTOPHER'S PLACE (24)
1 St. Christopher's Place, Oxford Street, W1

See Sofra Bistro–Mayfair, page 58, for full description. All other information is the same.

TELEPHONE: 020-7224-4080
TUBE: Bond Street

SOHO SPICE (46)
124–126 Wardour Street, Soho, W1

TELEPHONE
020-7434-0808
TUBE
Leicester Square, Tottenham
Court Road
OPEN
Daily
CLOSED
Christmas Day
HOURS
Mon–Thur 11:30 A.M.–
12:30 A.M., Fri–Sat till 3 A.M.,
Sun 12:30–10:30 P.M.,
continuous service
RESERVATIONS
Advised for dinner, especially
on weekends
CREDIT CARDS
AE, DC, MC, V
PRICES
À la carte, £18–20; set-price,
lunch daily, 3 courses including
tea or coffee, £9.50; lunch or
dinner monthly regional menu,
3 courses including tea or
coffee, £17
SERVICE
12½ percent service charge
MISCELLANEOUS
Nonsmoking section

Soho Spice is the red-hot, fast, fresh Soho Indian restaurant offering zest, color, and rich taste sensations in bright, cool, relaxing suroundings that you will enjoy. Featuring a Cuisine of the Month menu, the restaurant invites diners to tour the regional menus of the Indian subcontinent. Your dining travels will take you to Kashmir, known as the Switzerland of the East and famous for its flaming-red, yet mild tasting, chilies. Punjab, called the granary of India, is known for its earthy food, while Kerala, the Venice of the East, provides you with hot and spicy cuisine. From the exotic holiday paradise of Goa, the food will also be red-hot, but from the Northwest Frontier, made famous by the Khyber Pass and warrior tribesmen, you will dine on lustrous meat dishes. In addition to the regional menus, Soho Spice offers a set-price three-course lunch with both vegetarian and meat choices.

SOUP OPERA (35)
2 Hanover Street, Mayfair, W1

TELEPHONE
020-7629-0174
TUBE
Oxford Circus
OPEN
Mon–Sat
CLOSED
Sun, holidays
HOURS
Mon–Fri 7:30 A.M.–5 P.M.,
Sat 9 A.M.–5 P.M.
RESERVATIONS
Not accepted
CREDIT CARDS
None
PRICES
£3.50–8
SERVICE
Service discretionary
MISCELLANEOUS
No alcohol allowed, unlicensed

London soup bars have revolutionized on-the-run office lunches, and now represent somewhat of an underground growth industry in parts of the city filled with big office buildings and the workers who toil in them. The Soup Opera in Mayfair is virtuous for its austere simplicity. The antiseptic interior consists of a room wrapped in blond wooden bars with tall silver metal stools meant for precarious perching. Decor consists of a vast array of twigs, and a counter filled with bubbling soup vats kept hot by thermostatic temperature controls. Everyday there are a dozen or more vegetable, meat, and seafood soups served in three sizes: 12 ounce–*peckish,* 16 ounce–*hungry,* and 32 ounce–*ravenous.* Each one is rated to show if it is vegetarian, contains nuts, is gluten or dairy free, low-fat, or spicy. Can't choose between the sweet potato, chickpea and red pepper, vegetable, or the New England clam chowder? Ask for a sample taste . . . then decide. All soups come with a chunk of white, wheat, or ciabatta bread, or a baguette. Drinks consist of coffee, tea, soft drinks, and fruit smoothies.

SOUP WORKS (34)
9 D'Arblay Street, Soho, W1

In London, soup bars are the hottest craze for voguettes who have abandoned sandwiches as their midday refueling choice. SOUP Works features interesting and flavor-packed liquid meals with a menu that changes daily. The queue is out the door by noon for the multibean with roasted garlic soup, the Toulouse sausage and bean cassoulet, the English root vegetable soup, and the cream of shiitake mushroom soup. Every soup comes in four sizes and lists its vegetarian, fat, nut, gluten, and dairy particulars. Soup toppings are available, as are specialty breads, assorted desserts, and *froups*—otherwise known as smoothies. Arrive between 8 and 11:30 A.M. during the week and all day on the weekends and order their breakfast special: porridge with a choice of toppings that includes white and dark chocolate shavings, Greek yogurt, maple or golden syrup, and fruit compote.

TELEPHONE
020-7439-7687

TUBE
Oxford Circus

OPEN
Daily

CLOSED
Holidays

HOURS
Mon–Fri 8 A.M.–8 P.M., Sat–Sun 10 A.M.–6 P.M.

RESERVATIONS
Not accepted

CREDIT CARDS
None

PRICES
À la carte, £1.75–9; breakfast porridge special £2.50 includes coffee

SERVICE
Service discretionary

MISCELLANEOUS
No alcohol allowed, unlicensed

THE STAR CAFÉ (33)
22 Great Chapel Street, Soho, W1

The Star has been on the same site and under the same family ownership for more than sixty-five years. The owners pride themselves on having the oldest café in Soho. The food served is designed to inspire confidence in these hard economic times, and offers a concise, no-nonsense menu that is a varied catalog of pasta, meat, and fish dishes, omelettes, made-to-order sandwiches, and an all-day breakfast. In the summer, a salad bar is added. Aside from the daily specials, I think the sandwiches are the real stars. The selection seems endless, starting with a simple peanut butter and jelly or Marmite, to steak and sautéed onions, and a triple-decker layered with hot smoked bacon, roasted chicken, avocado, tomatoes, fresh basil, and lettuce and pesto dressing, all piled on bagels, freshly baked baguettes, or toasted ciabatta bread. The area is full of film and photo labs, and the employees from these offices make up the backbone of the clientele. The best seating is action central on the main floor, which contains tables covered

TELEPHONE
020-7437-8778

TUBE
Tottenham Court Road, Oxford Circus

OPEN
Mon–Fri

CLOSED
Sat–Sun, holidays

HOURS
Breakfast 7 A.M.–noon, lunch noon–4 P.M., afternoon snacks 4–6 P.M.

RESERVATIONS
Suggested for 2 or more at lunch

CREDIT CARDS
None

PRICES
À la carte, £4–7.50

SERVICE
Service discretionary

MISCELLANEOUS
Takeaway available

with red-and-white-checked oilcloths. Here you can also enjoy the impressive collection of pre–World War II enamel advertising signs that cover the walls. Service is swift, the food is reliable, and the prices are well within a Cheap Eater's budget.

STOCKPOT–SOHO (43)
18 Old Compton Street, Soho, W1

TELEPHONE
020-7287-1066
TUBE
Leicester Square, Tottenham Court Road
OPEN
Daily
CLOSED
Christmas Day
HOURS
Mon–Tues 11:30 A.M.–11:30 P.M., Wed–Sat 11:30 A.M.–11:45 P.M., Sun noon–11 P.M., continuous service
RESERVATIONS
Not accepted
CREDIT CARDS
None (no traveler's checks either)
PRICES
À la carte, £5–8; set-price, £4, slightly more on weekends
SERVICE
Service discretionary

There are several Stockpots in London, and each is individually managed. But all the locations operate on the same theory—volume. Stockpot diners fill up on lumberjack portions of international and British standards in areas of the West End and Chelsea where getting even a snack for under £15 can be a challenge. The Basil Street location (page 180) around the corner from Harrods in Knightsbridge is a welcome relief for shoppers who have spent a bundle at the famed department store. The Panton Street (page 158) and James Street restaurants (see below) are Cheap Eats near the theater district, and the King's Road site (page 179) offers respite from the many fast-food bars and cafés that infest this popular cruising ground in Chelsea.

The interiors of all the Stockpots are bare and somewhat harsh, with only green plants accenting the pine tables and hardwood chairs. The staff seem jolly and efficient, even when put to the test with a full house and a queue waiting to be seated. Daily mimeographed handwritten menus offer something for everyone, from pastas, dishes of the day, fish (mostly fried), omelettes, and salads to desserts with calories but little imagination. The best advice I can give is to stick with the daily specials or anything that must be cooked to order and served immediately. Stay away from any dish that sounds complicated, odd (such as Mexican stew), or seems clearly beyond the scope of the place. Please note that every Cheap Eater in London knows about the Stockpot's food bargains, so expect a wait and don't plan to linger over coffee if there is a crowd.

STOCKPOT–JAMES STREET (25)
50 James Street, W1

See Stockpot–Soho above for full description.
TELEPHONE: 020-7486-9185
TUBE: Bond Street
OPEN: Daily
CLOSED: Christmas Day

HOURS: Breakfast 7–11 A.M., lunch 11 A.M.–5 P.M., dinner 5–10 P.M.

RESERVATIONS: Not necessary

CREDIT CARDS: None

PRICES: Breakfast £2–3.25, lunch £4–6.50, dinner £5–7

SERVICE: 10 percent service charge

MISCELLANEOUS: Nonsmoking section

TOOTSIES (23)
35 James Street, W1

This is the newest in the Tootsies chain of restaurants that offer honest, good value meals geared toward families on a budget. They are all-purpose family Cheap Eats with three locations in London (see also pages 107 and 201) and several outside the city, serving the type of predictable food that welcomes ketchup. Their main claim to fame is their hamburger, which comes three ways: single, double, or vegetarian. It is served with lettuce, tomato, mayonnaise, french fries, and a dill pickle. For a few pence more you can dress it up with cheddar cheese, baked beans, a fried free-range egg, mesquite barbecue sauce, Mexican hot sauce, mushrooms, blue cheese sauce, or guacamole. Hearty breakfasts are served and include a glass of fresh orange juice and two cups of tea or coffee to go with your sausages and eggs or waffles, which are served with maple syrup and bacon. There are also salads, sandwiches, milk shakes, and desserts, of which the dark and deadly sticky chocolate pudding cake is my favorite. Children under ten have their own "Tots at Tootsies" menu, which they can color at the table with the crayons supplied.

TELEPHONE
020-7486-1611

TUBE
Bond Street

OPEN
Daily

CLOSED
Christmas Day, New Year's Eve

HOURS
Mon–Thur 11 A.M.–11 P.M., Fri–Sat 10 A.M.–11:30 P.M., Sun 10 A.M.–11 P.M., continuous service

RESERVATIONS
Not necessary

CREDIT CARDS
MC, V

PRICES
À la carte, £8–14

SERVICE
12½ percent service charge

MISCELLANEOUS
Nonsmoking section unavailable in this Tootsies

TOPO GIGIO (53)
46 Brewer Street, Soho, W1

I found Topo Gigio because I did not have any other choice. So many visitors to London had told me about it that—despite my impression that it was too touristy and I wouldn't like it—I finally gave in and had dinner here . . . and was happily surprised. Everyone was right— this is a good, family-owned, family-run Soho restaurant with modestly priced food. And it's not touristy.

Giuseppe and his older brother Maurizio are continuing the gracious traditions started by their father, who opened the restaurant almost forty years ago. The waiters in red vests and black pants are attentive without

TELEPHONE
020-7734-5931, 020-7437-8516

TUBE
Piccadilly Circus

OPEN
Mon–Sat

CLOSED
Sun, Christmas Day

HOURS
Noon–11:15 P.M., continuous service

RESERVATIONS
Suggested, especially for
pre-theater dining
CREDIT CARDS
AE, DC, MC, V
PRICES
À la carte, £20–25
SERVICE
10 percent service charge

being condescending, and service is brisk without feeling rushed. The tables, covered in bright red cloths, are turned several times an evening. The busiest times are just before the theater and just after the last curtain call. You will find a mixture of visitors and regulars, most of whom are served their favorite Italian dishes without ever consulting the menu. Management frowns on ordering just pasta and encourages you to ask questions if you don't see what you want on the menu. If the ingredients are in the kitchen, the chef will make the dish. The portions are modest, so you can safely have several courses plus dessert and not feel too full. When ordering, consult the long list of their specialties, and for dessert, try the *tartufo,* which is a scoop of creamy ice cream bathed in a dark chocolate coating.

UNION CAFÉ (21)
96 Marylebone Lane (north of Oxford Street), W1

TELEPHONE
020-7486-4860
TUBE
Bond Street
OPEN
Mon–Sat
CLOSED
Sun, holidays
HOURS
Lunch Mon–Fri noon–
2:30 P.M., Sat brunch 11 A.M.–
4 P.M.; dinner 6:30–10:30 P.M.
RESERVATIONS
Strongly advised
CREDIT CARDS
AE, MC, V
PRICES
À la carte, £20–30, minimum
charge at peak times: £12.50;
Sat brunch £6–15, no
minimum charge
SERVICE
12½ percent service charge

The minimalistically modern Union Café occupies a bright corner location a short stroll from the Oxford Street shopping jungle. Inside, plain white walls, open piping, big windows, and well-spaced tables on hardwood floors set the dining stage for the smart clientele, especially those coming from the nearby BBC offices during the lunch hour. The menu changes every Wednesday and remains the same for both lunch and dinner. The chef has a talent for intelligently preparing and presenting the freshest seasonal ingredients in portions that are just right. In the winter, a good starter is the soothing roasted tomato soup or warm goat cheese served on homemade walnut bread with roasted pears dressing the side. If you are in the mood for fish, try the smoked salmon with potato blini topped with crème fraîche or the seared cod with a side of spinach mash and creamed leeks. There is always a daily vegetarian pizza and a pasta, perhaps dressed with sun-dried tomatoes and wild mushrooms. Meat eaters need not worry with the chargrilled liver and bacon served with a side of roasted carrots, onions and new potatoes, or a roasted guinea fowl garnished with butternut squash and spicy cabbage. For dessert, the fresh fruit platter should placate dieters. Otherwise, the duo of dark and white chocolate mousses with chocolate sauce is my key pick.

VASCO & PIERO'S PAVILION (36)
15 Poland Street, Soho, W1

You don't have to splurge to eat dinner at Vasco & Piero's Pavilion, a solid Soho Italian choice in which the hospitality is warm and the Italian food is well prepared. It was recommended to me by another restaurant owner in the neighborhood as his favorite Soho Italian—and let me assure you there are scores of them. The family-run restaurant has a long track record . . . more than thirty years on this corner with a devoted following, who not only appreciate the good food value, but the warm, refined atmosphere and great selection of Italian wines. The best starter for both lunch and dinner is the grilled polenta served with fat asparagus spears and Parmesan cheese shavings. If you like calves' liver and it is featured, you won't be sorry you ordered it. The broccoli tortelloni in a buttery sage dressing or the spinach and ricotta pillows in a fresh tomato and basil sauce are only two of the pasta standouts. As for the desserts, I always order the lemon tart for the perfect finish to this special Cheap Eat in London.

TELEPHONE
020-7437-8774

TUBE
Oxford Circus, Tottenham Court Road

OPEN
Mon–Fri; Sat dinner only

CLOSED
Sun, Sat lunch, holidays

HOURS
Lunch noon–2:30 P.M., dinner 6–11 P.M.

RESERVATIONS
Advised

CREDIT CARDS
AE, MC, V

PRICES
À la carte, £20; set-price dinner only, £16.60, 2 courses, £19.50, 3 courses

SERVICE
12½ percent service charge

VECCHIA MILANO (22)
74 Welbeck Street (north of Oxford Street), W1

"What, another pasta place?" moaned my dining companions as we arrived at Vecchia Milano, an old-time Italian restaurant close to the shopping crowds surging along Oxford Street. "Trust me," I said, "this is one you are going to like and want to return to often!" Once our order of *bruschetta* (toasted bread with garlic and olive oil piled high with fresh tomatoes) arrived along with the trio of roasted peppers marinated with fresh anchovies and black olives in a very garlicky dressing, return visits were already being envisioned. Further seduction wasn't needed as we tucked into a warm goat cheese salad surrounded by roasted plum tomatoes and grilled marinated zucchini, followed by the heavenly *panzerotti alla ricotta* (huge pockets of fried ravioli stuffed with ricotta cheese and spinach, set off by a spicy tomato sauce). Next came one of their lighter dishes called *insalata de fegatini e pancetta* (lightly sautéed chicken liver and crisp bacon served on a bed of baby spinach with a balsamic vinaigrette). Main course pastas included the *pennette vegetariane* (a light mixture of zucchini, goat cheese, sun-dried tomatoes, and arugula tossed with

TELEPHONE
020-7935-2371

TUBE
Bond Street

OPEN
Mon–Sat

CLOSED
Sun, holidays

HOURS
Noon–11 P.M., continuous service

RESERVATIONS
Suggested during peak hours

CREDIT CARDS
AE, DC, MC, V

PRICES
À la carte, £16–22

SERVICE
10 percent service charge

olive oil and garlic) and a creamy tortelloni with wild mushrooms.

Certainly the fish and meat dishes do not take a back seat to any of the wonderful pastas, especially not the grilled tuna steak served on wilted radicchio with pesto sauce, or the *scaloppine Siciliana* (slices of veal flavored with fresh orange juice and served in a marsala wine sauce with a dusting of almonds on top). As for desserts, you are on your own here—all we could manage was a glass of sweet wine with a plate of crisp biscotti for dipping.

VERBANELLA RESTAURANT (14)
15–17 Blandford Street, Marylebone, W1

TELEPHONE
020-7935-8896
TUBE
Baker Street, Marble Arch
OPEN
Mon–Sat
CLOSED
Sun, holidays
HOURS
Lunch noon–3 P.M., dinner 6–10:30 P.M.
RESERVATIONS
Advised
CREDIT CARDS
MC, V
PRICES
À la carte, £18–25
SERVICE
12½ percent service charge

Verbanella is not the kind of chic watering hole that bursts on the scene and suddenly fades away when the glitz wears off. This is a two-room, family-owned neighborhood place that has a pleasant, unhurried atmosphere, service that comes with a smile, and a contented clientele who appreciate realistic prices for homespun Italian back-burner food, as well as the chefs' unique preparations of fresh fish. The well-prepared dishes include all of your Italian favorites: eggplant parmigiana, calves' liver with sautéed onions, saltimbocca, and at least six fresh fish renditions. One page of the menu is devoted to pasta, while another is devoted to Italian wines, which are very reasonably priced. Salads are not their strong suit, but I can't say that for their zabaglione—don't miss this, please!

VILLANDRY DINING ROOM (4)
170 Great Portland Street (corner of Weymouth Street), Marylebone, W1

TELEPHONE
020-7631-3131
TUBE
Great Portland Street
OPEN
Daily
CLOSED
Some holidays (call to check)
HOURS
Breakfast 8:30–11 A.M., lunch noon–3 P.M., tea 4–6 P.M., dinner 7–10 P.M.
RESERVATIONS
Essential

The Villandry Dining Room moved from its quirky, cramped location on High Street and now occupies a huge one-block-deep space in the northern tip of Marylebone, not too far from the beginning of Regent's Park. Frankly, I think a great deal of the restaurant's charm and appeal have been lost in the transition. Before, this French *épicerie*/deli/takeaway/bistro served dinner only two nights a month, and reservations for these eagerly awaited dining events were essential as far in advance as possible. Because it was primarily a grocery store selling French cheeses, pâtés, fruit tarts, bread, and some fresh produce, the dinner seating, which filled the front and back rooms, was makeshift at best. You were definitely crammed in at tables positioned with jigsaw-style precision to allow as many places to be set as is humanly possible. The close proximity allowed you to literally rub elbows with your neighbors, a well-heeled group clad in designer dresses and Savile Row suits that you wound up acquainted with by the end of the evening. Now the intimacy has given way to a barnlike space divided into a very expensive grocery, deli, meat, and produce section, and beyond it, a cavernous dining hall manned by a serious staff clad in black.

But the food, which covers the bases from breakfast through dinner, is hard to fault. The chefs continue to be inspired by seasonal products, and the creations are always memorable and seldom repeated. The menu clearly reminds guests that food made to order takes time to prepare, so plan accordingly. I don't know if that is an excuse for slow service or a ploy to get you to drink more wine between courses, but I can say that the food is worth the wait on most occasions. One of the best times to experience the new Villandry is on Saturday or Sunday for brunch, when many regulars combine it with a shopping trip to the market. You can begin with a glass of fresh grapefruit juice, or, if something more potent is in order, a bracing Bloody Mary. You can have butter-milk pancakes or a full English breakfast, but why not order the tortilla with black beans, peppers, and onions topped with a fried egg and accompanied by a salad? I also love the wild mushrooms, gently sautéed and served on toast, or you can try sharing a plate of charcuterie and assorted cheeses. For dessert skip the kiwi sorbet and head right for the rich chocolate cake with crème fraîche to ladle on, or the daily fruit tart. Lunch and dinner are more serious affairs, yet always imaginative. All main courses are nicely garnished and baskets of homemade breads are replenished throughout the meal. I loved the crisp broccoli artichoke and red onion salad with ginger dressing and a bit of garlic as a prelude to my grilled leg of lamb, which is served with cannelloni beans and a red wine sauce. Forget trying to count the calories in any of the desserts. If you didn't have the moist chocolate cake for brunch . . . here is your second chance. Otherwise, it is a toss-up between the apricot and almond tart or the cheesecake topped with fruit compote.

CREDIT CARDS
AE, MC, V

PRICES
À la carte, breakfast £10–20, lunch and dinner £20–28

SERVICE
12½ percent service charge

MISCELLANEOUS
No smoking allowed

WAGAMAMA (50)
12–26 Lexington Street, Soho, W1

TELEPHONE
020-7292-0990

TUBE
Piccadilly Circus

OPEN
Daily

CLOSED
Christmas Day through New Year's Day

HOURS
Mon–Sat noon–11 P.M., Sun 12:20–10:30 P.M., continuous service

RESERVATIONS
Not accepted

CREDIT CARDS
MC, V

PRICES
À la carte, £6–10

SERVICE
Service discretionary

MISCELLANEOUS
No smoking allowed

Welcome to Wagamama, where the philosophy is "positive eating, positive living." What is Wagamama? It's a Japanese noodle bar based on the *ramen* shops that have been popular in Japan for two hundred years. Ramen are Chinese-style thread noodles served in soups with various toppings, and they can't be eaten without slurping noises. It is said that the extra oxygen the slurping creates adds to the taste of the dish. Wagamama also specializes in fat white noodles called *udon,* and in addition, it offers a few rice dishes for those who aren't interested in noodles. Reservations are not taken, and dining is at long communal tables in a basement dining room with all the charm of a high school gym. Despite the spartan surroundings, the atmosphere is lively, especially at peak lunch and dinner hours, when the hordes queue to get in. The menu contains thorough explanations of each dish and reminds diners that quality is the first priority at Wagamama. The menu boasts that fresh noodles and produce are delivered daily and that "everyone concerned with Wagamama is actively involved in suggesting and implementing small improvements to the operation." The friendly waitstaff punch your order into handheld electronic keypads, which send it via radio signal to the appropriate station in the kitchen. When each dish is cooked, it is served immediately, meaning that individual dishes are delivered at different times to a group of diners. If your server has a red letter "L" on his or her badge, this means he or she is a new recruit in training, and the management asks, "Please be gentle with this person."

For most people, one bowl of noodles is enough with a side order of *gyoza*—the typical accompaniment to ramen—which are grilled dumplings containing a mix of cabbage, carrots, water chestnuts, and garlic, with a chili and garlic sauce on the side for an extra kick. The final plus for eating a nutritious, healthy meal at Wagamama is that they enforce a strict nonsmoking policy in both restaurants. And dishes can be prepared without MSG on request.

Cheap Eaters at the Lexington Street Wagamama arrive in a linear space from which they can view the kitchen before going into the basement restaurant, where dessert, juice, and drinks line the perimeter of the room.

This is the second Wagamama, and it opened in December 1995 and seats 176 people. It offers a range of yakitori and tempura dishes in addition to Wagamama's soup noodles and pan-fried noodles. A wider selection of their special merchandise is for sale here, too, including ramen bowls and ladles.

NOTE: There are currently three Wagamamas in central London (see also page 117), and another one planned for Kensington High Street (W8).

WAGAMAMA (20)
1010 Wigmore Street, Marylebone, W1

See Wagamama above for full description. All other information is the same.

TELEPHONE: 020-7409-0111
TUBE: Bond Street

YO! SUSHI (30)
52 Poland Street, Soho, W1

YO! Sushi is considered the coolest and grooviest sushi restaurant in London. It is also one of the most unusual, especially for Cheap Eaters who want to sit at an open counter, watch the food selections go by on a conveyor belt, and be served drinks by a self-propelled talking robot. What you see is what you get and at the end of your meal, a server will count your color-coded plates and drinks and hand you the bill. The futuristic surroundings are unbeatable, but what about the food? YO! Sushi only seems to prove that raw fish and seaweed have never been so fashionable. I think the food is marginal at best and downright terrible too much of the time. However, for a peek into what the dining future may hold, stop by and decide for yourself.

TELEPHONE
020-7287-0443

TUBE
Oxford Circus

OPEN
Daily

CLOSED
Christmas Day

HOURS
Noon–midnight, continuous service

RESERVATIONS
Not necessary

CREDIT CARDS
AE, DC, MC, V

PRICES
À la carte, £5–16

SERVICE
YO! Sushi states, "If you appreciate the service, then you can leave a tip, which is shared between all kitchen and floor staff."

MISCELLANEOUS
The YO! Sushi boutique sells T-shirts, hats, watches, sushi plates, YO!-yos, and sushi aprons.

YO! SUSHI (27)
Selfridges Food Hall, 400 Oxford Street, W1

See YO! Sushi above for full description. All other information is the same.

TELEPHONE: 020-7629-1234

TUBE: Bond Street

HOURS: Mon–Sat 10 A.M.–7 P.M., Sun noon–6 P.M.

YOUNG CHENG (54)
76 Shaftesbury Avenue, Soho, W1

TELEPHONE
020-7437-0237

TUBE
Leicester Square

OPEN
Daily

CLOSED
Christmas Day

HOURS
Noon–11:45 P.M., continuous service

RESERVATIONS
Not necessary

CREDIT CARDS
AE, MC, V

PRICES
À la carte, £6–15; set-price, £8, 3 courses, wine

SERVICE
Service discretionary

For many people, some of the best ethnic food in London is Chinese. For all of us, it is one of the Cheapest Eats we will find. At Young Cheng's storefront restaurant on Shaftesbury Avenue in the West End theater district, a crowd of mainly Chinese diners turns up from noon until almost midnight. The chef stands in a tiny corner kitchen in the front window, chopping, boiling, and stir-frying as fast as he can. If he runs out of any ingredients, he dashes two doors down to the Chinese greengrocer and grabs what he needs. Not every dish works, but if you stay with their specialties—baked spareribs, barbecued meats, and tofu dishes—you will have a pleasant, satisfying meal. Bear in mind that all lunches come with rice or noodles, thus keeping your Cheap Eats tab even lower.

The second location on Lisle Street (see page 142) is larger and a little tonier, but definitely not as authentic or full of interesting regulars as the Shaftesbury site. The abrupt service matches the atmosphere. The food, however, is just as good and the three-course set-price menus for around £12–15 per person offer good value. As with most Chinese restaurants, don't be overwhelmed by the compendium-style menu; usually the kitchen can do whatever you want, as long as they have the fixings.

Pubs

ARGYLL ARMS (29)
18 Argyll Street, Westminster, W1

Before the pub was built here in 1860, 18 Argyll Street was the home of the duke of Argyll. A gold sign stating, "In 1832 on this spot nothing happened," humorously reminds patrons that not much was going on here until the pub opened. Today the ivy-covered pub stands on a traffic-free pedestrian walkway by the Oxford Circus tube stop, and it's a large, lively example of the Victorian-era drinking house, with its separate bars, lovely acid-etched mirrors, and mahogany woodwork. It is also well known for its association with the theater world; in fact, the Palladium Theatre is just across the street. The pub is busy at lunch and packed in the afternoon, both inside and outside, with customers standing around the beer barrels out front. While hardly an oasis for fine dining, its pub grub is familiar, with the edge going to their hot salt-beef (corned beef) sandwich with mustard and pickles made to order on malted grain bread.

TELEPHONE
020-7734-6117

TUBE
Oxford Circus

OPEN
Daily

CLOSED
Christmas Day

HOURS
Noon–3 P.M.; sandwiches, 11 A.M.–9:30 P.M.

RESERVATIONS
Not accepted

CREDIT CARDS
MC, V

PRICES
À la carte, £4–8

SERVICE
No service charged or expected

MISCELLANEOUS
Nonsmoking section in back

THE GUINEA (58)
30 Bruton Place, Mayfair, W1

Everything about the Guinea pub is exceptional, including the loo, which is nicknamed "The Shrine." I will say no more, just see it for yourself.

Since the early 1400s, there has been a pub on this site. In the early days it catered to the servants and stable hands from the nearby mansions. Today, the pub is run by Carl Smith and his wife, Pauline, who also run the Windmill (see below), and it's one of the most successful in the city thanks to its award-winning food. After one or two meals in a pub you will no doubt agree that the food isn't much to write home about, unless you want to bemoan the fact that it is basically boring, tasteless, and totally uninspired. Not so at the Guinea, where the food is the main draw. In fact, the pub has won the best steak and kidney pie in Britain award three years running. It also nabbed the best pub sandwich award in 1991 and placed second in the same competition in 1992.

If you want one of the limited daily editions of their famed pies, the best plan is to arrive early to get a table.

TELEPHONE
020-7499-1210

TUBE
Green Park

OPEN
Mon–Sat

CLOSED
Sun, holidays

HOURS
Bar: 11 A.M.–11 P.M., lunch only Mon–Fri noon–2:30 P.M.; restaurant: Mon–Sat noon–2 P.M., 6:30–11 P.M.

RESERVATIONS
Accepted in restaurant only

CREDIT CARDS
AE, DC, MC, V

PRICES
Bar: à la carte, £6–9; restaurant: à la carte £15–25; set-price, lunch only, £18, 2 courses, £20, 3 courses

SERVICE
In restaurant only: £1 cover charge for dinner, 12½ percent service charge

Otherwise you will be milling around ten deep outside waiting for your lunch. Not having the pie? Then order the Mirabeau, the 1991 winner of the best sandwich. This creation is a triple-decker on grilled ciabatta bread featuring chargrilled Angus steak, lettuce, tomatoes, tarragon, anchovies, olives, and a dollop of mayonnaise. The 1992 sandwich runner-up award was presented to their Chicken Siciliano: grilled chicken, bacon, cream cheese, fresh parsley, oregano, black olives, and sun-dried tomatoes piled on ciabatta bread.

NOTE: If you wander through the pub's lounge to the formal restaurant, the Guinea Grill, you will be in for a Big Splurge meal in one of London's most exclusive grill rooms.

THE WINDMILL (51)
6–8 Mill Street (off Conduit Street), Mayfair, W1

TELEPHONE
020-7491-8050
TUBE
Oxford Circus
OPEN
Mon–Fri; Sat afternoon only
CLOSED
Sun, Sat dinner, holidays
HOURS
Mon–Fri 11 A.M.–11 P.M., Sat noon–4 P.M.; lunch noon–2:30 P.M., dinner 6–9:30 P.M.
RESERVATIONS
Not accepted
CREDIT CARDS
MC, V
PRICES
À la carte, £6–10
SERVICE
No service charged or expected in the pub, service discretionary in the restaurant
MISCELLANEOUS
Nonsmoking upstairs

The Windmill, a pub managed by Carl and Pauline Smith (who also run the Guinea, see above), is what most visitors to London are hoping to find and never do. As with the Guinea, the food is the main reason to be here. The Windmill serves the same award-winning dishes featuring steak and kidney pie and chargrilled sandwiches. In addition, watch for such British favorites as black pudding with mash, fried cabbage, and bacon; a mixed grill; fat sausages with onion gravy; and liver and bacon. Also, you don't have to belly up to the bar for your meal; you can actually get table service in a non-smoking area downstairs, or sit upstairs in their more formal dining area, where Oriental rugs dot the hardwood floors and interesting prints adorn the walls.

From Monday to Friday between 6 and 9:30 P.M. you can sample their bar snacks and sandwiches downstairs, or order a proper full-course dinner, starting with soups such as broccoli and Stilton, wild mushroom, or bacon. Or begin with a little potato salad, and then try their sausage from the National Sausage Champion Muffs of Bromborough, or their free-range loin of pork served with applesauce and crackling. The curries are another of the chef's specialties, but you are forewarned: they are hot and require *at least* two beers to put out the fire. Most pubs don't bother with desserts, but at the Windmill, you can dig into their Dorset apple cake with hot custard sauce or a scoop of frosty lemon sorbet laced with vodka.

Tearooms/Pâtisseries

AMATO (41)
14 Old Compton Street, Soho, W1

If you are looking for a slice of heaven, go directly to Amato, where everything is baked on the premises in a basement kitchen the size of the restaurant. All the pastry temptations are here and beckoning. All you have to do is look in the magnificent case and try to decide what will keep you off the diet for today. If you want a light bite, Amato will serve you a club sandwich, a two-egg omelette with a choice of fillings, two daily hot dishes, and filled croissants.

TELEPHONE
020-7734-5733

TUBE
Leicester Square, Tottenham Court Road

OPEN
Daily

CLOSED
Christmas Day

HOURS
Mon–Sat 8 A.M.–10 P.M., Sun 10 A.M.–8 P.M.

RESERVATIONS
Not necessary

CREDIT CARDS
AE, MC, V

PRICES
Pastries £1.50, light meals £5–10

SERVICE
Service discretionary

PÂTISSERIE VALERIE (45)
44 Old Compton Street, Soho, W1

The tearooms under the Pâtisserie Valerie umbrella are considered to be the best in London, and after one or two visits, you will see why. The original one in Soho first opened its doors in 1926, when Belgian-born Madam Valerie decided to introduce continental pastries to the English. It was an instant success and remains popular to this day. When the Germans bombed the shop during the war, the management moved around the corner to the present location. The impossibly crowded room, with renditions of Toulouse-Lautrec posters painted on the walls, has shared tables, people standing in the aisles, and rushed waitresses reaching over diners' heads and under their noses. This shop is known for its wedding and birthday cakes.

No matter which location you visit, you will mix in the early morning with a group of regulars sipping cups of coffee and enjoying the warm danishes being brought from the kitchen. During the noon rush, creamy omelettes, salads, club sandwiches, and other light fare are the choices. Everyone knows they must save ample room for the best part: dessert. The fresh fruit tarts, heavenly

TELEPHONE
020-7437-3466

TUBE
Piccadilly Circus, Tottenham Court Road

OPEN
Daily

CLOSED
Christmas Day, Easter Sunday, some holidays (call to check)

HOURS
Mon–Fri 8 A.M.–8 P.M., Sat 8 A.M.–7 P.M., Sun 10 A.M.–6 P.M.

RESERVATIONS
Not necessary

CREDIT CARDS
AE, MC, V

PRICES
À la carte, £3.50–10

SERVICE
Service discretionary

MISCELLANEOUS
Takeaway available for pastries

macaroons, mousse- and whipped cream–filled cakes and éclairs will quickly force you to give up the impulse to be virtuous with your diet. And, don't forget teatime, which is considered a must and worth queuing for.

NOTE: In addition to the two other locations below, see Café Valerie in Covent Garden, page 144, and Pâtisserie Valerie in Knightsbridge, page 183.

PÂTISSERIE VALERIE–SAGNE (9)
105 Marylebone High Street, Marylebone, W1

See Pâtisserie Valerie above for full description. Pâtisserie Valerie at Sagne, Marylebone, has been an elegant tearoom for decades. It was established in 1921 by a famous chocolatier and *pâtissier,* M. Sagne from Verlay, Switzerland. The café is magnificent, with its original mural documented in the book *Discovering London's Period Interiors.* Pâtisserie Valerie took over in 1993, extending the main room but maintaining the glorious thirties atmosphere. All other information is the same.

TELEPHONE: 020-7935-6240
TUBE: Baker Street, Bond Street
OPEN: Daily
CLOSED: Christmas Day, Easter Sunday, some holidays (call to check)
HOURS: Mon–Sat 8 A.M.–7 P.M., Sun 9 A.M.–6 P.M.
CREDIT CARDS: AE, MC, V

PÂTISSERIE VALERIE–REGENT'S PARK (3)
66 Portland Place, Regent's Park, W1

See Pâtisserie Valerie above for full description. Pâtisserie Valerie on Portland Place is on the first floor of the Royal Institute of British Architects (RIBA) building and has a large terrace that is lovely in the summer. All other information is the same.

TELEPHONE: 020-7631-0467
TUBE: Great Portland Street
OPEN: Mon–Sat
CLOSED: Sun, Christmas Day, Easter Sunday, holidays
HOURS: Mon, Wed, Fri–Sat 8 A.M.–7 P.M., Tues, Thur 8 A.M.–9 P.M.
CREDIT CARDS: AE, MC, V

RICHOUX–MAYFAIR (57)
41a South Audley Street, Mayfair, W1

These three rather old-world tearooms have been owned and operated by the same family for thirty years. The detailed menu has something for every taste, every time of day, and every budget. Whether it's breakfast, morning coffee, lunch, afternoon tea, dinner, or late supper—if you are hungry, Richoux will serve you. Richoux occupies key locations across from Harrods in Knightsbridge (see page 184), near Piccadilly Circus (see below), and in the heart of Mayfair near the American Embassy, making them even more attractive for shoppers, cinemagoers, and sightseers who want a dignified place to relax over a full meal or just a simple cup of herbal tea. The restaurants began in 1909 as pâtisseries and candy shops, with the exception of the Piccadilly location, which originally was a Chinese restaurant. If you look, you will still see some of the remnants of this early beginning.

NOTE: The company has expanded with two Richoux Coffee Company pit stops next to the Piccadilly and Kensington branches. I thought these were terrible . . . bad coffee and worse pastries, not to mention the noise and impersonal surroundings.

TELEPHONE
020-7629-5228

TUBE
Bond Street, Green Park

OPEN
Daily

CLOSED
Christmas Day

HOURS
Mon–Fri 8 A.M.–11 P.M.,
Sat 8 A.M.–11:30 P.M.,
Sun 9 A.M.–11 P.M.

RESERVATIONS
Not necessary

CREDIT CARDS
AE, DC, MC, V

PRICES
À la carte, £6–18

SERVICE
Service discretionary

MISCELLANEOUS
Takeaway available, including pastries, candies, and preserves; nonsmoking sections in all restaurants

RICHOUX–PICCADILLY (67)
172 Piccadilly, W1

See Richoux–Mayfair above for full description. All other information is the same.

TELEPHONE: 020-7493-2204
TUBE: Piccadilly Circus, Green Park
OPEN: Daily
CLOSED: Christmas Day
HOURS: Mon–Fri 8 A.M.–11 P.M., Sat 8 A.M.–11:30 P.M., Sun 9 A.M.–11 P.M., afternoon tea 3–6 P.M.

Wine Bars

ANDREW EDMUNDS WINE BAR AND RESTAURANT (38)
46 Lexington Street, Soho, W1

Andrew Edmunds is billed as a wine bar, but if you arrive at mealtime, you are expected to order a meal, not just a glass of wine with an appetizer.

TELEPHONE
020-7437-5708

TUBE
Piccadilly Circus

OPEN
Daily

CLOSED
Christmas Day, Easter Sunday

HOURS
Lunch Mon–Fri 12:30–
2:45 P.M., Sat–Sun 1–3 P.M.;
dinner Mon–Fri 5:30–
10:45 P.M., Sat–Sun 6–
10:30 P.M.

RESERVATIONS
Essential

CREDIT CARDS
AE, MC, V

PRICES
À la carte, £16–22

SERVICE
Service discretionary, but an
optional 12½ percent service
charge for bills over £50

But don't worry—the prices for lunch and dinner are as appealing as the food, and consequently, the place has a following and is usually full. The seasonally changing dishes are prepared with equal amounts of flair and care and with liberal amounts of imagination tossed in for good measure. Depending on the season, you might consider starting with the roasted fennel, artichoke, and bacon salad, the pumpkin and carrot soup with polenta croutons, or the crab cakes and guacamole. Main dishes might be baked chèvre on polenta for the vegetarians and rabbit in cider for others; or Cajun salmon with sweet potatoes and avocado salsa; or roast pheasant with parsnip mash, roasted sweet potatoes, and braised endive. If you want a really sweet ending, go for the chocolate mousse cake or the tiramisu. The varied wine list is reasonably priced and includes specially featured wines of the moment.

All the prints you see hanging in the restaurant are from the owner's print shop next door (open Monday to Friday from 10 A.M. to 6 P.M.), and they can be yours for the right price.

W2

Paddington and Bayswater

Bayswater runs along the northern end of Hyde Park and includes Paddington Station, a major train terminal with connections to the north as well as direct links to Heathrow for nine major airlines. The area is full of Cheap Sleeps and lots of Indian and Pakistani restaurants. Across Bayswater Road is Hyde Park, which joins with Kensington Gardens to form a 634-acre park, the largest in London. Speaker's Corner, on the northeast corner of Hyde Park, is a must. If you have an orange crate and something to say that is not obscene, or you have an urge to breach the peace, then you can do so at Speaker's Corner. The best time to see the real nutcases is on a Sunday around 2 to 3 P.M.

RESTAURANTS in W2

Hafez	**80**
Halepi	**80**
Kahn's	**81**
Kam Tong	**82**
Luscious	**82**
Makhni's Taj	**83**
Mandalay	**83**
New Culture Revolution	**84**
Norrman's Restaurant	**84**
Poons	**85**
Veronica's	**85**
Winton's	**87**

TEAROOMS/PÂTISSERIES

Pâtisserie Française	**88**

W2, W8, W11

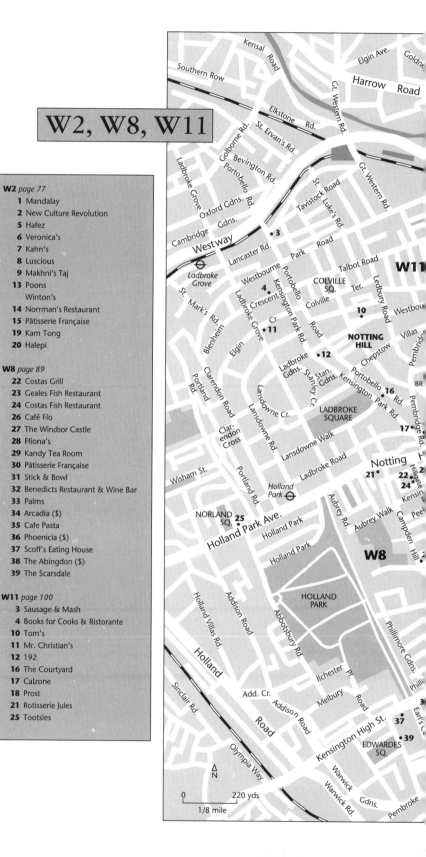

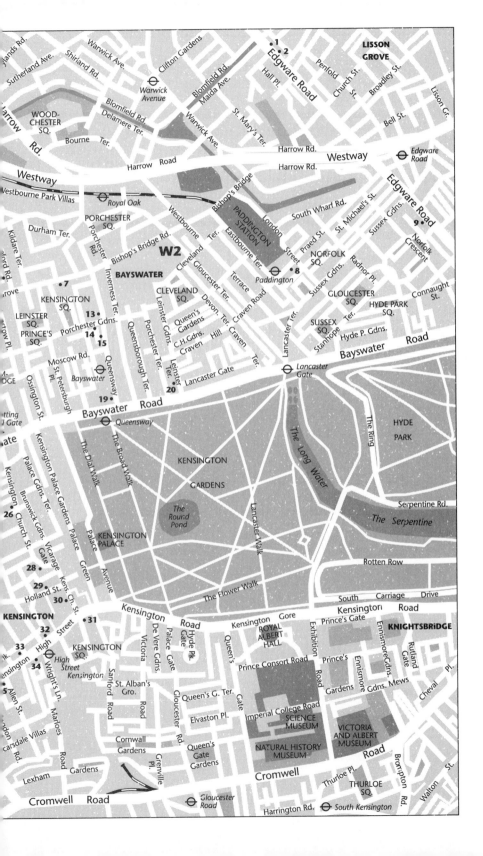

Restaurants

HAFEZ (5)
5 Hereford Road, Westbourne Park, W2

TELEPHONE
020-7229-9398, 020-7221-3167

TUBE
Bayswater, Queensway, Notting Hill Gate

OPEN
Daily

CLOSED
Never

HOURS
Noon–midnight, continuous service

RESERVATIONS
Advised

CREDIT CARDS
None

PRICES
£12–18

SERVICE
10 percent service charge

Fresh food, carefully cooked using quality ingredients and served at a fair price never goes out of style, and certainly not at Hafez—a twenty-year-old standby not too far from Notting Hill Gate. It is a small place, dominated by a mosaic bread oven and a few well-set tables. The bread oven will play an important part in your meal, as you watch the chef roll out the dough, swing it like a pizza, stretch it over an oblong pillow, and toss it onto a stone slab inside the oven, in which it cooks for five minutes and is removed with foot-long tongs and brought piping hot to your table. Careful, don't fill up because there is more to come. If you're sharing plates, order the *mazah* (a selection of five starters), and follow this with the mixed grill of lamb filet, lamb chops, minced lamb, and spring chicken. With the spring chicken you absolutely must have the fluffy, buttery rich saffron rice, which could be an entire meal in itself for many people. Skip the fish . . . it is all frozen.

You might be able to save much room for dessert, because, as the chef told me, "our portions are too big for the English, but just right for Americans." If you do, try their baklava.

HALEPI (20)
18 Leinster Terrace, Bayswater, W2

TELEPHONE
020-7262-1070, 020-7723-4097

TUBE
Bayswater, Queensway, Lancaster Gate

OPEN
Daily

CLOSED
2 days at Christmas

HOURS
Noon–1 A.M., continuous service

RESERVATIONS
Essential for dinner

CREDIT CARDS
AE, DC, MC, V

PRICES
À la carte, £22–28

SERVICE
12½ percent service charge

Halepi is not mentioned in many guidebooks or listed in London dining directories, and that is the way its loyalists want to keep it. Owned and run by the Kazolides family since 1966, Halepi offers typical Greek-Cypriot food in a rustic setting with long rows of closely placed tables covered with bright cloths. Greek bouzouki music plays in the background, and a native crowd arrives for both business lunches or long party evenings. The main difference between Greek mainland cooking and Greek-Cypriot food is that Cyprus has more Middle Eastern influences due to its historic links with Turkey and its proximity to Lebanon, Syria, and Israel. The emphasis is always on meats and grilled food.

If you are starved, or with a group prepared to share several dishes, start with an order of *meze* (assorted appetizers). Otherwise, concentrate on the grilled kebabs of chicken, lamb, or beef, or perhaps one of their specialties. If you like lamb, you are in heaven. Try the *klefticon* (oven-cooked baby lamb seasoned with aromatic spices), the minced lamb and eggplant moussaka layered with béchamel sauce, or the *afelia* (pork filet cooked in wine and spices served with both potatoes and rice). Not to be overlooked are their dolmas (grape leaves stuffed with lamb and rice). For dessert? Naturally you will have their homemade baklava, those melt-in-your-mouth layers of flaky pastry filled with honey and ground nuts. Theirs, made by the owner's mother and touted as the best in London, are so big that one serving will feed two people.

MISCELLANEOUS
Takeaway available

KAHN'S (7)
13–15 Westbourne Grove, Bayswater (west of Queensway), W2

Kahn's still maintains its reputation for cheap, mass-produced Indian food served by a corps of waiters who have been called "diabolically rude" and who answer the criticism with "Well, what do you expect when we are busy? Some guests even come because of us!" The jammed-together seating is uncomfortable, and there are long weekend queues, but despite all this, everyone seems to have a good time in this big, bustling, noisy restaurant, which can seat 350 diners at one time under a cloudlike ceiling mural.

A great deal of food is prepared ahead, which enables lightning service and encourages speed eating. The turnover is fast, so you are not likely to get something that has languished past its prime in a lukewarm pot on the back burner. The astonishingly cheap tandoori chicken is wonderful; so is the house specialty, butter chicken, prepared in a butter, cream, nut, and marsala sauce. Hardy taste buds should consider the chicken *jalfrezi,* a hot curry dish that requires an extra beer to put out the fire. In addition to the chicken dishes, look for those containing lamb, mutton, vegetables, fish, and seafood. You won't find anything on the menu with beef or pork in it. Desserts here are a tough call, with the lemon or orange sorbet being the best of the lot.

TELEPHONE
020-7727-5420

TUBE
Bayswater

OPEN
Daily

CLOSED
Christmas Day

HOURS
Lunch noon–3 P.M., dinner 6–11:45 P.M.

RESERVATIONS
Advised for large parties

CREDIT CARDS
AE, MC, V

PRICES
À la carte, £6.50–12; set-price, under £7

SERVICE
10 percent service charge

MISCELLANEOUS
Takeaway available

KAM TONG (19)
59–63 Queensway, Bayswater, W2

TELEPHONE
020-7229-6065

TUBE
Queensway, Bayswater

OPEN
Daily

CLOSED
Never

HOURS
Noon–11:15 P.M., continuous
service

RESERVATIONS
Suggested for Sun lunch

CREDIT CARDS
AE, minimum charge £10

PRICES
À la carte, £7–18; set-price, 5
meals, £11–22, 2-person
minimum, minimum charge
£7.80

SERVICE
12½ percent service charge

MISCELLANEOUS
Takeaway available

When I first walked by Kam Tong on a wet Sunday around four in the afternoon, the place was packed with local Chinese. This is always a good sign. We aren't talking about a five-stool, mom-and-pop take-out joint, but an auditorium-size restaurant that is perpetually busy from noon until almost midnight. It would be a stretch to call it gourmet or posh, but it is a reliable Cheap Eat in London if you're in the mood for Chinese and want to eat a meal at an odd hour, or at anytime for that matter.

If you have seen one basic Chinese menu, you have probably seen them all. This one is no different. There are 151 dishes, not counting eight more noodle offerings and five set-price meals. You name it and it is here, served with lightning efficiency. For dessert, treat yourself to a scoop or two of Winton's homemade ice cream, located down the street in the Whiteley's Shopping Center.

LUSCIOUS (8)
150 Praed Street, Paddington, W2

TELEPHONE
020-7723-6464

TUBE
Paddington

OPEN
Daily

CLOSED
Holidays

HOURS
Mon–Fri 8 A.M.–7:30 P.M.,
Sat–Sun 9 A.M.–6 P.M.

RESERVATIONS
Not accepted

CREDIT CARDS
None

PRICES
À la carte, £2.50–5.50

SERVICE
Service discretionary

Luscious is London's first café with a mission to help people consume less, simplify their lives, and treasure the things that count. The Luscious experience offers pure indulgence with its all low-fat menu, which promises pleasure without the guilt. The clean, fresh interior has a blue leather sofa and one table with two chairs in the back and a window bar counter with high-backed seats that allow you to watch all the people flocking into the McDonald's across the street. Of course, *those people* are not eating fat-free . . . you are, and you will be surprised at how good your Luscious reduced-fat cakes, muffins, yogurts, soup, salads, and fat-free coffee drinks can be. To help you get started on the road to a healthier, fat-free diet, Luscious offers a series of Low Fat Facts that tell you how many grams of fat a croissant will cost you (sixteen for a large one) and remind you that the Burger King Whopper means forty-two fat grams, which is one more gram than the average woman should consume in an entire day!

MAKHNI'S TAJ (9)
143 Edgware Road, Paddington, W2

Kuldeep Makhni has a resume most chefs can only dream about. He can trace his history back through eight generations of royal chefs from the Moghul Era to the present day. He began his career at fourteen, when he worked with Buddhist monks in Bhutan. From them, he learned patience and the secret of blending spices with natural ingredients to create the best taste and aroma. During his distinguished thirty years of cooking, he has served heads of state (including four American presidents), numerous members of royalty from around the world, Mother Teresa, and a host of Hollywood celebrities. Now he is cooking for those of us lucky enough to find him on Edgware Road. Every person on his staff has been personally trained by Kuldeep to uphold his rigorous standards of food preparation and serving. His menu lists over seventy-five Indian possibilities . . . a daunting choice for anyone to cope with. I recommend discussing your dining choices with him or one of his staff, while keeping an eye on several of his specialty dishes. One of these is the Goa stuffed crab, of which he proudly notes, "If you don't eat this dish in my house, you have not tasted my food." He treats all of his guests like royalty and says that "when you smile after your meal, I know it has been a success." When you dine at Makhni's Taj, there will be many smiles.

TELEPHONE
020-7262-9906

TUBE
Edgware Road

OPEN
Daily

CLOSED
Christmas Day

HOURS
Lunch noon–3 P.M., dinner 6 P.M.–midnight

RESERVATIONS
Suggested

CREDIT CARDS
AE, DC, MC, V

PRICES
À la carte, £15–25

SERVICE
12½ percent service charge

MANDALAY (1)
444 Edgware Road, near Lisson Grove, W2

If you are curious about Burmese food, Dwight Altaf Ally's Mandalay is a Cheap Eat that is worth the schlep from the tube stop. Voted one of London's best Cheap Eats, the restaurant is a family-run affair that feeds a mix of Burmese and smart Cheap Eating locals who arrive with children in tow for the two set-price lunches served Monday through Saturday. For under £4, you will have your choice of chicken, meatball, vegetable, or shrimp and potato curry served with rice and a salad. For less than £7, you will have the same curry choices plus a vegetable spring roll, banana fritters, and tea or coffee. If you decide on the à la carte menu, be sure to try the *calabash*—fritters made from squash strips rolled in a rice-flour batter flavored with turmeric and fresh ginger— or the coconut noodles and chicken, which is a Burmese staple.

TELEPHONE
020-7258-3696

TUBE
Edgware Road, Bakerloo Line

OPEN
Mon–Sat

CLOSED
Sun, holidays

HOURS
Lunch noon–2:30 P.M., dinner 6–10:30 P.M.

RESERVATIONS
Not necessary

CREDIT CARDS
AE, DC, MC, V

PRICES
À la carte, £8–12; set-price lunch £5–7

SERVICE
Service discretionary

MISCELLANEOUS
No smoking allowed

NEW CULTURE REVOLUTION (2)
442 Edgware Road, near Lisson Grove, W2

TELEPHONE
020-7402-4841

TUBE
Edgware Road, Bakerloo Line

OPEN
Daily

CLOSED
Christmas Day

HOURS
Noon–11 P.M.

RESERVATIONS
Not necessary

CREDIT CARDS
MC, V

PRICES
À la carte, £8–15

SERVICE CHARGE
Service discretionary

MISCELLANEOUS
Takeaway available, nonsmoking section

What is this revolution? At the New Culture Revolution it is "serving people's food and breaking away from high cholesterol dishes to give you a healthy and pleasurable experience of good eating." Chinese cooking has always placed an emphasis on the art of balancing the proper combination of ingredients to promote good health, long life, and energy. At the New Culture Revolution, Northern Chinese food is served and reflects a delicate balance of starch, fiber, and protein. Wheat is a staple rather than rice, which does not grow in the region. Thus, there is a wide variety of dumplings and noodles. The menu is typically long, but each section carefully describes what a diner can expect. No MSG is used. Starters are light and appetizing and are chosen to stimulate good digestion and cleanse the palate. Vegetarian crispy dumplings are filled with wood ear mushrooms, glass noodles, Chinese leaves, water chestnuts, and bamboo shoots. Twelve noodle dishes mingle meat or seafood with varied accompaniments. Home-style Northern Chinese dishes combine chilies, garlic, sesame, and other spices with lightly cooked ingredients that retain their natural flavors and qualities. The New Culture Revolution is a victory for you, allowing you to eat well, stay healthy, and still have a great Cheap Eat in London.

NORRMAN'S RESTAURANT (14)
Porchester Gardens (opposite Whiteley's Shopping Center), Bayswater, W2

TELEPHONE
020-7727-0278

TUBE
Bayswater, Queensway

OPEN
Daily

CLOSED
Christmas Day

HOURS
8:30 A.M.–11:30 P.M., continuous service

RESERVATIONS
Not necessary

CREDIT CARDS
None

PRICES
À la carte, £4–9; set-price, £7, full English breakfast £4

SERVICE
Service discretionary

Set in a fifties' time warp that includes the decor, food, and prices, Norrman's is about as real a café experience as you will have in this part of London. As you walk down Porchester Gardens, look for the placard standing outside listing daily specials, go down three steps, and enter the knotty-pine room with fourteen Formica-topped tables surrounded by velvet-covered, black metal chairs. Bridie, who has been at the helm for forty-plus years, sits by the phone booth at the end of the banquettes and greets the old-timers, who arrive for early morning coffee, the daily special, a teatime treat, or breakfast any time of day. Don't look for upscale dishes or sophisticated veal preparations. The menu leans heavily toward battered and fried foods, emphasizing fried liver with bacon, onions, or sausage, fried fish, pork chops, and hamburger steak with fried eggs. Other less health-inhibiting choices are the roast leg of lamb with mint sauce, the roast chicken, or a freshly cut sandwich. All dishes include potatoes and one vegetable and are served in heaping portions.

POONS (3)
205 Whiteley's Shopping Center, 151 Queensway, Bayswater, W2

For the best Chinese food in London, most people go to Chinatown, where no fewer than thirty restaurants lie huddled in a maze of streets just behind Leicester Square. One of the most famous of these is Poons, which has branches in several other parts of the city. The location on Lisle Street in Chinatown is the original. It is still an unpretentious hole-in-the-wall that is a favorite with the old Chinese. On my last few visits I was shocked at the low level of cleanliness and food sanitation, and thus do not recommend it for any Cheap Eater in London. Ditto their second location on Leicester Street. The other Poons—which are not in Chinatown but on Woburn Place (see page 116), in the City (see page 232), and here at Whiteley's Shopping Center—are modern, clean, and worthwhile.

At the City location, the menu goes beyond functional Chinese food, offering many dishes that have never been prepared in the U.S. before. In addition to a serene dining room, there is an eighty-seat fast-food section dedicated to nearby office workers who haven't time for a more leisurely lunch. The location on Woburn Place is large and rather formal, while the one at Whiteley's is open and sleek, just like most mall restaurants in the U.S. Plans are in the works to add a traditional sushi bar along the mall side of the restaurant. The food at all three recommended places is good; the service is typically abrupt; and prices won't kill the budget if you stick to the simple dishes, the set-price meals, or the daily dim sum served Monday to Friday from noon until 4 P.M. and Saturday and Sunday until 4:45 P.M. MSG is omitted on request.

TELEPHONE
020-7792-2884

TUBE
Bayswater, Queensway

OPEN
Daily

CLOSED
3 days at Christmas

HOURS
Noon–11 P.M., continuous service

RESERVATIONS
Suggested for dinner

CREDIT CARDS
AE, DC, MC, V, minimum charge £10

PRICES
À la carte, £12–22; set-price, £16–25, 2-person minimum

SERVICE
12½ percent service charge

MISCELLANEOUS
Takeaway available

VERONICA'S (6)
3 Hereford Road, Westbourne Park, W2

Since the turn of the century, a restaurant has occupied this historic Victorian building at 3 Hereford Road. Noted caterer Veronica Shaw took over in 1982 and began to experiment with English dishes when English

TELEPHONE
020-7229-5079 (24 hours), 020-7221-1452

TUBE
Bayswater, Queensway, Notting Hill Gate

OPEN
Mon–Fri; Sat dinner only
CLOSED
Sun, Sat lunch, holidays
HOURS
Lunch noon–2:30 P.M., dinner
6–11:30 P.M.
RESERVATIONS
Essential
CREDIT CARDS
AE, DC, MC, V
PRICES
À la carte, £20–25; set-price,
Mon–Fri lunch £14, Mon–Thur
dinner £18
SERVICE
10 percent service charge, £1
cover charge if no starter
ordered
MISCELLANEOUS
Catering available

food was far from fashionable. She emphasized a return to her British culinary heritage, introducing regional and historical themes to her food. The result is her award-winning restaurant that definitely proves it is possible to eat well and eat British.

The inside reminds me of a charming country house, with its cozy, warm, flower-filled interior decorated in warm yellow stripes in the front room and a garden setting in back with church pews for seating and candlelight for romance. Local London artists are featured in changing exhibitions and together with the hurricane candles, copper pots, and light classical music, they create an intimate atmosphere. Even the ladies' room is worth a trip to see the newspaper clippings of the many reviews Veronica has received, as well as the unusual light pull.

The menus change three or four times a year and besides offering imaginative interpretations of unusual and classic favorites from early English cooking, such as a recipe for field mushrooms with port and orange from Hannah Wolley's Receipt from the 1650s (a mixture of mushrooms, herbs, and garlic accompanied by fresh orange and drizzled with port and horseradish sauce). The double-roasted duck with thyme, oregano, and parsley combined with sorrel and garlic—or orange and Grand Marnier—has been a favorite of Veronica's guests since she opened. The standbys of steak and kidney pie with oysters, side dishes of raisin and celery mash, cinnamon roast potato, or buttery carrots in dill never fail to bring back pleasant dining memories. Desserts such as Elizabethan Chocolate Cream with almond puffs, served with double cream, rum, and toasted almonds, or warm gingerbread baked with rhubarb and paired with cinnamon ice cream and a port wine sauce, encourage everyone to save a little room at the end of the meal. The menu also touches on the new style of English cooking with filets of sea bass in a parcel with fresh peach dressing. Veronica's presents regional specialties from Dorset, Sussex, and Yorkshire as well as from Scotland, Ireland, and Wales. Holidays may include a Victorian Christmas dinner or a traditional English meal with all the trimmings.

Another constant at Veronica's is the commitment to healthy eating. The fat in the sauces is reduced; honey and brown sugar replace white sugar; salt is kept to a minimum; and fresh herbs and lemon are used as substitutes. Appropriate dishes are marked low-fat, high fiber, and suitable for vegetarians or vegans. Only the freshest and best meats, produce, and cheese are used, and wherever possible, organic products are chosen. Wild produce, gathered by Veronica herself on countryside trips, is used abundantly in the summer, when dishes display the bounty collected and include a profusion of wild mushrooms, elderflowers, blackberries, daisies, and dandelions. There is a small, well-balanced choice of wines. The restaurant also pioneered the inclusion of nonalcoholic wines and beers and has introduced a selection of organically produced wines.

From the start of your meal, when you are offered a complimentary nutty dip with fresh vegetables and a fresh roll, to the finish, when you sip your coffee and nibble on homemade sweetmeats, you will have a wonderful dining experience that you will want to repeat often. I can't wait to go back.

WINTON'S (13)
Whiteley's Shopping Center, 151 Queensway, Bayswater, W2

The ice cream at Winton's defies resistance. Care for some dark, bitter chocolate pudding ice cream? Or perhaps Dime Bar (made with bits of chocolate and caramel pieces), fresh fruit, or lemon mousse? All are natural and have no preservatives (and they don't contain an ounce of butterfat . . . well, maybe just a little). They also do frozen fruit yogurts, shakes, floats, and hot Belgian waffles topped with ice cream and swimming in their homemade hot fudge, butterscotch, or milk chocolate and caramel sauces. Chocoholics' fantasies will come immediately true with the Dark Fantasy: three scoops of chocolate ice cream with dark chocolate fudge sauce topped with whipped cream and sprinkled with dark Belgian chocolate. Whiteley's Dream allows you to create your own sundae with three scoops of any ice cream, covered with fruit, nuts, and whipped cream. Have I convinced you? When you go, please have an extra scoop of Pooh Bear's Delight for me—that's rich vanilla with a honey swirl.

TELEPHONE
020-7229-8489

TUBE
Bayswater, Queensway

OPEN
Daily

CLOSED
Christmas Day

HOURS
Sun–Thur 11 A.M.–10 P.M., Fri–Sat 11 A.M.–11 P.M., continuous service

RESERVATIONS
Not necessary

CREDIT CARDS
None

PRICES
£1.50–5

SERVICE
Service discretionary

MISCELLANEOUS
Takeaway available

Tearooms/Pâtisseries

PÂTISSERIE FRANÇAISE (15)
127 Queensway, Bayswater, W2

TELEPHONE
020-7229-0746

TUBE
Bayswater, Queensway

OPEN
Daily

CLOSED
2 days each at Christmas,
New Year's, Easter

HOURS
Pâtisserie: Mon–Wed 7 A.M.–
7 P.M., Thur–Sat 7 A.M.–8 P.M.,
Sun 7:30 A.M.–7 P.M.;
restaurant: Mon–Wed 8 A.M.–
6:45 P.M., Thur–Sat 8 A.M.–
7:45 P.M., Sun 8 A.M.–6:45 P.M.,
continuous service

RESERVATIONS
Not accepted

CREDIT CARDS
None

PRICES
Pâtisserie: £1.50 and up;
restaurant: à la carte, £3–8

SERVICE
Service discretionary

MISCELLANEOUS
Takeaway available for pastries

At Pierre Péchon's Pâtisserie Française, you will be drawn to the tempting window display of all your favorite French goodies: big, buttery croissants, pain au raisin, pain au chocolate, brioche, glistening fruit tarts, and creamy mousse-filled cakes. Once inside, there is more: everything from apple strudel to scones and a variety of fabulous wholemeal breads. In back is a dining section where you can sit and enjoy one of these bakery treats, or order breakfast from 8 A.M. to 3 P.M. They also serve quiche lorraine, hot soup, salads, a plat du jour, triple-decker sandwiches on their great bread, and savory and sweet crêpes. Given the high quality of the food, which is all made right here and is head and shoulders above almost everything else on this street, it is no wonder it is usually SRO every day from morning to night.

NOTE: There is a second location at 27 Kensington Church Street (see page 99).

W8

Kensington

This is a gracious and sheltered residential area that includes Kensington Palace, where Queen Victoria was born and Princess Diana lived. When visiting the palace you can see the Royal Court Dress collection, which displays clothes worn to regal gatherings from 1750 until today; the State Apartments including the room where Queen Victoria was baptized; and the King's Gallery, which exhibits seventeenth-century paintings. Kensington High Street is regarded as one of London's major shopping areas, and is a magnet for some of the newest, weirdest, and wildest clothing you can buy in London. Kensington Church Street is an important street for the antique collector with big bucks.

RESTAURANTS in W8 (see map page 78)

The Abingdon ($)	90
Arcadia ($)	90
Café Flo	91
Cafe Pasta	92
Costas Fish Restaurant	92
Costas Grill	92
Ffiona's	93
Geales Fish Restaurant	94
Palms	94
Phoenicia ($)	95
Scoff's Eating House	96
Stick & Bowl	96

PUBS

The Scarsdale	97
The Windsor Castle	97

TEAROOMS/PÂTISSERIES

Kandy Tea Room	98
Pâtisserie Française	99

WINE BARS

Benedicts Restaurant & Wine Bar	99

($) indicates a Big Splurge

Restaurants

THE ABINGDON (38, $)
54 Abingdon Road, Kensington, W8

TELEPHONE
020-7937-3339
TUBE
High Street Kensington
OPEN
Daily
CLOSED
Christmas Day
HOURS
Restaurant:
lunch Mon–Sat noon–2:30 P.M.,
Sun noon–3 P.M., dinner Mon–
Sat 6:30–11 P.M., Sun 6:30–
10:30 P.M.; bar:
Mon–Sat noon–3:30 P.M., 5:30–
11 P.M., Sun noon–3 P.M., 6:30–
10:30 P.M.
RESERVATIONS
Advised
CREDIT CARDS
AE, MC, V
PRICES
À la carte, £23–30; set-price,
lunch Mon–Sat, £11, 2 courses;
lunch Sun, £12.50, 2 courses,
£15, 3 courses
SERVICE
12½ percent service charge

The Abingdon is a stylish addition to Kensington. Open seven days a week for lunch and dinner, it offers a small, thoughtful menu of modern French food that's worth the higher prices. The interior has a coolly modern, big city feel with a central bar, sanded pine tables, a line of striped banquettes, and booths in the back. When reserving a table, request a booth. If you are seated along the banquettes in front, or at one of the round tables by the bar, the bar noise will drown out any table conversation you hoped to have.

A nice feature of the Abingdon is that the set-price lunch menus include many of their best dishes. For instance, for Sunday lunch you could start with a salad of mustard-crusted pork medallions on a bed of roasted peppers and rocket (arugula), or a bowl of *moules marinières* (mussels, white wine, garlic, shallots, and parsley). Follow this with the roast leg of lamb—pink, juicy, and very tender. If you are going vegetarian, the pumpkin and spinach tortelloni in a caper and sage butter sauce is delightful and so is the asparagus and goat cheese roulade dressed with a cherry tomato vinaigrette. Dessert treats are the Tunisian orange cake with yogurt or the homey bread and butter pudding with an apricot glaze and vanilla ice cream. For a lighter ending to the meal, try some homemade ice cream—orange, cinnamon, coffee, or passion fruit.

ARCADIA (34, $)
35 Kensington High Street, Kensington, W8

TELEPHONE
020-7937-4294
TUBE
High Street Kensington
OPEN
Mon–Fri; Sat dinner only
CLOSED
Sun, Sat lunch, holidays
HOURS
Lunch noon–2:30 P.M., dinner
6:30–11 P.M.
RESERVATIONS
Advised
CREDIT CARDS
AE, DC, MC, V

The atmosphere is clubby and life is good at Arcadia. You can sit at a table on the entry level, which is lined with old prints from *Le Petit Journal*. From here you will have a bird's-eye view—along with the two fifteen-year-old blue and red parrots, Stanley and Sally, who occupy a corner perch—of the suited businessfolk at lunch and of the coiffed women of a certain age accompanied by men of sympathy who dine in the evening. The downstairs is romantic and certainly more unusual. The small room contains mirror-painted murals by artist Liz Reber, who accomplished the impressive assignment in only twenty-four hours, including the walls in the WC.

Cheap Eaters in London who want just a little more style and atmosphere when dining will appreciate the one-, two-, and three-course set-price menus available for lunch. (Dining at the Arcadia at night, when there is only an à la carte menu, is a definite Big Splurge.) The food has a sophisticated cast to it, but frankly, not everything is equally matched. For starters, it is hard to miss the caramelized onion and thyme tart or the creamy spinach and mushroom soup. The pan-fried lamb sweetbreads in a raspberry vinegar sauce will probably have limited appeal, which is too bad because it is an interesting starter. Main courses to look out for include the braised leg of rabbit or the smoked haddock baked with an herb crust. The one to watch out for and avoid is the Oriental belly pork stir-fried with vegetables and served with coconut basmati rice, all doused in teriyaki sauce. The only thing you will have to watch out for in the dessert selection is your waistline. Conservatives will order the mango ice cream, but I recommend the dark chocolate mousse with a rum sauce. In the evening, the à la carte menu is more expansive. Longtime favorites are the pumpkin and pistachio risotto cake served with Parma ham, and the warm goat cheese and shiitake mushroom terrine. Main courses include salmon, braised lamb shank with roasted parsnip and zucchini couscous, marinated honey-roasted quail, a filet of beef and char-grilled, corn-fed chicken breast with a wild mushroom *rösti,* which is similar to a potato pancake.

NOTE: The entrance to Arcadia is off the footpath leading from Kensington High Street to Kensington Court.

PRICES
À la carte, £25–30; set-price, lunch only, £9.95, 1 course, £13.95, 2 courses, £16.95, 3 courses

SERVICE
£1 cover charge if ordering à la carte and at dinnertime; 12½ percent service charge

CAFÉ FLO (26)
127–129 Kensington Church Street, Notting Hill, W8

There are several locations, but I like this one because it is large and more relaxing. See Café Flo on page 37 in W1 for full description.

TELEPHONE: 020-7727-8142
TUBE: Notting Hill Gate
OPEN: Daily
CLOSED: 2 days at Christmas
HOURS: Breakfast Mon–Fri 9 A.M.–noon, brunch Sat–Sun 10 A.M.–1 P.M., lunch noon–3 P.M., snacks 3–5 P.M., dinner 5–11:30 P.M., Sun until 11 P.M.
RESERVATIONS: Suggested on weekends

CREDIT CARDS: MC, V
PRICES: À la carte, £12–20; set-price, £8.50–12
SERVICE: 12½ percent service charge

CAFE PASTA (35)
229–231 Kensington High Street, Kensington, W8
See Cafe Pasta on page 128 for full description. All other information is the same.
TELEPHONE: 020-7937-6314
TUBE: High Street Kensington
OPEN: Daily
CLOSED: Christmas Day

COSTAS FISH RESTAURANT (24)
18 Hillgate Street, Notting Hill, W8

TELEPHONE
020-7727-4310
TUBE
Notting Hill Gate
OPEN
Tues–Sat
CLOSED
Sun–Mon, holidays
HOURS
Lunch 12:30–2:30 P.M., dinner 5:30–10:30 P.M.
RESERVATIONS
Not necessary, but suggested on Fri
CREDIT CARDS
None
PRICES
À la carte, £5–10
SERVICE
Service discretionary
MISCELLANEOUS
Takeaway available

Budget-conscious Londoners have been noshing on fish-and-chips for decades. The fish is usually cod, haddock, plaice, or any other whitefish, batter-dipped and deep-fried until golden. It comes to you crunchy on the outside and moist inside. Accompanied by an order of chips (french fries), mushy peas, and a splash or two of vinegar, it makes a satisfying Cheap Eat in London.

Costas Fish Restaurant is a local fish-and-chips destination owned and managed by Andreas Papadopoulos. It is a spotless fish takeaway in front with a few Naugahyde booths in back. The fish is delivered daily from Grimsby, the batter is made here, and only pure vegetable oil is used to cook the fish. After your fish-and-chips, order one of their apple or banana fritters with strawberry sauce and you will know why the neighbors eat here almost daily. For grilled fish, or a Greek meal, try the sister restaurant next door, Costas Grill (see below).

COSTAS GRILL (22)
14 Hillgate Street, Notting Hill, W8

TELEPHONE
020-7229-3794
TUBE
Notting Hill Gate
OPEN
Mon–Sat
CLOSED
Sun, holidays
HOURS
Lunch noon–2:30 P.M., dinner 5–10 P.M.
RESERVATIONS
Advised

Costas Grill and its sister restaurant next door, Costas Fish Restaurant (see above), are in a pretty London neighborhood. From the Notting Hill Gate tube stop, walk along Uxbridge Street toward Hillgate and Campden Hill Road and admire the brightly colored mews houses, many with flower-filled window boxes and tiny street-side gardens. Costas Grill is one of the old neighborhood standbys, exuding a feeling of familiarity and friendliness. London is not a bastion of fine Greek food, but here you can eat plenty of the basics and still spend less than £20. In fact, the owner told me, "You can't spend £20 unless you drink a lot of wine!" Neither the menu, nor the decor, nor George, the all-purpose owner, waiter, and greeter, have ever changed. The food will appeal to carnivores: try the garlic sausages, lamb kidneys cooked in wine, souvlaki (kebabs), or *kefthedes* (meatballs). If you like your fish chargrilled, try their trout, salmon, or sea bass, which all come with rice, potatoes, and vegetables, and sell for under £10 per plate. You can fill up on everything but the desserts, which are on the disappointing side, unless you would be happy with their homemade yogurt and honey or a fruit fritter.

FFIONA'S (28)
51 Kensington Church Street, Kensington, W8

If you happen to be dining alone, ask to be seated at the long table. I promise you it won't be long before you are talking with your neighbors and making plans to return here often. That is how I met the two people sitting next to me. "How did you find out about Ffiona's?" I asked. "Oh, friends from Chicago told us about it, and we live across the street. Now we eat here at least two or three times a week." The small restaurant is casual, friendly, comfortable, and above all, fun, and it's run by Ffiona, who does the cooking, and her attractive red-haired sister, Althea, who takes the orders and serves on weekends. Together they make everyone feel welcome and at home. Ffiona's friends say that she never met a stranger, and I believe it.

Before opening this restaurant, Ffiona had quite a career. She sold investment bonds, managed the Chicago Rib Shack, and cooked at the Park Lane Hotel. The inside is homey: faded fabric-covered walls match the banquette and chair cushions and sheets of musical scores line the ceiling. There are bleached wood tables, three old clocks, a caricature of Marlene Dietrich, green plants, wine bottles with dripping candles, and soft music in the background. It's a mixed approach to decorating, but it is pure Ffiona, and you wouldn't want to change a thing.

The menu is handwritten in white chalk on a blackboard. I like her eggplant fritters served with a small green salad loaded with red onions, red peppers, and cucumbers. Watch for homemade fish cakes, roast duck, wild salmon, pasta with fresh vegetables, and boiled

CREDIT CARDS
None

PRICES
À la carte, £12–20

SERVICE
Service discretionary

TELEPHONE
020-7937-4152

TUBE
High Street Kensington

OPEN
Daily for dinner; Sun lunch also

CLOSED
4 days at Christmas and Easter

HOURS
Lunch Sun noon–3 P.M., dinner Mon-Sat 6:30 P.M.–midnight, Sun 7–10 P.M.

RESERVATIONS
Advised

CREDIT CARDS
AE, MC, V

PRICES
À la carte, £12–20; set-price, Sun lunch only, £14

SERVICE
Service discretionary

ham in parsley and white wine. On Sundays, there is always a roast for lunch. For dessert anytime, think lemon tart. It is everyone's favorite.

GEALES FISH RESTAURANT (23)
2 Farmer Street, Notting Hill, W8

TELEPHONE
020-7727-7969

TUBE
Notting Hill Gate

OPEN
Tues–Sat

CLOSED
Sun–Mon, holidays, 2 weeks at Christmas, first 2 weeks of August

HOURS
Lunch noon–3 P.M., dinner 6–11 P.M.

RESERVATIONS
Accepted for more than 8

CREDIT CARDS
AE, MC, V

PRICES
À la carte, £9–16

SERVICE
Service discretionary, 15 pence cover charge

Geales serves only deep-fried fish in a two-room country-style dining room near Kensington Palace. Their fish-and-chips are not only relatively inexpensive but touted by many as the best in London . . . if you like your fish batter-dipped and fried. The fish is sold according to size and weight and the selection is basic: cod, haddock, plaice, and salmon being the best sellers. The beef fat used for deep-frying gives the fish a distinct, crusty texture that doesn't overpower it. Everything you order will be charged on an à la carte basis, from appetizers and main courses to chips, salad, a spoonful of tartar sauce, a side of pickles, and dessert. And you are asked to pay separately when you are served your drinks and your food. This and the 15 pence cover charge per person may seem strange to some of us, but it has been working here for years.

PALMS (33)
3–5 Campden Hill Road (off Kensington High Street), Kensington, W8

TELEPHONE
020-7938-1830

TUBE
High Street Kensington

OPEN
Daily

CLOSED
2 days at Christmas

HOURS
Coffee and pastries 10 A.M.–noon, noon–11:30 P.M., continuous service

RESERVATIONS
Accepted for more than 8

CREDIT CARDS
MC, V

PRICES
À la carte, £12–18

SERVICE
12½ percent service charge

Pasta is still a key buy at Palms, but the menu now includes weekend breakfast, more starters and meal-size salads, plus meat, fish, and chicken entrées.

The appetizers are every bit as interesting as the new main course meat dishes. I like to order several appetizers and share, starting with *crostini* (Italian toast with caramelized onions, crumbled feta cheese, and sun-dried tomatoes), a plate of deep-fried calamari and zucchini, and finally, the avocado and spinach salad dotted with raw mushrooms and crispy bacon. For lunch, the *chèvre* salad or the *salade de Provence*—a warm mix of bacon, mushrooms, potatoes, and spring onions on a bed of mixed greens—will definitely fill you to the brim. You might add an order of hot garlic bread or a freshly baked baguette if you need just a little extra.

The chicken dijonnaise, a grilled breast of chicken with a grain mustard sauce, is as tender as butter, and the *pommes* puree that comes with it soaks up the juices wonderfully. The lamb steak marinated in rosemary is another good choice, and so are the *moules marinière* (mussels) bathed in a broth of white wine, garlic, and herbs.

Please don't overlook their pastas, made with their own additive- and preservative-free sauces. The choices include a *penne chorizo*, a simple *spaghettini a la rustica* (thin pasta topped with fresh tomatoes, garlic, basil, and olive oil), and everyone's favorite, *spaghetti carbonara*. Their two specialty desserts will definitely test your willpower . . . the banana and caramel tart or the tiramisu.

One caveat: It is up to you, but I would avoid the house wine. I do not like the fact that the waitstaff pour the house red and white into empty bottles with a Palms label, stuff a cork in it, and deliver it to your table, which suggests that they want you to *think* they just opened it for you.

NOTE: There is another location at Covent Garden (see page 135).

PHOENICIA (36, $)
11–13 Abingdon Road, Kensington, W8

Middle Eastern meals do not follow the Western pattern of three courses plus coffee or tea. They start and end with *meze*: a variety of small dishes of vegetables, salads, meat, and pastries, accompanied with olives and unleavened pita bread to scoop up the food. Lebanese food, in particular, is a delightful collection of flavors from all over the Middle East.

The outstanding Cheap Eats attraction at Phoenicia, a Lebanese restaurant, is the all-you-can-eat meze buffet lunch served every day. Other bargains are either of the pre- or after-theater dinners, which include coffee and dessert. For the lunch buffet, huge tables are laden with salads, tabbouleh, hummus, pita bread (made here in a clay oven), lamb, chicken fixed numerous ways, vegetables, cheeses, and sweets. If you have never tried Lebanese food, this is the perfect place to start. If you don't get to the lunch buffet and decide to go for a regular dinner, there are meze meals for two that include eight dishes as well as grills, but budgeteers should be wary of ordering mostly from the à la carte menu; your bill can get way out of hand if you aren't careful.

TELEPHONE
020-7937-0120

TUBE
High Street Kensington

OPEN
Daily

CLOSED
Christmas

HOURS
Noon–midnight, continuous service; meze lunch buffet Mon–Sat 12:15–2:30 P.M., Sun and holidays 12:15–3:30 P.M.

RESERVATIONS
Essential for lunch, advised otherwise

CREDIT CARDS
AE, DC, MC, V

PRICES
À la carte, £18–35; set-price, Mon–Sat meze buffet, £11.95, Sun £12.95, other set-price meze from £15–35 per person

SERVICE
£1.50 cover charge, 15 percent service charge

MISCELLANEOUS
Takeaway and catering available, half price for children under 8

SCOFF'S EATING HOUSE (37)
267 Kensington High Street, Kensington, W8

TELEPHONE
020-7602-6777
TUBE
High Street Kensington
OPEN
Daily
CLOSED
Christmas Day
HOURS
Breakfast Mon–Sat 7 A.M.–
noon, Sun 9 A.M.–noon,
lunch 11:30 A.M.–6 P.M.,
dinner 6–11 P.M.
RESERVATIONS
Not necessary
CREDIT CARDS
AE, DC, MC, V
PRICES
À la carte, breakfast, £3–7,
lunch or dinner, £7–12; set-
price, £5 for any pasta or pizza
with a choice of two fillings, £6
for the daily roast, 2 courses,
lunch only £7
SERVICE
Service discretionary

Everything is out of date at Scoff's Eating House, especially the prices, which hark back to a time before most Cheap Eaters in London were born. The name doesn't have much pizzazz and neither does the interior. The original rustic beams strung with wine bottles compete with a stuffed deer head mounted on a wooden wall. Career waitresses in red shirts and short black skirts keep everyone served and happy. Luigi Sbuttoni owns the restaurant, and he doesn't put on airs. Nor does he stint on the Italian and English food, which is served in mega portions. The food scores high for value, just as long as you arrive before 6 P.M. when you can order all the pasta and pizza you can eat for less than £6. The roast of the day with two vegetables and potatoes will be a pound or so more. The Chicken Sophia Loren costs a mere 5 pence more than the roast, but look what you get—an eight-ounce breast of chicken with artichoke hearts covered with cheese and a light tomato sauce. This comes with potatoes and a vegetable. If you open the place at 7 A.M., you can tank up on Luigi's full English breakfast, which consists of an egg, bacon, sausage, mushrooms, two pieces of toast, and tea or coffee for less than £3. If you can find the equivalent in tony Kensington, please send me the address.

STICK & BOWL (31)
31 Kensington High Street, Kensington, W8

TELEPHONE
020-7937-2778
TUBE
High Street Kensington
OPEN
Daily
CLOSED
Christmas Day
HOURS
11:30 A.M.–11 P.M., continuous
service
RESERVATIONS
Not accepted
CREDIT CARDS
None
PRICES
À la carte, £4–8; set-price,
£4.80; minimum charge per
person £2
SERVICE
No service charged or expected
MISCELLANEOUS
Takeaway available

With only four tables downstairs and as many communal bar tables upstairs, you can see this is not the place to settle in for the long term. It is, however, absolutely unbeatable for a fast Chinese Cheap Eat while shopping along Kensington High Street. One of the most expensive meals (No. 10) costs around £5. For that you will get one spring roll, one prawn, two spareribs or sweet-and-sour pork, fried rice, and a vegetable. There are dozens of other possibilities ranging from soup (sweet corn, wonton, or chicken noodle) to nuts (litchi served in a bowl or made into a drink).

Pubs

THE SCARSDALE (39)
23a Edwardes Square, Kensington, W8

The Scarsdale is a respectable pub next to Edwardes Square, named in honor of William Edwardes, the first baron of Kensington. The square was designed by a Frenchman as living quarters for French officers in the belief that England would eventually be invaded and occupied by Napoleon. Work began in 1811. A year later the builder went bankrupt and Napoleon began his retreat from Moscow. So much for the invasion of England. Now that you can pass the history quiz, what about the pub?

First of all, it is very pretty. In the past, it has been named the best pub in London with the best city garden. If you go in the spring or summer, you will agree, and best of all, the inside is free from blasting music and clanging pinball machines. There is smoke (this is a pub, after all), but the seating inside around the two fireplaces is comfortable, especially on a cold London day. And finally, the food is above the usual pub grub stuff. Go for Sunday lunch when you have a choice of three roasts served with two vegetables, potatoes, and Yorkshire pudding. At other times the cook dishes out a varied line that includes chicken wings with barbecue sauce, cheeseburgers and fries, chargrilled tuna steaks, grilled lamb with minted garlic sauce, and spinach and ricotta cannelloni.

TELEPHONE
020-7937-1811

TUBE
High Street Kensington

OPEN
Daily

CLOSED
Christmas Day, holidays

HOURS
Mon–Sat noon–11 P.M., Sun noon–10:30 P.M.; lunch noon–2:30 P.M., dinner 6:30–9:30 P.M.

RESERVATIONS
Accepted for more than 6

CREDIT CARDS
MC, V

PRICES
À la carte, £7–15

SERVICE
Service discretionary

THE WINDSOR CASTLE (27)
114 Campden Hill Road, Notting Hill, W8

Tucked away between Notting Hill Gate and Kensington High Street is the Windsor Castle, which has the atmosphere of a traditional English country pub. It was built in 1828, during the reign of King George IV, on top of Campden Hill, from where the Royal Windsor Castle could be seen twenty miles away. Over the years, little has changed. It still has three small bars with the original plank floors and authentic furniture rather than mock Victorian. Conversation flourishes because pinball machines, jukeboxes, and screaming children have been banished (from the pub area, anyway). Behind the pub lies a leafy, secluded garden with lime, plane, and cherry trees shading the wooden chairs and

TELEPHONE
020-7234-9951

TUBE
Notting Hill Gate

OPEN
Daily

CLOSED
Christmas Day

HOURS
Pub: Mon–Sat noon–11 P.M., Sun noon–10:30 P.M.; food service: noon–10 P.M., continuous service

RESERVATIONS
Not accepted

CREDIT CARDS
AE, MC, V

PRICES
À la carte, £5–12

SERVICE
Service discretionary

MISCELLANEOUS
Nonsmoking section at lunch only

tables, making it a relaxing place to spend a warm Sunday afternoon. The appetizing English food is made here and ranges from sandwiches, ploughman's lunches, and steamed steak and kidney pudding to bangers and mash featuring Mrs. O'Keefe's famous homemade British regional sausages of wild boar, Cumberland (spicy pork), Yorkshire (spicy pork with herbs), and Lincolnshire (mild pork with herbs). There are Sunday roast lunches, a game pie served hot or cold, and the house specialty: oysters or steamed mussels. You can have homemade puddings such as treacle tart or apple pie—but only on Sunday.

Tearooms/Pâtisseries

KANDY TEA ROOM (29)
4 Holland Street, Kensington, W8

TELEPHONE
020-7937-3001

TUBE
High Street Kensington

OPEN
Tues–Sun

CLOSED
Mon, 2 weeks at Christmas, last 2 weeks in August

HOURS
Tues–Thur 10:30 A.M.–5:30 P.M., Fri–Sat 10:30 A.M.–6:30 P.M., Sun 11 A.M.–6 P.M., light lunches served 11:30–3:30 P.M.

RESERVATIONS
Not necessary

CREDIT CARDS
None

PRICES
À la carte, £4.50–9; afternoon tea, £5.50

SERVICE
Service discretionary

MISCELLANEOUS
No smoking allowed

Inspired by childhood memories of the tearooms of his native city of Kandy, Sri Lanka, Ananda Wijesiri opened his tearoom where he serves "nice tea for nice people."

His is a proper tea with scones, clotted cream, jam, and a pot of tea served on Royal Crown Derby china. Six varieties of tea along with sandwiches on his homemade bread made from organic flour, scones, quiche using free-range eggs, and salads are also available. The photographs you see around the room of Queen Elizabeth in her thirties, Sir Noël Coward, and Ananda's three young daughters in their ballerina costumes were taken by the photographer four doors down the street. The cast-iron teapot over the kitchen door belonged to Wijesiri's family and was used daily between 1933 and 1979, when it sat on a wooden fire, filled with water, always ready for a visitor to have a cup of tea.

PÂTISSERIE FRANÇAISE (30)
27 Kensington Church Street, Kensington, W8

See Pâtisserie Française on page 88 for full description. All other information is the same.

TELEPHONE: 020-7937-9574
TUBE: High Street Kensington
OPEN: Daily
HOURS: 8 A.M.–6 P.M.

Wine Bars

BENEDICTS RESTAURANT & WINE BAR (32)
106 Kensington High Street, Kensington, W8

Directly opposite the High Street Kensington tube station is Benedicts. The second-floor wine bar and restaurant delivers much more than first appearances from the street would suggest. After entering a small open doorway, you climb two sets of stairs lined with old photos of Kensington High Street. Halfway up, there is a sign of encouragement: "Just a little further . . . it's worth the climb!" It is worth the climb, and you eventually find yourself in a darkly paneled, rather dimly lit room. The theme is Irish, thus the pictures of well-fed monks and priests adorning the walls and a valuable set of monk cartoons displayed along the hallway between the kitchen and the loo. The best thing about eating here is that you can order an appetizer or a salad with a glass of wine for either lunch or dinner and be treated as well as if you ordered the most expensive three-course meal. The place is run by Bernard Molloy, whose brother runs a similar bar in Warwick, Rhode Island, called Matt Molloy's.

The seasonal menu offers few exciting surprises, but everything is nicely served and tastes good. The best appetizer is always the golden-fried mushrooms stuffed with cream cheese, herbs, and garlic. Main courses range from a short list of daily and weekly specials to the usual grilled steaks, beef Wellington, chicken, fish, meat pies, omelettes, and lasagna. All dishes are garnished with vegetables and potatoes. Desserts are made elsewhere. A better choice is the excellent Irish coffee.

TELEPHONE
020-7937-7580
TUBE
High Street Kensington
OPEN
Mon–Sat, Sun dinner only
CLOSED
Holidays
HOURS
Mon–Fri noon–3 P.M., 5–10:30 P.M.; Sat noon–11 P.M., Sun from 1–8 P.M., continuous service
RESERVATIONS
Not necessary
CREDIT CARDS
AE, DC, MC, V
PRICES
À la carte, £10–18
SERVICE
Service discretionary

W11

Notting Hill and Portobello Road

North of Kensington, Notting Hill was once a slum and a haunt of drug dealers and prostitutes. Today, W11 is one of London's most stylish addresses, affordable to anyone able to spend up to five or six million pounds on a place to call home. Those who can are film and media personalities, bankers, and trust-fund yuppies who somehow manage to scrimp by on £200,000 per year. One of the best reasons for visiting the area is the famous Portobello Road Market, one of London's best antique and bric-a-brac hunting grounds, especially early Saturday morning. The market dates back to the nineteenth century when gypsies traded horses here. The street is lined with stalls selling everything from good quality items to cheap imports. In the neighborhood, there is an interesting mix of art galleries, restaurants, and shops. Westbourne Grove, off Portobello Road, is an up-and-coming area of trendy boutiques and overpriced restaurants.

RESTAURANTS in W11 (see map page 78)

Restaurants

BOOKS FOR COOKS & RISTORANTE (4)
4 Blenheim Crescent, Notting Hill, W11

Books for Cooks was started in 1983 by Heidi Lascelles, who became aware of the need for a specialist cookbook store when she searched London's bookshops in vain for a book of German recipes she hoped to recreate for her family. Little did she know that her Georgian terrace house on Blenheim Crescent would go on to become a gourmet mecca for cooks, culinary professionals, and food lovers from all over the world. With eight thousand books on the shelves, Books for Cooks stocks London's largest inventory of cookbooks—old, new, obscure, well known, ethnic, and gourmet, written in Yiddish, French, German, English, and countless other languages. If it has to do with cooking, Books for Cooks stocks it or knows about it, and they will order it for you and have it shipped if it isn't on the shelf. In addition to the books, a series of forty-four cooking workshops takes place on Sundays when the shop is closed. Classes run for three hours, and you receive a printed recipe booklet of what has been prepared, a glass of wine and, of course, a taste of the dishes cooked. It costs £22–30 depending on the course; bring a pen and your undivided attention.

Even if you are not in the market for a cookbook or can't attend one of their classes, you should never consider leaving London without sampling lunch served in the tiny, fifteen-seat Books for Cooks Ristorante in the back of the shop. The menu changes daily according to the whims of the chef, who uses only the best seasonal ingredients to create the deliciously inventive dishes, many of which are listed in their own series of cookbooks written by the resident French chef, Eric Treuillé. Reservations are essential for lunch, which is served only between 12:30 and 1:30 P.M. on weekdays, and for the two seatings on Saturdays at noon and 1:45 P.M. To avoid disappointment, I always telephone for my reservation the minute I arrive in London. In the morning and after lunch until around 4 P.M., coffee and pastries are served.

NOTE: Because they are unlicensed, they suggest stopping by Corney & Barrow wine merchants around the corner on Kensington Park Road to purchase a bottle of good wine to have with your lunch.

TELEPHONE
020-7221-1992

FAX
020-7221-1517 (for ordering books)

EMAIL
info@booksforcooks.com (book orders and inquiries)

TUBE
Notting Hill Gate, Ladbroke Grove

OPEN
Mon–Sat lunch only; Sun for workshops only (call to check)

CLOSED
Sun, holidays

HOURS
Lunch Mon–Fri 12:30–1:30 P.M., Sat lunch 2 seatings, noon and 1:45 P.M., coffee and pastries in the morning and after lunch until around 4 P.M.

RESERVATIONS
Essential

CREDIT CARDS
AE, DC, MC, V

PRICES
À la carte, £12–18; set-price, £12, 2 courses, £15, 3 courses

SERVICE
Service discretionary

MISCELLANEOUS
BYOB, no corkage fee

CALZONE (17)
2a–2b Kensington Park Road, Notting Hill, W11

TELEPHONE
020-7243-2003

TUBE
Notting Hill Gate

OPEN
Daily

CLOSED
4 days at Christmas

HOURS
Sun–Thur noon–11:45 P.M.,
Fri–Sat until 12:45 A.M.;
coffee and panini served
10 A.M.–5 P.M.; continuous
service

RESERVATIONS
Not necessary

CREDIT CARDS
AE, MC, V

PRICES
À la carte, £6–10

SERVICE
Service discretionary

MISCELLANEOUS
Takeaway available

The menu at the sprightly green and white Calzone is created around dressed-up regular or wholemeal, thin-crust pizzas, a smattering of pastas, and a garden variety of salads designed to either fill you on their own or complement the rest of your meal. The simple yet tasty range of pizzas all come in for under £7.50, and they appear at first glance to be too large to finish in one sitting. But the light, thin base makes them easy to consume, because they are not weighed down with a laundry list of gooey toppings. If you are here before 5 P.M. and are not in the mood for pasta or pizza, you can order Calzone *panini*—Italian sandwiches made with a choice of freshly baked focaccia or ciabatta bread spread with tuna and onion, mozzarella, tomato, ham or salami, and basil or grilled vegetables. The customers seem to be on the short side of forty, happy in the knowledge that they have found a nifty spot that serves fresh, well-priced food they can afford, whether eating it here or getting it to go.

NOTE: There is another Calzone on Fulham Road in South Kensington (see page 204).

THE COURTYARD (16)
59a Portobello Road, Notting Hill, W11

TELEPHONE
020-7221-8016, 020-7221-7689

TUBE
Notting Hill Gate

OPEN
Mon–Sat; Fri night also

CLOSED
Sun, holidays, Christmas Day
through New Year's Day

HOURS
Mon–Sat 9 A.M.–5 P.M., Fri
7–10 P.M., continuous service

RESERVATIONS
Not necessary

CREDIT CARDS
None

PRICES
À la carte, £4–10

SERVICE
Service discretionary

The room where you will be eating was built in 1862 as a church school "for the education of children of the labouring, manufacturing, and other poor classes in the Notting Hill parishes of St. John and St. Peter," and it continued as such until the 1920s. Until 1992, the church school created fine art prints, reproducing the works of David Hockney and Henry Moore. Today it serves as an arts café with all the local artwork you see available for sale. Because the Notting Hill parishes still own the building, the license does not allow them to be open to the public at night. This has been cleverly circumvented by charging a 50 pence *yearly* "membership fee," which allows the café to serve wine and beer and remain open on Friday evenings.

There are tables on the patio, and inside are pews and church chairs surrounding shared wooden tables. On the mezzanine are cushioned rattan armchairs, suitable for settling in with a cup of tea and an interesting magazine or the daily newspaper. Coffee, tea, and pastries are served in the morning and afternoon. Lunch begins at noon and lasts until it is gone, usually around 2 P.M. On Thursdays, there is a specially priced lunch for OAPs (unfortunately known as old age pensioners, their version of "senior citizens"), and on Friday nights between 7–10 P.M. there is music, poetry readings, mime, or other artistic performances.

NOTE: To get there, walk along Portobello Road from the Notting Hill Gate tube; it will be on the left before Chepstow Villas.

MISCELLANEOUS
A yearly 50 pence "membership fee" allows the café to remain open on Friday night and to serve wine and beer.

MR. CHRISTIAN'S (11)
11 Elgin Crescent, Notting Hill, W11

The waitstaff at Mr. Christian's state: "We make people want to come back." Now celebrating more than a quarter of a century in this location, it is clear that they certainly do! After a Saturday morning spent braving the crowds at the Portobello Road Market, I urge you to join the queue at Mr. Christian's and sample one of the best sandwiches in London.

During the week this is a delicatessen serving morning croissants and muffins, midday sandwiches, salads, and hot specials alongside a stunning assortment of salamis, cheeses, pâtés, sixteen varieties of olives, and vintage olive oils. On Saturday, when the Portobello Road Market is in full swing, Mr. Christian's hits its stride—the food spills onto the sidewalk in a dazzling display of international breads, which are sold whole or sliced into sandwiches and wolfed down by hungry shoppers. If it is available, be sure to sample their English sourdough bread—a specialty that takes five days to make and lasts up to eight days. Another bread to try is the Innes bread, studded either with raisins and walnuts or sun-dried tomatoes.

NOTE: The Portobello Road Market operates as an antique/flea market on Friday and Saturday, but it is best on Saturday mornings from 8 A.M. to 1 P.M., when the street stalls are open.

TELEPHONE
020-7229-0501

TUBE
Ladbroke Grove, Notting Hill Gate

OPEN
Daily

CLOSED
Christmas Day

HOURS
Mon–Fri 6 A.M.–7 P.M., Sat 5:30 A.M.–6 P.M., Sun 6 A.M.–4 P.M., continuous service

RESERVATIONS
Not accepted

CREDIT CARDS
AE, MC, V

PRICES
À la carte, £5–10

SERVICE
No service charged or expected

MISCELLANEOUS
No seating, all takeaway

192 (12)
192 Kensington Park Road, Notting Hill, W11

TELEPHONE
020-7229-0482

TUBE
Notting Hill Gate, Ladbroke Grove

OPEN
Daily

CLOSED
August, Christmas Day, holidays

HOURS
Bar: Mon–Fri 12:30–11 P.M., Sun until 10:30 P.M.; lunch Mon–Fri 12:30–3 P.M., Sat–Sun until 3:30 P.M., dinner Mon–Sat 6:30–11:30 P.M., Sun 7–11 P.M.

RESERVATIONS
Advised

CREDIT CARDS
AE, DC, MC, V

PRICES
À la carte, £15–25; set-price, £12.50, lunch only, 2 courses including tea or coffee

SERVICE
Service discretionary, 12½ percent service charge for 6 or more

With twenty-five wines available by the glass and a wine list with eighty-plus bottles from France, Spain, Italy, Portugal, Australia, and New Zealand, you would think 192 would bill itself as a wine bar. While the upstairs is a wine bar at night, the wine is not the true drawing card here—the first-rate food is. The inside, which can seat a hundred on spindly metal chairs, is minimal, with lavender, yellow, and turquoise walls offsetting the green cotton-velvet banquettes. A touch of glitter is added at night when the bar is outlined with tiny sparkling fairy lights. The prices and attitude of the staff are refreshingly humble and the food is consistently varied and well presented.

The menu changes weekly and offers a wide range of choices, with portions generous enough to allow grazing through a selection of appetizers and a glass or two of an unknown wine. Consider an order of the broccoli and blue cheese tart or a small order of tagliatelle with shiitake mushrooms, courgettes (zucchini), and tomatoes to start. Perhaps the double-baked Stilton soufflé with pears and *bitey roquette* or the Thai beef salad with sweet chili and lime, along with a glass of good wine will be all you want. The seasonal salad of grilled vegetables and grilled Haloumi cheese goes nicely with either the roast pheasant with braised cabbage and celeriac puree or the roast cod paired with artichoke mash and lemon butter. Just like the rest of the menu, desserts change with the seasons and are listed with suggested wines, sherries, and ports to accompany them. If the time is right, there will be a pear *tarte tatin* (warm upside-down tart) served with cinnamon ice cream. Always on is a hot pudding, something with chocolate, and assorted cheeses.

PROST (18)
35 Pembridge Road, Notting Hill, W11

TELEPHONE
020-7727-9620

TUBE
Notting Hill Gate

OPEN
Mon–Fri dinner only, Sat–Sun all day

CLOSED
Holidays

German restaurants in London are few and far between, and good ones that are reasonably priced *and* good are almost impossible to find. Prost is the delightful exception. With an interesting menu that features only organically produced food, Prost offers German and Eastern European dishes, served in a pleasant atmosphere. The two-level restaurant is just intimate enough to invite long stays and serious conversation. Owner

David Parker is on deck—behind the bar making the coffees, pouring the wine and beer, and generally running a tight ship. During the week he opens only for dinner. Because it is close to the Portobello Road antique/flea market, he also opens on Saturday and Sunday early enough to catch the brunch/lunch crowd and the afternoon tea and cake trade.

On Saturday mornings I like to order two scrambled eggs with spinach and a warm baguette with melted brie dripping out the edges. If I arrive for dinner, I never miss the blini with smoked salmon, sour cream, and caviar. The house specialty, pork filet on *späetzle* (German dumplings) topped with mushroom sauce and gratinéed with cheese, never fails to win praises. The woodland mushroom Stroganoff with toasted pine nuts will appeal to some, but you will never go wrong with the braised chicken paprika in a rich sour cream horseradish sauce. Dessert? No question here . . . the apple strudel, and don't forget the cream. If you like schnapps, Mr. Parker has quite a collection, including the famous Liniaquivit, the Norwegian schnapps that must cross the equator two times to be so labeled.

ROTISSERIE JULES (21)
133 Notting Hill Gate, Notting Hill, W11

It's simple, it's good, it's cheap—it's free-range chicken sliced onto a sandwich, made into a salad, or at its best, roasted and sold by the quarter, half, or whole. To go with your juicy chicken, order a side of creamy potatoes, french fries, corn on the cob, ratatouille, or a salad, with homemade apple tart or chocolate mousse to top it all off. Everything is made here, nothing is frozen, and preservatives are not in the larder. With one-and-a-half-hour notice they will roast a whole or half leg of lamb, and with two days notice, they will roast a goose or suckling pig for you. You can eat your feast here or call for free delivery in most parts of London (see below). A dinner for twenty will be delivered piping hot to your door in one hour.

They deliver in SW1, SW3, SW5, SW6, SW7, SW10, SW11, and W2, W8, W10, and W14. There is a £20 minimum delivery order, or £3 delivery charge, for Mayfair, Pimlico, W2, W11, and W14. They deliver daily: Monday to Saturday from 6–10:30 P.M. and all day on Sunday. Please note they recommend that the roasted meats be eaten straight away and they do not recommend

HOURS
Mon–Fri 5:30–11 P.M.,
Sat 10 A.M.–11 P.M., Sun
11 A.M.–11 P.M., continuous
service

RESERVATIONS
Suggested on weekends

CREDIT CARDS
AE, MC, V

PRICES
À la carte, breakfast £6–9,
lunch and dinner £16–22

SERVICE
Service discretionary

TELEPHONE
020-7221-3331 (deliveries
only)

TUBE
Notting Hill Gate

OPEN
Daily

CLOSED
Christmas Day

HOURS
Mon–Sat noon–11:30 P.M., Sun
until 10:30 P.M., continuous
service; delivery hours Mon–
Sat 6–10:30 P.M., all day Sun

RESERVATIONS
Not necessary

CREDIT CARDS
AE, MC, V

PRICES
À la carte, £5–10, whole
chicken £10 (serves 3–4), whole
duck £18 (serves 3–4), whole
lamb £25 (serves 4–6)

delivery orders of the fries as they get soggy quickly. Get the creamed potatoes instead.

NOTE: Other locations are in SW3 (see page 178) and SW7 (see page 200).

SAUSAGE & MASH (3)
268 Portobello Road, Notting Hill, W10

If you can't get to the East End to sample an English soul food dish, try your luck at Sausage & Mash at the end of Portobello Road, which is officially in W10, not W11. The location, under a freeway overpass and tube track, is hardly inspiring, but their sausages are first rate provided you stick with the traditional combinations and avoid off-the-wall creations such as duck and black cherry sausage served with a cinnamon, ginger, and allspice mash. Vegetarians have two choices, but again, if you aren't prepared to sit around communal tables and tuck into a plate full of real pork sausages with mash and gravy, eat someplace else.

TOM'S (10)
226 Westbourne Grove, Notting Hill, W11

While browsing through the rapidly changing shopping scene along Westbourne Grove, keep Tom's in mind for a reviving cappuccino, a large deli sandwich, or a hot lunch served Monday to Saturday from noon to 5 P.M. It is easy to spot: just look for the Texaco station next to the post office at which the No. 23 bus stops. Date and walnut bread, toasted *tartines* or panettone, scrambled eggs, cream cheese and chives on a toasted bagel, all remind you that this is a trendsetting corner of London. Kippers and beans on toast tell you that London eating habits have not really changed that much. British farmhouse cheeses, olive oils, wines, a small selection of fruits and vegetables, and even Skippy peanut butter (smooth or crunchy) are all available from the deli portion of Tom's.

RESERVATIONS
Not necessary
CREDIT CARDS
MC, V, minimum
charge £10
PRICES
À la carte, £4–9
SERVICE
Service discretionary

TOOTSIES (25)
120 Holland Park Avenue, Holland Park, W11

See Tootsies in W1, page 63, for a full description. All other information is the same.

TELEPHONE: 020-7229-8567
TUBE: Holland Park
HOURS: Sun–Thur 9 A.M.–11:30 P.M., Fri–Sat until 12:30 P.M.
MISCELLANEOUS: Nonsmoking section

WC1

Bloomsbury

Known as intellectual London, this is a good location with a quiet atmosphere for being so central. It is the former home of the famed Bloomsbury Group, which included biographer Lytton Strachey, novelists Virginia Woolf and D. H. Lawrence, and economist John Maynard Keynes. The cornerstones of the area are the British Museum and Russell Square, which is the largest in London after Lincoln's Inn Fields. University of London buildings are scattered throughout the area, as are many fine antiquarian bookshops and print and map specialists.

Restaurants

COSMOBA (6)
9 Cosmo Place (off Southampton Row), Bloomsbury, WC1

It is reassuring to return to a favorite Cheap Eat and find it better than it was. That is how I always find Cosmoba, situated on the same side of a pedestrian lane that sports a trendy wine bar and a haunted pub. Cosmoba is the one the locals recommend as having good value for money. It is a plain, family-run restaurant, with the same chef for twenty-five years, who serves homey Italian food that is definitely worth a second trip. The menu is comfort reading for all Italian food fans. There is a long list of antipasti with everything from stuffed zucchini and homemade pâté to a mixed salami plate or melon with Parma ham. Follow that with veal, chicken, steak, or one of the daily specials, such as grilled calves' liver, osso bucco (veal shanks) and rice, or lamb steak in a tomato, garlic, and olive sauce. Pasta is well represented, with lasagna, ravioli, spaghetti, tagliatelle, penne, and their homemade fusilli, all served with a variety of sauces. When I am feeling virtuous, I order the oranges in caramel sauce, thinking it is a slightly healthier alternative to their profiteroles (cream puffs) slathered in chocolate or the fat-gram-rich zabaglione (custardlike dessert made in a copper pot).

TELEPHONE
020-7837-0904

TUBE
Russell Square

OPEN
Mon–Sat

CLOSED
Sun, holidays

HOURS
Lunch 11:30 A.M.–3 P.M., dinner 5:30–11 P.M.

RESERVATIONS
Suggested on weekends

CREDIT CARDS
MC, V

PRICES
À la carte, £10–20

SERVICE
Service discretionary

THE FRYER'S DELIGHT (10)
19 Theobald's Road, Bloomsbury, WC1

Fast food British-style began with fish-and-chips, and today you can find fish-and-chips shops all over London that vary little in price but are oceans apart in quality. One of the best is the Fryer's Delight. When Joan Rivers is in London, this is where she eats her fish-and-chips. So do many *Cheap Eats in London* readers, one of whom wrote to me stating, "The fresh tender cod was one of the best fish dishes we've ever had anywhere, including meals at expensive fish restaurants." You will know you are close when you pass people in the street munching their cod wrapped in unlined newsprint. You will also recognize it by the line of people on the sidewalk waiting to get to the counter, and by the cars double-parked in front with drivers dashing in to pick up an order.

TELEPHONE
020-7405-4114

TUBE
Holborn

OPEN
Mon–Sat

CLOSED
Sun, holidays

HOURS
Restaurant noon–10 P.M., takeaway noon–11 P.M., continuous service

RESERVATIONS
Not accepted

CREDIT CARDS
None

SOMERS TOWN

King's Cross,
St. Pancras

Phoenix Road

Chalton St.

BRITISH
LIBRARY

ST.
PANCRAS
STATION

St.
Chad's St.

Gray's Inn

EUSTON
STATION

Cardington St.

Everholt Street

Euston

Road

Euston

ARGYLE
SQ.

Argyle St.

Belgrove

Argyle St.

Robert St.

Hampstead

N. Gower St.

William Rd.

Duke's
Road

Upper Woburn Pl.

Mabledon Pl.

Bidborough St.

Hastings St.

Judd St.

Thanet St.

Leigh St.

Cromer St.

1

REGENT
SQUARE Sidmou

Drummond

Road

Euston

Burton St.

Gardens

Cartwright

Leigh St.

2

WC1

Euston
Square

Tavistock St.

Endsleigh Pl.

Endsleigh St.

TAVI-
STOCK
St. SQ.

Tavistock

Herbrand St.

Woburn Place

Marchmont St.

Hunter St.

Place

MECK
BU

Warren
Street

Gordon St.

Coram
St.

3

Bernard St.

BRUNSWICK
SQUARE

COR
FIEL

Warren St.

FITZROY
SQ.

Grafton Way

UNIVERSITY
COLLEGE

Torrington Pl.

Bedford Way

Russell
Square

Guilford St.

Cleveland Street

Whitfield St.

Maple St.

Gower Street

Huntley St.

Torrington Pl.

Ridgmount
Gardens

Malet St.

Gower St.

RUSSELL
SQUARE

Southampton Row

QUEEN
SQUARE

5

Cosmo
Pl.

Great Ormon

Howland St.

Charlotte St.

Ridgmount
St.

UNIV.
OF
LONDON

6

Old Gloucester St.

Boswell St.

8

Foley St.

House St.

Goodge St.

Chenies St.

7

Alfred Pl.

Gower
Mews

Bedford Place

Montague St.

BLOOMSBURY

Goodge
Street

Store St.

Great Titchfield St.

Gt. Portland St.

Riding

Gt. Mortimer St.

Newman St.

Percy St.

Morwell St.

BEDFORD
SQUARE

BRITISH
MUSEUM

Bloomsbury St.

Great Russell St.

13

BLOOMS-
BURY SQ.

BLOOMS-
BURY SQ.

Regent Street

Titchfield St.

Berners St.

Wells St.

Rathbone Pl.

14

Coptic

Museum

15

Bloomsbury Way

Castle St.

Oxford

Great Russell St.

Streatham St.

17

16

St.

Holborn

Oxford
Circus

Street

Tottenham
Court Rd.

New

Oxford

18

High Holborn

Newton St.

Drury

Macklin St.

PALLADIUM

Noel St.

SOHO
SQ.

St. Giles High St.

19

20

Endell

Neal's

Shorts

Gdns.

21

24

Acre
St.

Grt. Queen St.

Wild

Gt. Marlborough St.

SOHO

Wardour St.

Dean St.

Greek St.

Charing

Avenue

22

23

Earl

25

Long Acre

26

29

Kingly St.

Beak St.

Broadwick St.

Old Compton St.

28

Shelton

ham St.

30

31

Monmouth St.

32

Covent
Garden

Bow St.

Russell

36

37

Regent Street

GOLDEN
SQUARE

Brewer St.

Shaftesbury

New-
port

38

St. Martin's

Long Acre

Floral St.

35

Langley

34

COVENT
GARDEN

40

King St.

41

44

Tavist

Conduit St.

Glasshouse St.

Lisle

St.

52

Cranbourn St.

39

Garrick

St.

46

45

47

Henrietta

48

Exeter

50

49

St.

Clifford St.

Vigo
St.

Coventry

St.

53

Leicester
Square

51

Maiden
La.

Bedford St.

Old Bond Street

ROYAL
ACADEMY
OF ARTS

PICCADILLY
CIRCUS

Piccadilly
Circus

LEICESTER
SQUARE

54

William IV St.

55

Strand

Savoy

Dover Street

Piccadilly

Jermyn St.

Regent Street

Haymarket

Orange

NATIONAL
GALLERY

56

57

CHARING
CROSS STATION

Duke St.

ST. JAMES'S
SQUARE

Pall Mall East

TRAFALGAR
SQUARE

Charing
Cross

Northumberland Av.

58

Embankment

Hungerfor

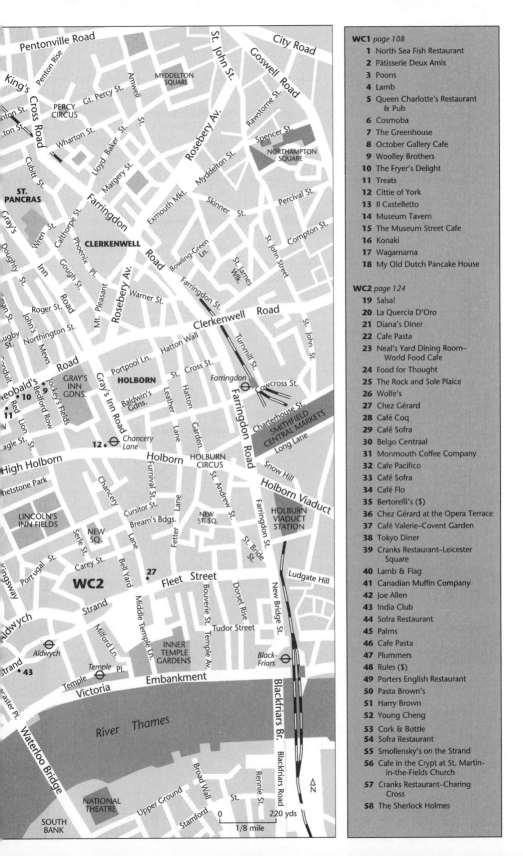

PRICES
À la carte, £3.50–6.50

SERVICE
No service charged or expected

MISCELLANEOUS
Takeaway available

The cooking is done right in front of you by a team consisting of a father, uncle, and two sons in a tiny room with zero decor, other than a wall lined with various write-ups about the place, bottles of vinegar and ketchup, and a salt shaker on each table. What counts is their specialty: deep-fried chicken or fish-and-chips served in heaping portions that you will have a hard time finishing. When I asked how much fish-and-chips they sell on a daily basis, I was told, "At least ten to twelve bags of potatoes, each weighing twenty-five kilos, and seven to nine stones of cod." (To do the math, remember that one kilo equals 2.2 pounds and one stone equals 14 pounds.) If you order takeaway, it will be wrapped in plain white paper and handed to you. If you are eating your food here, place your order at the counter, find a seat at one of the five plastic-covered booths with bright orange tabletops, and your heaping plate will be brought to you by the motherly waitress. An order of rock cod and chips with a huge slab of buttered bread will set you back less than £5 and will be one of the best Cheap Eats you will enjoy in London.

THE GREENHOUSE (7)
16 Chenies Street (basement of Drill Arts Center), Bloomsbury, WC1

TELEPHONE
020-7637-8038

TUBE
Goodge Street

OPEN
Mon–Sat; Sun lunch only

CLOSED
Sun dinner, holidays

HOURS
Mon–Fri 11 A.M.–8:30 P.M., Sat 11 A.M.–8 P.M., Sun noon–4:30 P.M., lunch daily 12:30–2 P.M., continuous service

RESERVATIONS
Not accepted

CREDIT CARDS
None

PRICES
À la carte, £5–8

SERVICE
No service charged or expected

MISCELLANEOUS
No smoking allowed, BYOB, no corkage fee, unlicensed; Monday nights are reserved for women only; 10 percent off from 2–5:30 P.M. for students

Interest in vegetarian food has increased considerably in London, and there are a number of specialty restaurants that offer excellent vegetarian cuisine at prices most Cheap Eaters can afford. The Greenhouse, in the basement of the Drill Arts Center, is one of the most popular, despite its laid-back, vaguely hippie air. Seating is around shared bare wooden tables in a white-washed room filled with ads and posters for fringe plays, offbeat art exhibitions, New Age meetings, and yoga classes. I think the best time to go is for lunch, when the selection is at its freshest and best. There is no written menu, but the dishes, which change daily, are listed on a blackboard behind the counter. In addition to the specials of the day, there is usually quiche, a selection of salads, pizza, and one vegan soup. The desserts are special, particularly the carrot walnut cake or the chocolate loaf.

IL CASTELLETTO (13)
17 Bury Place, Bloomsbury, WC1

Some of the most reliable restaurant tips come from owners of family-run bed-and-breakfast hotels that are recommended in *Cheap Sleeps in London*. These are people who have lived in the neighborhood and are always on the lookout for good value meals, not only for their guests, but for themselves. One of the best family-run budget B&Bs near the British Museum is St. Margaret's Hotel (see *Cheap Sleeps in London*). Italian owners Mr. and Mrs. Marazzi have been in this area for decades, and they know what they are talking about when suggesting a good Italian restaurant. They told me about Il Castelletto, run by the Bragoli brothers, headed by the affable Luigi. It is a comfortable sort of place where nothing has changed for years: not the waitstaff, the pink-and-white table linens, the swag curtains, the Windsor armchairs with thin cushions, and certainly not the lusty Italian food.

Regulars begin with the hearty Tuscan bean soup or the quickly fried zucchini and aubergines (eggplant). Most of the vegetables served come from one brother's garden, so you know they will be fresh. Pastas are plentiful and filling and start with the plainest garlic, basil, and olive oil rendition on up to sauces made with fresh seafood. *Crespelle* (crêpes) with spinach and ricotta cheese in a tomato sauce or stuffed with pumpkin they grew themselves are two other special dishes to consider. Veal dishes are tender. Just be sure to order the simple versions, as those drenched in cream sauce tend to get a little heavy. A light finish is the warm *zabaglione al marsala* (custardlike dessert made in a copper pot), which you will have to share because it is only made for two or more—but let me assure you, you will wish you had the velvety soft custard all to yourself.

TELEPHONE
020-7405-2232

TUBE
Holborn

OPEN
Mon–Fri; Sat dinner only

CLOSED
Sun, holidays

HOURS
Lunch noon–3 P.M., dinner 5:30–11 P.M.

RESERVATIONS
Advised (ask for a table by the window)

CREDIT CARDS
AE, DC, MC, V

PRICES
À la carte, £15–25; set-price, lunch only £7, pasta of the day and salad, £12, 2 courses

SERVICE
£1 cover charge, 12½ percent service charge

KONAKI (16)
5 Coptic Street, Bloomsbury, WC1

Konaki is located about a two-minute walk from the British Museum. The interior is serene, compared to most Greek restaurants, with beamed ceilings, comfortable seating, appropriate background music, and lights on each table in the evening. The food is filling and generously served, especially the *meze* (assorted appetizers) for two at £28. This gargantuan feast is composed of three courses with a choice of ten to fifteen starters; lamb

TELEPHONE
020-7580-9730, 020-7580-3712

TUBE
Tottenham Court Road

OPEN
Mon–Fri, Sat dinner only

CLOSED
Sun, Sat lunch, Christmas Day

HOURS
Lunch noon–3 P.M., dinner
Mon–Thur 6–11 P.M.,
Fri–Sat 6 P.M.–midnight

RESERVATIONS
Advised on weekends

CREDIT CARDS
AE, MC, V

PRICES
À la carte, £12–18; set-price,
lunch, £7, 2 courses, dinner,
£10, 3 courses, meze for
two, £28

SERVICE
50 pence cover charge,
12 percent service charge

cutlets, chicken or pork souvlaki (kebabs) for the main course; and all the fresh pita bread you can eat and dessert. If you order à la carte, the moussaka is one of their specialties and one of the best I have had in London. Vegetarians are not left out in the cold. There is always a *poly pikilo*—a Greek hot pot, which is a spicy vegetable casserole cooked with wine, or a stew of tender white beans simmered in tomato sauce.

THE MUSEUM STREET CAFE (15)
47 Museum Street, Bloomsbury, WC1

TELEPHONE
020-7405-3211

INTERNET
www.museumstreetcafe.com
(for mail orders)

TUBE
Tottenham Court Road,
Holborn

OPEN
Mon–Fri

CLOSED
Sat–Sun, holidays

HOURS
Breakfast 8 A.M.–noon, lunch
noon–3 P.M., afternoon tea
3–6 P.M.

RESERVATIONS
Essential (1–2 days ahead) for
lunch

CREDIT CARDS
AE, MC, V

PRICES
À la carte, breakfast £4–8,
lunch £5–15, afternoon tea
£5–8

SERVICE
Service discretionary, 12½
percent service charge for 5 or
more

MISCELLANEOUS
No smoking allowed

Open for breakfast, lunch, and afternoon tea, the Museum Street Cafe draws enlightened diners to its elegant, minimal space. The small dining room holds a few bare tables and hard-seated bistro chairs. Coat hooks, a large vase of fresh flowers, a baker's rack holding their own jams and other sweets you can purchase, and a gray terrier named Frank complete the spartan scene. The all-vegetarian food, however, is anything but spartan. Everything you see on your plate is expertly prepared here, using top-quality ingredients, resulting in bold flavors that will soon convince you that modern British vegetarian food can be *very* gourmet.

If you arrive for breakfast, you will want to start with one of their designer coffees and a glass of fresh orange juice. Further choices include porridge with brown sugar and cream, boiled or scrambled organic eggs served with vegetarian sausages and toast. The strawberry, raspberry, black currant jams and orange marmalade are home-made, and so is the coconut banana bread and the cinnamon toast. At lunchtime, start with an invigorating glass of fresh carrot and ginger juice, elderflower lemonade, or a glass of blood orange juice. For something stronger, the wines are fairly priced, and one of the two beers is one of the best in the world: Budweiser Budvar from Czechoslovakia. The roasted aubergine soup with herbed feta cheese, the warm goat cheese salad with roasted red peppers, carrots, and sunflower seeds, or the grilled polenta served with oven-roasted green beans and beetroot, with a tangy Gorgonzola and walnut dressing are only a few of the imaginative seasonal dishes that await you. By all means you must save room for dessert . . . all of which are homemade, of course. My dining companion and I couldn't decide between their famous Valrhona chocolate cake, the carrot cake, or the caramel ice cream, so we had all three, which was a good decision. Teatime treats are equally as wonderful, especially their Earl Grey fruitcake, which has developed such a following that it is now shipped around the globe to its addicted devotees.

MY OLD DUTCH PANCAKE HOUSE (18)
131 High Holborn, Bloomsbury, WC1

True to its name, this restaurant serves 105 varieties of those 1½-foot-wide Dutch pancakes, stuffed with everything under the sun and presented on genuine Delft blue pancake plates to hungry people who love a hearty bargain. In these *pannekoeken,* prepared to order with wholemeal or plain flour, the ingredients are cooked into the batter rather than being rolled inside or spooned over the top. The many fillings include cheese, ham, sausage, bacon, chicken, vegetables, herbs, ice cream, and fresh fruit. It is true: some people actually have room for dessert, and those who do can select from thirty sweet pancake and eight waffle creations, including a summer-time treat with fresh strawberries, ice cream, and whipped cream piled on top. There is even a waffle version of the banana split: a fresh banana waffle with cream, nuts, and chocolate sauce. Whew!

There are two restaurants, and both boast interiors with a high degree of Dutch kitsch—scrubbed-pine tables, blue-and-white-tiled fireplaces, and displays of wooden shoes and antiques throughout. Sometimes there are used (chipped or cracked) *pannekoeken* plates for sale.

NOTE: Each restaurant (see page 176 for King's Road location) runs separate promotions at different times of the year. Look for half-priced pancakes and drinks, two-for-one deals, and early-bird and lunch specials.

TELEPHONE
020-7242-5200

TUBE
Holborn

OPEN
Daily

CLOSED
2 days at Christmas

HOURS
Noon–11:30 P.M., continuous service

RESERVATIONS
Accepted for more than 5

CREDIT CARDS
MC, V

PRICES
À la carte, £8–15, minimum charge at peak times £3.50

SERVICE
10 percent service charge

NORTH SEA FISH RESTAURANT (1)
7–8 Leigh Street, Bloomsbury, WC1

For over two decades, charming Mark Felipe and his family have been running one of the best fish restaurants in this part of London. On one side of the North Sea Fish Restaurant is a fish-and-chips takeaway, on the other a neatly dressed dining room with pink velvet chairs and

TELEPHONE
020-7387-5892

TUBE
Russell Square

OPEN
Mon–Sat

varnished wooden tables. The only thing on either menu is fresh fish: sixteen varieties deep-fried in pure peanut oil, sautéed, or grilled and served with either homemade tartar sauce, chips, or boiled potatoes. The catch comes in every morning from the Billingsgate fish market. It arrives around 5 A.M., and the North Sea fishmonger spends the next few hours cutting it into serving-size filets. Best-sellers, in addition to the eighty fish cakes sold per day, are the cod, haddock, plaice, and skate, which is a bony fish that is an acquired taste for some. The portions are giant, leaving barely enough room for the slice of homemade truffle, tiramisu, or pineapple fritter for dessert.

NOTE: If you do not want your fish cooked in peanut oil, ask that it be prepared in vegetable oil.

OCTOBER GALLERY CAFE (8)
24 Old Gloucester Street, Bloomsbury, WC1

At the October Gallery Cafe, which is about five minutes from the British Museum, polished wooden tables are set in the back of an art gallery, which displays changing avant-garde art "from around the planet." In warm weather, you can sit outside in the plant-filled patio of this former Victorian school building. While the art may appeal to only a distinct few, let me assure you that the vibrant food will appeal to everyone.

Everything is made daily and in small quantities, so there are never any leftovers. For the best selection, arrive when they open (for lunch only) because the locals are on to this one. The choices change daily and can range from a bowl of parsnip soup or hummus with pita and a salad to baked trout on a bed of couscous. There is always one hot meat dish, two vegetarian dishes, and dessert finales such as the chocolate truffle tart. If you want a glass of wine, you will have to bring it with you because the café is unlicensed, but you can order a cup of their organic coffee.

POONS (3)
50 Woburn Place, Russell Square, Bloomsbury, WC1

See Poons in W2, page 85, for full description.
TELEPHONE: 020-7580-1188
TUBE: Russell Square
OPEN: Daily

CLOSED: Christmas Day

HOURS: Noon–11 P.M., continuous service

RESERVATIONS: Accepted for 6 or more

CREDIT CARDS: AE, DC, MC, V

PRICES: À la carte, £18–28; set-price, £10.50–25 per person, 2-person minimum; Sat–Sun dim sum lunch from £9

SERVICE: Service discretionary

MISCELLANEOUS: Takeaway available

TREATS (11)
13 Lamb's Conduit Passage, Bloomsbury, WC1

Treats is well named because eating here is a Cheap Eat treat for sure. Eli and Yannis Casanova are a dynamic international team. Eli is from Czechoslovakia and Yannis is Greek, and their restaurant's interior evokes a typical Greek café. The narrow, whitewashed space has a blue-tiled counter, framed Greek costumes, hanging green plants, and a painting of Pyrgi, a village on the island of Chios where Yannis was born. Eight small tables are crowded into the back and on warm days there are a few tables outside.

The Mediterranean food is what brings back the regulars, especially for the chargrilled kebabs wrapped in pita bread. *Taramosalata,* hummus, tzatziki, and *melitzanosalata* (eggplant) are also served with pita bread for dipping. Willpower bites the dust when it comes to their pastries, which according to Eli are made especially for them by a Greek granny. All of the breads are made in-house, as are the soups and the falafels, which are served with a green salad. They are officially open from Monday to Friday from 8 A.M. to 4 P.M., but Eli told me, "If the light's on, we are here."

TELEPHONE
020-7404-5505

TUBE
Holborn

OPEN
Mon–Fri

CLOSED
Sat–Sun, holidays

HOURS
8 A.M.–4 P.M., continuous service

RESERVATIONS
Not accepted

CREDIT CARDS
None

PRICES
À la carte, £3.50–7

SERVICE
No service charged or expected

MISCELLANEOUS
No smoking between noon and 2 P.M.

WAGAMAMA (17)
4 Streatham Street (off Bloomsbury Street), Bloomsbury, WC1

This is the original Wagamama in London. See Wagamama in W1, page 68, for full description. All other information is the same.

TELEPHONE: 020-7323-9223

TUBE: Tottenham Court Road

OPEN: Daily

CLOSED: Several days at Christmas

HOURS: Mon–Sat noon–11 P.M., Sun 12:30–10 P.M., continuous service

WOOLLEY BROTHERS (9)
33 Theobald's Road, Bloomsbury, WC1

TELEPHONE
020-7405-3028
TUBE
Holborn
OPEN
Mon–Fri breakfast and
lunch only
CLOSED
Sat–Sun, holidays
HOURS
7 A.M.–3:30 P.M. (usually sold
out by 2:30 P.M.), continuous
service
RESERVATIONS
Not accepted
CREDIT CARDS
None
PRICES
À la carte, £2–6
SERVICE
No service charged or expected
MISCELLANEOUS
All takeaway

Sandwich shops are a sixpence a dozen in central London. These popular food outlets appeal to office workers on tight schedules and cabbies on the run, and they offer a chance for visitors to rub elbows with the locals, or at least to exchange smiles.

On Theobald's Road there are several sandwich shops, but the one to remember is Woolley Brothers. Everything served in this spic-and-span, brightly painted orange spot is made according to their own recipes in the huge kitchen below, which also serves as action-central for their catering business. The ingredients are the best, the food creative, and the results worth many repeat visits. Because there is only one small table in the back courtyard, you should plan on taking your food with you.

Every day there are more than sixteen sandwich choices, plus two specials, and ten or more salads that come in small, medium, and huge. Salads range from "Hazeldorf, like his brother Wal, but with hazelnuts, celery, and raisins," to potato and leek (leeks cooked with herbs and a little oil and mixed with boiled potatoes and lemon mayonnaise dressing). Pies, pastries, baked potatoes with hot and cold toppings, breakfast sandwiches, cereals, danishes, croissants, and wonderful daily soups complete the food picture at this top-drawer Cheap Eat in London.

NOTE: After paying for your order at Woolley Brothers, walk through the restaurant to Lamb's Conduit Passage and see the flower shop across the way. It looks like many others in London—small, colorful, and fragrant—but the owner has a particularly interesting background. Josephine Ford's family has been in the flower business for generations. It started in the late 1800s with her grandmother, who sold roses at Oxford Circus, which was an actual circus at that time. Tradition held that on Alexandra Rose Day, the flower sellers gave up their "pitchers" (stalls or stands) to the queen's ladies-in-waiting, who stood and sold their roses for them. And the flower ladies went to Buckingham Palace, where they had tea with the queen. Ms. Ford still has the photo taken of her grandmother at the tea party.

If you are from Southern California or New York City, you will be interested to know that when Ms. Ford was not in the flower business, she worked at Casa del

Zorro in Borrego Springs near San Diego, and in New York at Goldfarbs and the Waldorf Astoria Hotel. Her shop hours are Mon–Fri 9 A.M.–6 P.M.; tel: 020-7242-7620.

Pubs

CITTIE OF YORK (12)
22–23 High Holborn Street, Holborn, WC1

The Cittie of York, which celebrated its three hundredth birthday in 1995, has more history per square centimeter than almost any pub you will visit in central London. I like it because everything is original. When you first enter, look up at the vats stacked on shelves around the ceiling. Each is capable of holding eleven thousand gallons of lager, and they were in full use until World War II, when they were emptied during the Blitz for fear that bombs would cause them to burst open and flood the pub and the tube station running underneath. The booths along the sides of the main room were confession boxes with curtains to shield them, but the curtains finally had to be removed due to the indiscreet liaisons that took place when they were closed. The coal fireplace, which dates back to Waterloo, once stood in the hall of Gray's Inn and has a secret chimney that lies under the floor. If the pub is not too busy, ask to see the brick cellar where the ale from the Samuel Smith brewery in Yorkshire is stored in wooden casks. The pub sells 450 gallons of this ale per week, not to mention just as much stout, lager, and cider. The lager is stored in aluminum casks, where it is tapped and vented for twenty-four hours, allowing the beer to settle before being dispensed at the bar through hundred-foot-long hoses.

Next to the pub is the gatehouse to Gray's Inn, where Charles Dickens's David Copperfield lived. Dickens himself worked as a clerk in Gray's Inn and drank at the Cittie of York pub. In addition to following in the footsteps of Dickens, you will join the past and present illustrious company of Dr. Samuel Johnson, Sir Thomas More, Sir Francis Bacon, and Aimee Jane Browning, whose pictures are displayed around the front bar. Who is Aimee Jane Browning? The young daughter of the present managers and the first child to be born in the Cittie of York. Quite a distinction, I think.

TELEPHONE
020-7242-7670

TUBE
Chancery Lane

OPEN
Mon–Sat

CLOSED
Sun, holidays

HOURS
Pub: Mon–Fri 11:30 A.M.–11 P.M., Sat noon–11 P.M.; lunch noon–2:30 P.M., dinner 5–10 P.M.

RESERVATIONS
Not accepted

CREDIT CARDS
AE, MC, V

PRICES
À la carte, £4–8

SERVICE
No service charged or expected

History aside, a pub is for eating and drinking, and you will do both well here. Cooking is taken seriously by Mrs. Browning, and she oversees the preparation of four daily hot dishes, beef and ale pie, chili con carne, pork sausages and mash, chicken with Stilton and broccoli, plus a host of sandwiches, salads, and homemade desserts—the best of which are St. Clement's Delight: an oh-so British concoction of orange Jell-O and lemon mousse topped with cream and the equally British jam roly-poly, which is a jam cake roll served with soft custard.

A final note of interest is the manager's hidden window where he can clandestinely keep an eye on the pub. The leaded stained-glass windows with the letters S. S. in the main bar provide the vantage point.

LAMB (4)
94 Lamb's Conduit Street, Bloomsbury, WC1

TELEPHONE
020-7405-0713
TUBE
Russell Square
OPEN
Daily
CLOSED
Christmas Day
HOURS
Pub: Mon–Sat 11 A.M.–11 P.M.,
Sun noon–4 P.M., 7–10:30 P.M.;
lunch daily noon–2:30 P.M.
RESERVATIONS
Not accepted
CREDIT CARDS
MC, V
PRICES
À la carte, £4–7
SERVICE
No service charged or expected
MISCELLANEOUS
Nonsmoking section

The Lamb is a magnificent pub in the heart of Bloomsbury, the part of London made famous in the twenties and thirties by the Bloomsbury Group of writers, which included Leonard and Virginia Woolf, Lytton Strachey, and John Maynard Keynes. Aside from the beautiful green-tiled exterior, the most striking feature of the pub is the horseshoe bar, with its original etched-glass "snob screens" still in place. These rotating screens were used in Victorian days to shield the pillars of society when they were drinking with women of dubious distinction. In the rest of the pub, the wood-paneled walls are decorated with a fascinating display of Hogarth prints and sepia photographs of half-forgotten stars of the Victorian music halls and theaters. On a more current note, there is a large photo of the Queen Mum with a glass of beer in her hand.

The seating throughout is comfortable, and you can always hear what is being said. The Lamb is one of the rare pubs that does not have piped-in music, a blaring jukebox, or banging flipper machines drowning out the gentle hum of conversation. The music you will hear comes from a late-eighteenth-century coin-operated music box, with all the money going to the Children's Hospital. In addition to the usual front sidewalk seating, on warm days, there is a secluded back patio where you can drink the afternoon away to your heart's content. Besides the great atmosphere, the Young's beer is good, the lunchtime food is above average and made here, there is a nonsmoking section, and the generally upscale crowd is very friendly.

NOTE: When you leave the pub, turn right on Lamb's Conduit Street and walk to the end and you will come to Coram's Fields, a park dedicated to children, where the sign by the entrance reads: "Adults may only enter with a child. If you see an adult who happens to be on their own, please contact a member of the Coram's staff." The park has recently undergone a huge renovation, making it an even more delightful place to while away an hour or so watching the children delight in their play.

MUSEUM TAVERN (14)
49 Great Russell Street, Bloomsbury, WC1

The Museum Tavern is a splendid pub with a long history. It is one of the oldest pubs in Bloomsbury, first opening for business in the early eighteenth century. For over 265 years it has continued to offer ales, wines, spirits, food, and hospitality to visitors and locals alike. Located opposite the British Museum, it was Karl Marx's watering hole during his London days, and it's also rumored to have been one of the gathering places for Virginia Woolf and her Bloomsbury Group, and for Oscar Wilde and his friends. The pub is known for its real ales, which you will find listed and explained on a board as you enter. Because it is such a convenient place for resting tired feet after tramping the corridors of the British Museum, it is wall-to-wall crowded at lunchtime, with most of the hot food gone by 2 P.M. So, for a good selection of their meat pies, the best cut on the Sunday roast, and a seat, plan to arrive early.

TELEPHONE
020-7242-8987

TUBE
Holborn, Tottenham Court Road

OPEN
Daily

CLOSED
Christmas Day

HOURS
Mon–Sat 11 A.M.–11 P.M., Sun noon–10:30 P.M.; hot lunch daily, noon–2 P.M. (or until it is gone)

RESERVATIONS
Not accepted

CREDIT CARDS
AE, MC, V

PRICES
À la carte, £6–9

SERVICE
No service charged or expected

QUEEN CHARLOTTE'S RESTAURANT & PUB (5)
1 Queen Square, Bloomsbury, WC1

The history of Queen Charlotte's Larder goes back to 1710, when the first tavern was licensed to operate on this site. When the mentally ill King George III was confined to a hospital on Queen Square across the street, his consort, Queen Charlotte, used the underground cellars at the pub to store delicacies to take to her sick husband. When the alehouse became a full tavern later in King George's reign, it was named the Queen's Larder in honor of Queen Charlotte. The cellars are now used to store beer kegs and are said to be haunted by ghosts. The present-day pub still has its original Georgian facade

TELEPHONE
020-7837-5627

TUBE
Russell Square, Holborn

OPEN
Daily, restaurant for dinner only

CLOSED
Christmas Day

HOURS
Pub: Mon–Fri 11 A.M.–11 P.M., Sat noon–11 P.M., Sun noon–10:30 P.M., lunch noon–3 P.M.; restaurant: dinner daily 6–9 P.M.

RESERVATIONS
Advised for restaurant, not
accepted in pub

CREDIT CARDS
MC, V

PRICES
À la carte, £3–10

SERVICE
Service discretionary in
restaurant, no service charged
or expected in pub

MISCELLANEOUS
No smoking in restaurant

with six bricked-up windows recalling the days of the window tax when property owners boarded up windows rather than be subjected to pay additional taxes per window.

History, ghosts, and taxes aside, the best part about this pub today is that it serves hot dinners in its upstairs dining room, highlighting the house specialty, home-made potpies. These meals-in-themselves are filled with vegetables, beef, lamb (the most popular), or chicken, and come garnished with potatoes and three seasonal vegetables or a salad. Lunch is served in the pub down-stairs and consists of above-average bar food, such as chili, steak and kidney pie, sandwiches, ploughman's platters, and fish-and-chips.

Tearooms/Pâtisseries

PÂTISSERIE DEUX AMIS (2)
63 Judd Street, Bloomsbury, WC1

TELEPHONE
020-7383-7029

TUBE
Russell Square

OPEN
Daily breakfast and lunch only

CLOSED
Holidays

HOURS
Mon–Sat 9 A.M.–5:30 P.M., Sun
9 A.M.–1:30 P.M.

RESERVATIONS
Not accepted

CREDIT CARDS
None

PRICES
À la carte, £2.50–5

SERVICE
No service charged or expected

MISCELLANEOUS
Mainly takeaway

Is lunch today to be an event or a snack on the run? If it's the latter, make it an elegant quick bite at the Pâtisserie Deux Amis. This is an appealing place to stop for a light bite . . . be it a sandwich made on a freshly baked baguette (they fly the dough in from Paris) or a bowl of soup and a slice of one of their seven specialty breads (rye, sesame, onion, golden grain, wholemeal, muesli, and walnut). In the morning, go for a frothy cappuccino and one of their special croissants filled with almond paste and glazed with a dusting of almonds outside. There are two or three tables inside and one outside at which you can enjoy your quick repast.

WC2

Charing Cross, Covent Garden, Leicester Square, and The Strand

All distances in London are measured from Charing Cross, the official center of London on the south side of Trafalgar Square. Book lovers won't want to miss a stroll down Charing Cross Road, which is loaded with fascinating secondhand booksellers. If Charing Cross is London's official center, Trafalgar Square is the sentimental heart of the city. It has a history as the setting for riots and demonstrations. Once the home of the royal horses, it was made into a square in 1829 to honor Lord Nelson with the 185-foot Nelson's Column. The square is framed by the National Gallery, the National Portrait Gallery, and the St. Martin-in-the-Fields church.

Covent Garden is where the slick and chic meet to eat and drink in an enticing variety of restaurants, which are close to most major West End theaters. By 1974, the Eliza Doolittle flower girls and the famous fruit and vegetable markets had moved to a new location at Nine Elms, outside of London. The market reopened as a collection of boutiques with a carnival atmosphere that is one of the liveliest parts of London.

Holborn was the thirteenth-century route for the transport of goods to the city, and it's now the heart and soul of Legal London, where you can walk around the Inns of Court and see the wigged and gowned lawyers heading for court.

Great people-watching is yours anywhere around Leicester Square (pronounced LES-ter). It is perpetually jammed with tourists flocking to one of the many cinemas that ring the square, eating greasy, overpriced junk food, or just standing around checking out the action. There's always a long line for half-price tickets at the Half-Price Ticket kiosk in the center of the square, but don't think you will get tickets for any of the top shows for a song, because they are rarely sold here. Tickets here are mainly for lesser-known or fringe shows.

The Strand is a commercial road with incessant traffic and pollution—not much to hold a visitor's interest.

($) indicates a Big Splurge

Restaurants

BELGO CENTRAAL (30)
50 Earlham Street, Covent Garden, WC2

What a place! If it was not a restaurant, this Belgian brewery hall/eatery would make a good indoor amusement park. Belgo Centraal serves unpretentious food in an—how should I phrase this?—architecturally stimulating environment. The name of the game is excess, and they manage to make some kind of statement at almost every metallic turn. Witness the lighted entry catwalks and zany lift going down to the arched-brick basement where there's an open kitchen and high-tech loo. There are two eating areas, and if you arrive without reservations, you will probably sit communal-style at long tables with hard benches in the eating halls. Reservation holders for the restaurant fare only marginally better from a comfort standpoint, if you view sitting on metal chairs with wooden seats as an improvement.

Don't worry—there are good reasons to eat here. They include, of course, the Belgian beers and the mussels, accompanied typically with french fries and mayo. Other good choices are the smoked wild boar sausages and mash, spit-roast chicken, grilled yellowfin tuna on a warm salad of green beans, new potatoes, and plum tomatoes, or grilled calves' liver served with celeriac mash and a Rodenbach beer sauce. Try desserts of crêpes or *gauffres* (waffles) with either caramelized apples and prunes or mixed forest fruits housed under a blanket of warm Belgian white chocolate sauce. Whipped cream can be had on request. All the ice cream is homemade.

For Belgo on a budget, the set-price menus are definitely Cheap Eat deals. Lunch for a fiver (£5), served between noon and 5 P.M. offers three choices: wild boar sausages, Belgian mash, and a soft drink or a beer; a half kilo (one pound) of *moules marinières* (mussels) served with a green salad and a bottle of sparkling water; or a *tartine de champignons* (toasted rye bread topped with wild mushrooms, cream, and chives, accompanied by a bottle of sparkling water). "Beat-the-Clock" runs Monday to Friday from 5–6:30 P.M. You pay the price at the time shown on your food order for one of the three listed food specials. For example, if you arrive at 5:05 P.M., order the *moules marinières* served with *frites* (fries) and a white beer and pay only £5.05. Come at 6:29 P.M., and the same

TELEPHONE
020-7813-2233

TUBE
Covent Garden

OPEN
Daily

CLOSED
Christmas Day

HOURS
Eating hall: noon–midnight (Sun till 10:30 P.M.), continuous service; restaurant: lunch noon–3 P.M., dinner 5:30 P.M.–midnight (Sun till 10:30 P.M.)

RESERVATIONS
Suggested for restaurant

CREDIT CARDS
AE, DC, MC, V

PRICES
À la carte, £12–22; set-price, lunch £5, 1 course and beverage; lunch and dinner £15, 2 courses, beverage or ice cream; "Beat-the-Clock" Mon–Fri 5–6:30 P.M.

SERVICE
15 percent service charge

MISCELLANEOUS
Their shops sell gift packs of beer and glasses and gifts (open daily noon–10 P.M.)

dish will cost you £6.29. After 8 P.M., you are looking at more than £13.50 for the identical meal. Finally, there is the Belgo Complet offered daily for both lunch and dinner. This includes a salad *liégeoise* followed by a kilo pot of *moules marinières* or *provençales* served with *frites* and mayo and a choice of beer, soft drink, or a dish of homemade vanilla ice cream.

NOTE: If you can't get to Belgo Centraal in London, maybe their newest outpost in New York City will be more convenient for you. It is located at 414 Lafayette Street, opposite the Crunch Gym, at the corner of Astor Place and the Joe Papp Public Theater (tel: 212-253-2828).

BERTORELLI'S (35, $)
44a Floral Street, Covent Garden, WC2

TELEPHONE
020-7836-3969
TUBE
Leicester Square, Covent Garden
OPEN
Mon–Sat, and on holidays when the Royal Opera has a performance
CLOSED
Sun, most holidays (call to check)
HOURS
Lunch noon–3 P.M., dinner 5:30–11:30 P.M.
RESERVATIONS
Advised
CREDIT CARDS
AE, DC, MC, V
PRICES
À la carte, £18–30; set-price, café only Mon–Sat lunch, pre-theater 5:30–7 P.M., and post-theater 10–11:30 P.M., 2 courses £10.95
SERVICE
12½ percent service charge
MISCELLANEOUS
Nonsmoking tables on request

Eat upstairs and splurge. Eat downstairs at the café/bar and pay half the price, but have all the upstairs quality in both food and service. The downstairs menu focuses on substantial Italian food that is well-prepared and -presented. A cornucopia of antipasti aims to please with warm spinach salad tossed with croutons, avocado, mushrooms, bacon, and shavings of pecorino cheese; roasted and marinated peppers; aubergines (eggplants); artichokes with Parmesan shavings; and a lusty minestrone of seasonal vegetables served with basil-flavored oil. Six pizzas compete for attention with as many pastas, which are dressed in sauces of clams marinated with garlic, *chorizo* (pork) sausage and french beans, or chicken livers, red-roasted onions, tomatoes, and chili cheese. Substantial main courses of sun-dried tomato polenta; lamb steaks with Swiss chard, oyster mushrooms, and a dried tomato *tapenade;* or roast breast of chicken with a wild mushroom ragout should fill gourmands and still leave room for one of their Italian ice cream creations.

CAFÉ COQ (28)
154 Shaftesbury Avenue, Covent Garden, WC2

TELEPHONE
020-7836-8635
TUBE
Covent Garden

In the mood for half of a French free-range chicken, straight off the spit? At Café Coq, it is brown and juicy with a selection of fresh sauces, or marinated and chargrilled in one of the following: barbecue spice, ginger, mustard and garlic, lemongrass, coriander and coconut, Jamacian jerk, or chili. Can't decide on a flavor? When in doubt, try a piece dipped in each. Red meat lovers are not left wanting here. Not with Welsh free-range lamb steak, Scotch Angus sirloin steak, seared duck breast, and a selection of herbed sausages and a side of Dijon mustard. All orders come with a side salad, masses of *frites* and mayonnaise.

OPEN
Mon–Sat

CLOSED
Sun, Christmas Day

HOURS
Lunch noon–3 P.M., dinner 5:30–11 P.M.

RESERVATIONS
Not necessary

CREDIT CARDS
AE, MC, V

PRICES
À la carte, £10–14; set-price, £9

SERVICE
Service discretionary

CAFÉ FLO (34)
51 St. Martin's Lane (next to Lumière Cinema), Covent Garden, WC2

See Café Flo on page 37 for full description. All other information is the same.

TELEPHONE: 020-7836-8289
TUBE: Leicester Square
OPEN: Mon–Sat; Sun lunch and dinner only
CLOSED: Christmas Day
HOURS: Mon–Sat 10–11:30 A.M., noon–11:30 P.M., Sun noon–11 P.M., continuous service

CAFE IN THE CRYPT AT ST. MARTIN-IN-THE-FIELDS CHURCH (56)
St. Martin-in-the-Fields Church, Trafalgar Square, WC2

St. Martin-in-the-Fields is the parish church for Buckingham Palace. You probably won't run into the queen taking tea at the Cafe in the Crypt, but you will meet countless others who have come to appreciate this roomy underground restaurant with its vaulted ceilings, plain wood-slat furniture, and nonsmoking section. The location on Trafalgar Square puts you across from the National Gallery and the National Portrait Gallery and in close walking distance to Piccadilly, Covent Garden, and many West End theaters.

The straightforward home-style cooking is varied, but not always consistent. I have had wonderful dishes on one visit, and run into fair sandwiches, a poor watercress soup, doughy apple crumble, and tasteless custard the next. Though it's generally excellent, I am just warning you that they don't always bat a thousand in the kitchen. The choices change for both lunch and dinner,

TELEPHONE
020-7839-4343

TUBE
Charing Cross

OPEN
Daily

CLOSED
Sun breakfast, Christmas Day

HOURS
Breakfast Mon–Sat 10 A.M.–noon, lunch daily noon–3:15 P.M., tea daily 2:30–5:30 P.M., dinner nightly 5–7:30 P.M.

RESERVATIONS
Not accepted

CREDIT CARDS
None

PRICES
À la carte, £5–10

SERVICE
Service included

so you won't strike out for long. In addition to soups and hot mains, there is a cold buffet counter with salads, filled-sandwich rolls, and desserts.

All the profits from the restaurant support the church's charities, especially those that take care of the poor and the homeless. Shoppers may want to devote a few minutes to the bookstore and take a very quick stroll through the Courtyard Craft Market directly behind the church (open daily from 9 A.M. to 6 P.M.). The merchandise is largely T-shirts, cheap Indian clothing, and junk, but now and then there is a stall with something of merit. There is also an art gallery next to the restaurant and the London Brass Rubbing Centre. Free lunchtime concerts are held at 1 P.M. on Monday, Tuesday, and Friday; choral services are held on Wednesdays at 1 and 5 P.M.; and evening concerts are held every night except Wednesday and Sunday starting at 7:30 P.M. Tickets cost around £15 and are available at the door, in advance from the box office, or through credit card booking agencies that will charge an additional booking fee.

CAFE PACIFICO (32)
5 Langley Street, Covent Garden, WC2

TELEPHONE
020-7379-7728
TUBE
Covent Garden
OPEN
Daily
CLOSED
Christmas Day
HOURS
Mon–Sat noon–11:45 P.M., Sun noon–10:45 P.M., continuous service
RESERVATIONS
Suggested for lunch
CREDIT CARDS
AE, MC, V
PRICES
À la carte, £14–22
SERVICE
12½ percent service charge

Let's face it—if you love Mexican food, going without it can cause deep longing. For years, the Mexican food scene in London ranged from grim to nonexistent. Not any longer. With Cafe Pacifico firmly entrenched on the scene, your Mexican favorites—margaritas, quesadillas, chimichangas, tacos, enchiladas, and fajitas—are all within easy reach in Covent Garden. To really appreciate the place, give it a chance to build some momentum and arrive after 8 P.M. The loud and active crowd will not appeal to the Sun City set, but for people mixing and matching, it's a knockout. If you are in London on Cinco de Mayo (May 5), there will be a live Mexican band to add to the festivities on this Mexican national holiday.

WARNING: Keep an eye on the tab—those margaritas can add up in a hurry.

CAFE PASTA (22)
184 Shaftesbury Avenue, Soho, WC2

TELEPHONE
020-7379-0198
TUBE
Covent Garden
OPEN
Daily

Cafe Pasta serves reliable Italian food that is perfect for a quick meal with little fanfare. While the dishes can hardly be labeled original, they are filling and inexpensive. Best choices include the fusilli with Gorgonzola sauce; penne in a spicy sausage and tomato chili sauce; lemon coriander chicken tossed with egg tagliatelle, ginger, lime, and garlic; or baked lasagna. Smoked mozzarella cheese melted on garlic bread is the best starter. Roasted artichoke salad with olives and an herb dressing is the best salad, and can be ordered as a main course or comfortably split between two for an appetizer. Daily specials and seasonal promotions add interest for the locals. If you go during an off-meal time, say in the morning or late afternoon, there is a small menu featuring designer coffees, sandwiches, pastries, and milk shakes. The ambience is pleasantly relaxed and friendly. Children are welcomed with coloring sheets and crayons and served half portions upon request.

CLOSED
Christmas Day

HOURS
Mon–Sat 9:30 A.M.–11:30 P.M., Sun 9:30 A.M.–11 P.M., pastas served beginning 11:30 A.M. until closing, continuous service

RESERVATIONS
Not necessary

CREDIT CARDS
AE, MC, V

PRICES
À la carte, snacks £3–6, meals £10–20

SERVICE
Service discretionary, 10 percent service charge for 6 or more

MISCELLANEOUS
Children's portions served on request

CAFE PASTA (46)
2–4 Garrick Street, Covent Garden, WC2

There are no snacks served at this Cafe Pasta. See Cafe Pasta above for full description. All other information is the same.

TELEPHONE: 020-7497-2779
TUBE: Leicester Square
OPEN: Daily
CLOSED: Christmas Day

CAFÉ SOFRA (29)
1 Bow Street, Covent Garden, WC2

See Sofra Bistro–Mayfair in W1, page 58, for full description. All other information is the same.

TELEPHONE: 020-7379-4554
TUBE: Covent Garden
OPEN: Daily
CLOSED: Never

CAFÉ SOFRA (33)
15 Catherine Street, Covent Garden, WC2

See Sofra Bistro–Mayfair in W1, page 58, for full description. All other information is the same.

TELEPHONE: 020-7240-9991
TUBE: Covent Garden
OPEN: Daily
CLOSED: Never

CANADIAN MUFFIN COMPANY (41)
5 King Street, Covent Garden, WC2

See the Brewer Street location in W1, page 38, for full description. All other information is the same.

TELEPHONE: 020-7379-1525
TUBE: Leicester Square, Covent Garden
OPEN: Daily
CLOSED: Christmas Day
HOURS: Mon–Fri 8 A.M.–7:30 P.M., Sat 9 A.M.–7 P.M., Sun 10 A.M.–6 P.M., continuous service

CHEZ GÉRARD (27)
119 Chancery Lane (off Fleet Street), Holborn, WC2

See the Charlotte Street location in W1, page 39, for a complete description. This Chez Gérard stays open longer and serves breakfast and a café menu in its wine bar in addition to its regular lunch and dinner menus. All other information is the same.

TELEPHONE: 020-7405-0290
TUBE: Chancery Lane
OPEN: Mon–Fri
CLOSED: Sat–Sun, holidays
HOURS: Breakfast 8–10:30 A.M., lunch noon–3 P.M., dinner 6–10 P.M., wine bar food 5:30–10 P.M.
PRICES: À la carte, breakfast £4–6, wine bar £6–12

CHEZ GÉRARD AT THE OPERA TERRACE (36)
The Market, The Piazza, Covent Garden, WC2

TELEPHONE
020-7379-0666

TUBE
Covent Garden

OPEN
Daily

CLOSED
Christmas Day

HOURS
Lunch 11 A.M.–3:30 P.M., dinner 5:30–11:30 P.M.

PRICES
À la carte, café: £5–12, restaurant: £18–30; set-price, daily dinner and Sat lunch £16, 3 courses, £4 extra for 4 courses

SERVICE
£1 cover charge, 12½ percent service charge

Because it is in the heart of Covent Garden, this Chez Gérard has both a restaurant side, called the Opera Terrace, and a café/bar geared to lighter fare. The café is *très français,* with plates of cheese and charcuterie, baguette sandwiches, assorted salads and the ever-popular *tarte tatin* (hot upside-down apple tart with ice cream). I recommend reserving a table with a terrace view, but the table will not be guaranteed. If you can manage to nail a table with a view, you will have a great perch from which to observe the swarms milling around the piazza below. At Chez Gérard's Opera Terrace, the same good value set-price menu is available for dinner from Monday to Saturday and for weekend lunches. Please see the Charlotte Street location in W1, page 39, for a full description. Otherwise the information is the same as in all the Chez Gérard restaurants regarding reservations, credit cards, and service.

CRANKS RESTAURANT–CHARING CROSS (57)
8 Adelaide Street, Charing Cross, WC2

This branch of Cranks is mostly a takeaway shop with only a few seats. See the Marshall Street location in W1, page 42, for full description. All other information is the same.

TELEPHONE: 020-7836-0660
TUBE: Charing Cross
OPEN: Mon–Sat
CLOSED: Sun, holidays

CRANKS RESTAURANT–LEICESTER SQUARE (39)
17–19 Great Newport Street, Soho, WC2

See the Marshall Street location in W1, page 42, for full description. All other information is the same.

TELEPHONE: 020-7836-5226
TUBE: Leicester Square
OPEN: Daily
CLOSED: Christmas Day, holidays

DIANA'S DINER (21)
39 Endell Street, Covent Garden, WC2

You will need a trucker's appetite (and an equal level of food sophistication) to do justice to the overflowing plates of food served at this meat-and-potatoes café on the fringe of Covent Garden. When you arrive, don't be put off by the diner's plainness, with its smoke-charred walls, narrow wooden tables, fake flowers, and a deli case positioned by the front entrance. Cafés like this have been around since time began and are havens for Londoners in search of plenty to eat for not much money. A cholesterol-laden full English breakfast is available all day. Entrées are a familiar lot: liver and onions with mashed potatoes, homemade fish cakes served with chips and a salad, beef, chicken, or turkey with two vegetables and a pile of chips, spaghetti with meat or fish sauce, homemade steak and kidney pie, sandwiches (best avoided), baked potatoes with ten or more fillings, their own jam roll, and fruit crumble slathered in cream. These are the English staples the neighborhood locals have been thriving on at Diana's for decades, and they have no intention of changing their dining ways at this point.

TELEPHONE
020-7240-0272

TUBE
Covent Garden

OPEN
Daily

CLOSED
Christmas Day

HOURS
Mon–Sat 7 A.M.–7 P.M. (8 P.M. in summer), Sun 8 A.M.–5 P.M., continuous service

RESERVATIONS
Not accepted

CREDIT CARDS
None

PRICES
À la carte, £4.50–8.50

SERVICE
No service charged or expected

MISCELLANEOUS
BYOB, no corkage fee, unlicensed

FOOD FOR THOUGHT (24)
31 Neal Street, Covent Garden, WC2

TELEPHONE
020-7836-0239
TUBE
Covent Garden
OPEN
Mon–Sat; Sun lunch only
CLOSED
Sun dinner, Christmas Day
HOURS
Mon–Sat noon–8:30 P.M.,
continuous service;
lunch noon–3:30 P.M.,
dinner 5:30–8 P.M.,
Sun noon–4 P.M.
RESERVATIONS
Not accepted
CREDIT CARDS
None
PRICES
À la carte, £4–9.50, minimum
charge at peak times: £2.50
SERVICE
No service charged or expected
MISCELLANEOUS
No smoking allowed, BYOB,
no corkage fee, unlicensed

On the street level, a small open kitchen vies for space with the cafeteria buffet, one table, and a counter seating three. The whitewashed downstairs dining room is a better place to eat, provided you can manage to find an empty chair, especially during the noon to 1:30 P.M. lunch trade, which starts lining up outside about fifteen minutes before the door opens. Food for Thought is a vegetarian restaurant, and too often vegetarian and vegan food blend together in bland forgetfulness. Although the vegetarian food is budget-priced here, it doesn't look or taste as though it's been done on the cheap.

The seasonal menu changes daily and offers balanced contrasts in color, taste, and texture. Each Sunday, "platter specials" reflecting different cuisines are served. I liked my Thai platter with spring rolls to dip in a chili sauce, white Thai curry and rice, and a refreshing lime and tomato salad. For dessert, taste the fruit scrunch, an oat-based fruit square with fruit yogurt, cream, honey, and chocolate, which is dribbled over it. It's better than it sounds. No booze is served, but fresh juices, sparkling water, barley cup, and soya milk are. Cheers!

NOTE: To create Food for Thought dishes in your own home, you can purchase their cookbook, which sells for £9.

HARRY BROWN (51)
4 New Row, Covent Garden, WC2

TELEPHONE
020-7240-0230
TUBE
Leicester Square
OPEN
Daily in summer; Mon–Sat in
winter
CLOSED
Sun in winter; Christmas Day
HOURS
Mon–Sat 7:30 A.M.–8 P.M., Sun
11 A.M.–6:30 P.M., continuous
service
RESERVATIONS
Not accepted
CREDIT CARDS
None
PRICES
À la carte, £2.50–7
SERVICE
No service charged or expected
MISCELLANEOUS
Takeaway available

Harry Brown is a sandwich bar with a little more zip than most. The neat and tidy interior displays an impressive collection of old-time radios. The made-to-order sandwiches, which can be ordered on granary baps (buns), baguettes, focaccia, or ciabatta bread are huge by any standard. They are known for their salt beef (corned beef) and the Hot Club, a gooey wonder filled with sausage, egg, mayonnaise, bacon, mushrooms, and melted cheese. If you are looking for breakfast anytime, try one of theirs. Their breakfasts are a notch above the mundane for their quality ingredients, including the same maize-fed eggs that the queen uses, their own sausage, and the best bacon on the market.

NOTE: Please see Pasta Brown's on page 136, which is under the same ownership. The photo on the Harry Brown menu is the owner Anthony Brown's grandfather.

INDIA CLUB (43)
143 The Strand, Covent Garden, WC2

If you like unadorned Indian food, this is the Cheap Eats address to remember when you are low on funds. Even though it is on the Strand, it is easy to walk right past it without a second look, as the India Club is hidden up a flight of dark stairs next to a fleabag Indian hotel. The clean but spartan canteen's interior has never changed, probably because there is nothing to it. The largely southern Indian food is not only cheap but authentic, and the high number of loyal Indian patrons who eat here daily attests to this. For the price of a prefab burger, larger fries, and a shake, you can have Mughlay chicken or chicken curry Madras—their specialties—along with rice, mango chutney, and Indian tea. A vegetarian meal is equally reasonable, with vegetable or egg curry, *dal* (lentils), and *chille bhajias* (fritters) all costing less than £3.50 per dish. The eccentric service from long-suffering white-coated waiters is courteous.

TELEPHONE
020-7836-0650

TUBE
Temple, Aldwych

OPEN
Mon–Sat

CLOSED
Sun, holidays

HOURS
Lunch noon–2:30 P.M., dinner 6–10 P.M.

RESERVATIONS
Accepted for 6 or more

CREDIT CARDS
None

PRICES
À la carte, £6.50–10, minimum charge: £4

SERVICE
Service discretionary

MISCELLANEOUS
BYOB, no corkage fee, unlicensed

JOE ALLEN (42)
13 Exeter Street (corner of Burleigh), Covent Garden, WC2

Joe Allen is a fashionable restaurant in a dark alley near Covent Garden. Accessible only to the determined (look for the brass plaque by the door), the popular restaurant is a faithful copy of branches in New York, Miami Beach, and Paris: brick walls, red-and-white-checked tablecloths, photos of film and theater stars, and a stuck-up waitstaff serving good American food. The big crowd comes in after the theater to order bowls of chili con carne, plates of barbecued ribs with black-eyed peas, wonderful main course salads (try the Caesar), slabs of pecan pie, and oversize chocolate chip or oatmeal cookies and ice cream. At lunch, they make a great eggs Benedict, and the popular Joe Allen—half of a baked potato with spinach, a poached egg, hollandaise sauce, and a grilled tomato on the side. Insiders order the hamburger with everything; it's not on the menu, so you have to ask for it. Even though the late-night diners often seem too chic and the noise levels seem too loud, this is still a great place to grab a late meal and people-watch to your heart's content.

TELEPHONE
020-7836-0651

TUBE
Covent Garden

OPEN
Daily

CLOSED
2 days at Christmas

HOURS
Mon–Sat noon–1 A.M., Sun noon–midnight, continuous service

RESERVATIONS
Essential at night and on Sun

CREDIT CARDS
MC, V

PRICES
À la carte, £10–22; set-price, Mon–Sat noon–4 P.M., £12, 2 courses, £14, 3 courses; pre-theater menu, Mon–Sat 5–6:30 P.M., £14, 2 courses, £16, 3 courses

SERVICE
Service discretionary

MISCELLANEOUS
T-shirts and baseball caps for sale

LA QUERCIA D'ORO (20)
16 Endell Street, Covent Garden, WC2

TELEPHONE
020-7379-5108

TUBE
Covent Garden

OPEN
Mon–Fri; Sat dinner only

CLOSED
Sun, Sat lunch, Christmas Day

HOURS
Lunch noon–3 P.M., dinner
5:45–11:30 P.M.

RESERVATIONS
Not necessary

CREDIT CARDS
AE, MC, V

PRICES
À la carte, £10–20

SERVICE
£1 cover charge for bread;
10 percent service charge for
large groups, otherwise service
discretionary

Italian food is good in London, despite the fact that its popularity has had more ups and downs than the Italian government. New wave Italian cooking is now the hot new thing—but you need a scorecard to keep track of the chefs and restaurants as they jockey to stay abreast of the latest fads.

Enter La Quercia D'Oro, which is as old-world Italian as they come. This Covent Garden *trattoria* doesn't pay heed to fads, calorie counts, or decorating improvements. It does listen to its portly customers, who are happy with plastic-covered tables and paper napkins, and who come back day after day for mama's *cucina*. Olives and bread and butter start the meal; chocolates, mints, and biscotti end it. In between are big servings of every Italian dish you know and love: steamed mussels in garlic and white wine, minestrone soup, pastas with tomato, clam, carbonara, or pesto sauces, shrimp scampi, chicken and veal either sautéed with a few herbs or buried in a decadent cheese and cream sauce. Desserts? Frankly, these are easily forgotten. Wind up instead with a glass of *vin santo* or a bracing espresso.

MONMOUTH COFFEE COMPANY (31)
27 Monmouth Street, Covent Garden, WC2

TELEPHONE
020-7836-5272, 020-7379-
4337

TUBE
Covent Garden

OPEN
Mon–Sat

CLOSED
Sun, holidays

HOURS
9 A.M.–6:30 P.M.

RESERVATIONS
Not accepted

CREDIT CARDS
MC, V

PRICES
Cup of coffee £1.50, bag of
coffee per pound £4.75–9

SERVICE
Service discretionary

MISCELLANEOUS
No smoking allowed

The wave of espresso bars and designer coffeehouses are fast replacing the greasy café for discerning Londoners. Nowhere is this more evident than around Covent Garden, where it seems you can get a cappuccino in a dozen forms, including decaf, flavored, and low-fat. It is hard to recognize the Monmouth Coffee Company as a coffee bar because its four tables, one of which seats only one very small person, are buried in the back behind bags of fresh coffee beans from around the world. All the roasting is done here and every coffee can be sampled in individually filtered cups before you buy it in bulk. How much bulk coffee do they sell a week? In excess of one ton!

NEAL'S YARD DINING ROOM–WORLD FOOD CAFE (23)
14 Neal's Yard (first floor), Covent Garden, WC2

Neal's Yard Dining Room–World Food Cafe is an upstairs haven for Cheap Eaters searching for healthy dishes at prices that won't take big bites out of their budget. It is located above the Neal's Yard Remedies shop and overlooks the Neal's Yard courtyard ringed with juice and sandwich bars, a New Age walk-in back-rub spot, and the Neal's Yard Bakery, which uses their own stone-ground wholemeal flour in all their breads. The whole atmosphere is a throwback to the hippie movement of the sixties. The open kitchen/dining room serves international vegetarian and vegan dishes to diners who sit at a horseshoe bar facing the cooking and food prep area, or at small tables positioned around the edge of the room. The wonderful travel photos displayed on the walls are the work of one of the owners and his wife.

To eat here you must be an adventurous diner willing to try new food combinations and able to tackle oversize portions. The menu features dishes from Mexico, Turkey, India, Sri Lanka, West Africa, and the Middle East, with the occasional British pudding thrown in for good measure. If you opt for the West African meal, you will have a stew made from sweet potatoes and vegetables cooked in a creamy peanut sauce and served over steamed rice. Accompanying this will be beet salad and a fresh banana on the side. Lighter appetites can be satisfied by filled tortillas, several salad and soup choices, or an assortment of Greek appetizers. The Polish lemon and raisin cheesecake is always tempting if it is available, and so is the flourless French chocolate cake.

TELEPHONE
020-7379-0298

TUBE
Covent Garden

OPEN
Mon–Sat

CLOSED
Sun, holidays (call to check)

HOURS
Noon–5 P.M.

RESERVATIONS
Not accepted

CREDIT CARDS
MC, V

PRICES
À la carte, £6–9; minimum charge during lunch: £5

SERVICE
Service discretionary

MISCELLANEOUS
No smoking allowed, BYOB, no corkage fee, unlicensed

PALMS (45)
39 King Street, Covent Garden, WC2

The Covent Garden Palms follows the same basic menu as the Kensington Palms in W8, but adds weekly specials and lunch and dinner set-price menus. See Palms, page 94, for full description. All other information is the same.

TELEPHONE: 020-7240-2939
TUBE: Covent Garden
OPEN: Daily
CLOSED: Christmas Day
HOURS: Noon–midnight, continuous service
PRICES: À la carte, £9–17; set-price, lunch £8, 2 courses, dinner £10, 2 courses plus coffee or tea

PASTA BROWN'S (50)
32 Bedford Street, Covent Garden, WC2

TELEPHONE
020-7836-7486
TUBE
Covent Garden, Leicester
Square
OPEN
Daily
CLOSED
Christmas Day
HOURS
Mon–Sat 8 A.M.–midnight, Sun
noon–6:30 P.M.; breakfast
8–11:30 A.M., full menu served
11:30 A.M.–closing; continuous
service
RESERVATIONS
Accepted for more than 4
CREDIT CARDS
None
PRICES
À la carte, £10–20; all pasta
dishes are £5 for takeaway
SERVICE
12½ percent service charge
MISCELLANEOUS
Takeaway available

Facelifts are great, especially when they turn out well, and Pasta Brown's has had another good one . . . leaving just enough character intact to keep it interesting. The new look is highlighted by metal sculptures of wine being poured into a glass, a bowl of pasta, and Andy Warhol–style poster art. The chairs still look like back-breakers, but actually aren't—once you've had a glass or two of wine, that is. The tables, sporting a blue bottle with a sprig of fresh flowers, and the up-tempo jazzy music give the restaurant a trendy feel. Softening the decor is a photo of the owner's grandmother by the door. (If you have been around the corner to their other restaurant, Harry Brown, page 132, you will remember that the owner's grandfather is pictured on that restaurant's menu.)

Beneath all the new look is still a restaurant with Italian heart and soul. This is evidenced by the almost thirty pastas, ranging from spaghetti Napoli—"simply tomato sauce, but very good"—to tortelloni Alfredo, or spinach pasta filled with ricotta and served with cream and freshly grated Parmesan cheese. The rest of the menu tempts with side orders of salads, garlic bread, homemade soups, assorted chicken dishes, and desserts for which you will extend your caloric boundaries, especially the tiramisu and banoffee (banana and toffee) pie. In the morning, coffee and pastries are served to local office workers, who keep watch on the passersby from the window and outside tables.

PLUMMERS (47)
33 King Street, Covent Garden, WC2

TELEPHONE
020-7240-2534
TUBE
Covent Garden, Leicester
Square
OPEN
Daily
CLOSED
Holidays
HOURS
Lunch noon–2:30 P.M.,
dinner 5:30–11:30 P.M.
(Sun till 10:30 P.M.)
RESERVATIONS
Essential after 8 P.M.
CREDIT CARDS
AE, DC, MC, V

Plummers is perfect for a romantic dinner or a long, leisurely lunch with someone you are just getting to know. It looks small from the street, but there are actually two spacious rooms in the restaurant, all nicely done in cream-colored cloths with white paper overlays, linen napkins, fresh flowers, candles at night, and a back room with green hanging plants and a pitched, stained glass skylight.

The well-priced set-price menus offer choice and value for the money. For £6 you can have a choice of the lunch special of the day . . . maybe a seared breast of chicken in a creamy leek sauce with pesto mash, the pasta of the day, or chargrilled lamb chops with a potato garnish. The expanded lunch and pre-theater menus offer any starter or dessert from the à la carte menu and a choice of four main courses, including a vegetarian course. This allows you to sample popular apple and Stilton or curried parsnip soups as well as their legendary banana and toffee pie or steamed butterscotch sponge cake with a light custard sauce, otherwise known as spotted dick. Main courses might include a grilled rump steak, a filet of haddock with an herb crust, or a caramelized onion, artichoke, and pecorino cheese tart with a tomato and avocado salad.

PRICES
À la carte, £15–25; set-price, lunch £6, main course only; lunch and pre-theater meal 5:30–6:45 P.M. every evening except Sat, £10.90, 2 courses

SERVICE
12½ percent service charge

PORTERS ENGLISH RESTAURANT (49)
17 Henrietta Street, Covent Garden, WC2

Porters is an attractive restaurant decorated with Covent Garden memorabilia, that's great for the whole family or for visitors in search of something typically English. Sure, it's on the touristy side, but the food and prices are good and no one leaves feeling fleeced. Arrive hungry, forget your diet, and order one of their famous potpies or special monthly dishes, and you will not go away disappointed.

The best starters are soups, served with a chunk of crusty white or wholemeal bread. In the winter, try their brown onion ale and cheddar cheese soup, and on warmer days try the chilled carrot and orange for a refreshing starter. But make sure to leave plenty of room for the main event, which is their filling potpie ranging from steak and kidney or Cumberland minced beef and vegetables cooked with ale and herbs, to more offbeat ones like lamb and apricot, or a fish pie made with cod, salmon, and prawns. Sausage and mash, bubble and squeak, spotted dick . . . no, these are not names from nursery rhymes, but some of the other dishes worth trying at Porters. For the novice, these translate as sausage and mashed potatoes; fried mashed potatoes, cabbage, and onions; and sponge cake with raisins and warm custard sauce. New on the menu are five grills: steak, chicken breast, lambs' kidneys or lamb steak, and salmon. They are all good, but frankly, when having a meal at Porters, you should order their famous potpies and bypass the rest. In the afternoon, Porters, here and in their casual bar next door, serves both a luxurious full tea with finger sandwiches, warm fruit scones, and cakes, and a traditional cream tea with warm fruit scones. If you have an early curtain call for the theater and plan to eat afterward, these afternoon teatimes are lifesavers.

TELEPHONE
020-7836-6466

TUBE
Covent Garden

OPEN
Daily

CLOSED
Christmas Day

HOURS
Noon–11:30 P.M. (Sun till 10:30 P.M.), continuous service

RESERVATIONS
Advised and essential during peak hours

CREDIT CARDS
AE, DC, MC, V

PRICES
À la carte, £15–22; set-price, £17, 2-person minimum, any soup, any pie served with a side dish, and any dessert (except ice cream), half-bottle of house wine, tea, coffee, and the tip included!

SERVICE
Service discretionary, 10 percent service charge for 5 or more

MISCELLANEOUS
May impose a 2-hour table limit during peak times

THE ROCK AND SOLE PLAICE (25)
47 Endell Street, Covent Garden, WC2

TELEPHONE
020-7836-3785
TUBE
Covent Garden
OPEN
Daily
CLOSED
Christmas Day
HOURS
11:30 A.M.–10:30 P.M. (Sun till
9 P.M.); takeaway 11:30 A.M.–
11:30 P.M.; continuous service
RESERVATIONS
Not accepted
CREDIT CARDS
None
PRICES
À la carte, £6–10
SERVICE
Service discretionary
MISCELLANEOUS
Takeaway available

Regulars come from the neighborhood and around the globe to eat Ismet Hassan's excellent fish-and-chips. I have met people from northern Cyprus, New Jersey, and people who live two blocks away when I have eaten here. My mail indicates that many *Cheap Eats in London* readers also count themselves among the faithful. There are other things on the menu: steak and kidney pie, hamburgers, sausages, and some unadventurous desserts. Ignore these and pay attention only to the halibut, cod, salmon, plaice, skate, or Dover sole—or any other daily fish that is offered. Whether you enjoy eating your fish-and-chips (with a side of mushy peas to be really authentic) at one of the seven indoor tables next to the kitchen, sitting at a picnic table on the sidewalk, or as you walk down the street, you can always be assured of fresh deep-fried fish that is so good that you, too, will be back many times.

RULES (48, $)
35 Maiden Lane, Covent Garden, WC2

TELEPHONE
020-7836-5314
TUBE
Covent Garden
OPEN
Daily
CLOSED
Christmas Day
HOURS
Noon–midnight, continuous
service
RESERVATIONS
Essential
CREDIT CARDS
AE, DC, MC, V
PRICES
À la carte, £30–35; set-price,
Mon–Fri 3–6 P.M., £17.95,
2 courses
SERVICE
Service discretionary,
12½ percent service charge for
6 or more

In 1798, the year Napoleon opened his campaign in Egypt, Thomas Rule opened his oyster bar in Covent Garden. In all its years, spanning the reigns of nine monarchs, Rules has been owned by only three families, and it still flourishes as the oldest restaurant in London and is certainly one of the most well-known and loved. Throughout its long history, Rules has been the haunt of writers, artists, lawyers, journalists, actors, and great literary talents. The past lives on in the hundreds of drawings, paintings, and cartoons displayed on the walls. The late Sir John Betjeman, then poet laureate, described the ground-floor interior as "unique and irreplaceable, and part of the literary and theatrical history of London." The restaurant seats over two hundred people on its three floors, employs a staff of eighty, and serves an average of 450 people a day.

Rules has always made quality and value its priorities, and it continues to maintain its reputation for solid, dependable food with service that is not just excellent but friendly. The kitchen specializes in classic game cookery. Rules owns an estate in the High Pennines, known as England's last wilderness, which supplies the game for the restaurant and where it is able to exercise its own quality controls and determine how the game is treated. The other meat and poultry served comes from lean, healthy, free-range animals, and the fresh fish includes both wild salmon and sea trout.

I am saving the best for last . . . their incredibly priced afternoon and pre-theater suppers, of which any starter and main course will be only £17.95. This has to qualify as one of London's better gourmet Cheap Eat steals, considering where you are and the quality of the food.

NOTE: The afternoon meals and pre-theater suppers are served from 3 to 6 P.M. Monday to Friday and are not available in December. For any of these meals, you can select from the entire menu including their special dishes prepared for two, which are prime rib, rack of lamb, whole roast pheasant, and grilled Dover sole. All main courses include potatoes and a vegetable.

SALSA! (19)
96 Charing Cross Road, Soho, WC2

Salsa! is one hot ticket—a South America–themed restaurant that draws the young, the bold, and the beautiful. These stylish patrons sample tapas, sip exotic cocktails, and dance the night away. There are live bands six nights a week, an eighty-foot-by-eight-foot video screen and satellite TV, and a DJ with a sixteen-channel sound mixer. For those who need to brush up their rusty sambas, lambadas, bossa novas, or merengues, there are Spanish dance lessons between 6:30 and 7 P.M. every night. If it's rhythmic and sexy, they dance to it here, and believe me, after a pitcher or two of margaritas or a few San Miguel beers, the place is alive, moving, and uninhibited. The live music starts at 9 P.M. (for which there is a cover charge every night but Wednesday), and there may be queues. However, if you are here before 8 P.M., there are no lines, no cover charges, and you can partake of the 40-percent-off Happy Hour drinks (from 5:30 to 8 P.M. nightly), with a dance lesson thrown in. For the best effect, go with a group and spend the evening munching on chips, dips, thin pizzas, potato skins, crab cakes, barbecued riblets, and tiny fajitas. During busy times there is a minimum charge of £10 per person seated at a table and a limit of two hours at the table. When your time is up, just head for the bar and dance till you drop.

TELEPHONE
020-7379-3277

TUBE
Tottenham Court Road

OPEN
Mon–Sat dinner only

CLOSED
Sun, holidays

HOURS
5:30 P.M.–2 A.M., meals served Mon–Thur 5:30 P.M.–12:30 A.M., Fri–Sat until 1:30 A.M.

RESERVATIONS
Essential for 6 or more, strongly advised otherwise

CREDIT CARDS
AE, MC, V

PRICES
À la carte, £15–25; set-price, £15, selection of tapas, 2-person minimum

SERVICE
Service discretionary, 10 percent service charge for 6 or more; cover charge after 9 P.M., £4 on Mon, Tues, Thur; free Wed; £8 on Fri, Sat

MISCELLANEOUS
Happy Hour daily 5:30–8 P.M. (call to check)

SMOLLENSKY'S ON THE STRAND (55)
105 The Strand, Covent Garden, WC2

TELEPHONE
020-7497-2101
TUBE
Charing Cross
OPEN
Daily
CLOSED
2 or 3 days at Christmas
HOURS
Mon–Wed noon–midnight,
Thur–Sat noon–12:30 A.M.,
Sun noon–5:30 P.M., 6:30–
10:30 P.M.; special children's
events Sat–Sun noon–4 P.M.
RESERVATIONS
Advised, especially on
weekends for children's events;
essential on Sun nights for jazz
if you want to see the stage
CREDIT CARDS
AE, DC, MC, V
PRICES
À la carte, £20–25, children
£7–9
SERVICE
Service discretionary
MISCELLANEOUS
Nonsmoking policy on Sat–Sun
from noon–4 P.M. during
children's activities

Looking for a great place to take your family for a treat? The American-owned and -inspired Smollensky's is the ticket. Providing a taste of home for all ages, it will surely offer something for every member of your party. Starting with the small fry, the children's menu is highlighted by "Kids' Kocktails" and "Kids' Dessert Konkoktions." On weekends, from noon to 4 P.M., entertainers keep the kids busy, and at 2:30 in the afternoon, all the little ones are invited for a Punch and Judy or magic show. There is also a clown who paints willing faces, free helium balloons, and a variety of T-shirts for sale. If this isn't enough, there is also a play area for tots under seven and Nintendo games for the older ones.

For the grown-ups, there are two sets of live jazz on Sunday evenings starting at 8:15 P.M. with a £5 cover charge. From Monday to Saturday nights at 7 P.M. there is a piano player, singer, and guitarist, no cover charge, and on Thursday, Friday, and Saturday nights, DJ dancing starts at 10 P.M., again, with no cover charge.

Mom and Dad can relax Monday through Friday from 5:30–7:30 P.M. during the half-price Happy Hour, then slip into a comfortable banquette and enjoy one of the main draws on the menu: perfectly grilled steak served with one of eight sauces and golden-fried potatoes. Dieters must beware of the dazzling dessert lineup, starring a large bowl of Erna's chocolate mousse. If you finish your first helping, there is no charge for the second.

SOFRA RESTAURANT (54)
17 Charing Cross Road (opposite Garrick Theatre), WC2

See Sofra Bistro–Mayfair in W1, page 58, for full description. All other information is the same.
TELEPHONE: 020-7930-6090
TUBE: Leicester Square

SOFRA RESTAURANT (44)
36 Tavistock Street, Covent Garden, WC2

See Sofra Bistro–Mayfair in W1, page 58, for full description. This location is somewhat less hectic than others and has a *meze* (assorted appetizers) bar by the entrance. All other information is the same.
TELEPHONE: 020-7240-3773, 020-7240-3972
TUBE: Covent Garden

TOKYO DINER (38)
2 Newport Place, Chinatown, WC2

The Tokyo Diner is an outpost of Japanese fast food in London. The concept is carried out in a simple bi-level interior where the speedy turnover allows diners to enjoy affordable, satisfying food featuring Japanese rice, filtered water, and fresh ingredients. They have a no-tips policy and are open 365 days a year from noon until midnight.

The menu is explicit, with each dish and its history explained. *Bento* meals (box lunches served in sectioned dishes filled with noodles, rice, sashimi, pickles, and perhaps one or two other tidbits) are featured. Curries, sushi, seasonal dishes, and soba noodles or rice with countless toppings are washed down with Kirin beer, sake, or Japanese tea. Slurping is encouraged, at least when it comes to eating the noodles.

TELEPHONE
020-7287-8777

TUBE
Leicester Square

OPEN
Daily

CLOSED
Never

HOURS
Noon–midnight, continuous service

RESERVATIONS
Not accepted

CREDIT CARDS
MC, V

PRICES
À la carte, £5–10

SERVICE
No service charged or expected

MISCELLANEOUS
Nonsmoking section

WOLFE'S (26)
30 Great Queen Street, Covent Garden, WC2

There is now only one Wolfe's in London, around the corner from the New London Theater on Drury Lane, where the musical *Cats* has been performing for years. It is a very smart, clubby sort of place, with dark paneling, upholstered banquette seating, little table lights, a mirrored ceiling, and a long bar at which the singles seem to greet, drink, and eat, hoping to meet someone interesting. Most of the staff have been serving the loyal patrons for more than twenty years.

Long recognized as the salvation of many a famished diner, Wolfe's is best enjoyed for what it is: a great place for a cooked-to-order designer hamburger, a large salad, or a guilt-inspiring dessert. If you wander too far from these choices, prices increase significantly. The big draw has always been the Wolfeburger, which is removed from the fast-food ghetto thanks to the quality of their naturally fed Scottish beef and the charbroiling cooking process. You can have yours bare (without its toasted sesame seed bun), but with a generous helping of cottage cheese and a salad instead. Or, step up to the Continental Wolfeburger accessorized with fresh vegetable puree and your choice of potato garnish—creamed, baked, fried, or

TELEPHONE
020-7831-4442

TUBE
Covent Garden

OPEN
Mon–Sat

CLOSED
Sun, 2 days at Christmas

HOURS
Noon–midnight, continuous service

RESERVATIONS
Advised

CREDIT CARDS
AE, DC, MC, V

PRICES
À la carte, £15–20

SERVICE
No service charge for bills under £40, 12½ percent service charge for bills over £40

croquettes. The chef recommends ordering the hamburgers to be cooked "medium" and reminds you that they are not in the fast-food business; therefore, please allow more time to prepare your food properly. For the under-twelve set, Wolfe's has a children's menu with a small Wolfeburger or fried eggs with chips (french fries) and a salad. For everyone, there is a page devoted to desserts with a dozen or more ice cream creations, along with cakes, pies, tarts, and their unbelievably good specialty, a Waffle-Wolfe: two scoops of vanilla ice cream sandwiched between warm waffles and smothered in hot chocolate and whipped cream.

You might be interested to know that Wolfe's popular Knightsbridge location, across from Harrods, was bought out by Mohamed Al Fayed, Harrods's owner, who also purchased every other business on the block in order to expand Harrods's parking and administrative offices. At last report, the wealthy neighbors were mounting a significant campaign to prohibit Mr. Al Fayed from installing a helicopter pad on top of his new structure . . . with his excuse for it being that he needed fast access to his store and there was never any place to park. Let's hope the neighbors prevail!

YOUNG CHENG (52)
22 Lisle Street, Leicester Square, WC2

This is the dressier version of their Shaftesbury Avenue Cheap Eat (see page 70). It has polished floors and comfortable seats, the waitstaff are dressed in black pants, white shirts, and maroon vests, and you will pay slightly higher prices. The window is lined with dripping ducks and you can see the cooking and chopping going on in front of you. The food is just as good, though: try the crab, lobster, or crispy duck, or for a much Cheaper Eat, the rice with pork spareribs, or beef, all for under £8. While here, check out the Chinese herbalist two doors away . . . things haven't changed in this shop for centuries.

TELEPHONE
020-7287-3045

TUBE
Leicester Square

OPEN
Daily

CLOSED
Christmas Day

HOURS
Noon–midnight, continuous service

RESERVATIONS
Not necessary

CREDIT CARDS
AE, MC, V

PRICES
À la carte, £5–10; set-price, £8–20

SERVICE
Service discretionary

Pubs

LAMB & FLAG (40)
33 Rose Street (off Garrick Street), Covent Garden, WC2

The Lamb & Flag is a pub that has remained largely unchanged since it opened in 1623 and was called the Coopers Arm. Later, it became the Bucket of Blood after the poet John Dryden was attacked out in front. Today it is quiet, and just hidden enough to escape the Covent Garden hordes. Its charm lies in its old wooden floors and wainscoted walls. Hot pub food is served for lunch and on Sundays, toasties, doorstops, ploughman's, and a roast. No food is served at night.

TELEPHONE
020-7497-9504

TUBE
Covent Garden

OPEN
Daily

CLOSED
Christmas Day

HOURS
Pub: Mon–Sat 11 A.M.–11 P.M., Sun noon–10:30 P.M.; food service: daily noon–3 P.M.

RESERVATIONS
Not necessary

CREDIT CARDS
None

PRICES
Sandwiches from £3.50, daily specials and roasts from £6.50

SERVICE
No service charged or expected

THE SHERLOCK HOLMES (58)
10 Northumberland Street, Charing Cross, WC2

No self-respecting Sherlock Holmes devotee will be able to resist this pub, a shrine to the great detective and his creator, Sir Arthur Conan Doyle. Inside are countless mementos that will thrill any fan, including photos of famous actors who have played the role of the sleuth on stage and screen. The first-floor restaurant has a perfect replica of Holmes's cluttered 221b Baker Street study, with its book-lined walls, his deerstalker hat and cloak hanging on a hook, handcuffs, a syringe, a sofa covered with his papers, and a model of the man himself. Why is a pub so totally devoted to Sherlock Holmes so far from Baker Street? As all real Holmes buffs will tell you, this was the site of the Northumberland Hotel, which is mentioned in the novel *The Hound of the Baskervilles.*

One must be reminded that this is a pub, and food and drink are served. Downstairs is primarily for basic pub food, sandwiches, and serious drinking. The upstairs serves proper meals in a more formal setting. The

TELEPHONE
020-7930-2644

TUBE
Charing Cross, Embankment

OPEN
Daily

CLOSED
Never

HOURS
Bar: Mon–Sat 11 A.M.–11 P.M., Sun noon–10:30 P.M.; pub food: Mon–Sat 11 A.M.–11 P.M., Sun noon–2:30 P.M., 6–10 P.M., continuous service; restaurant: Mon–Thur noon–3 P.M., 5:30–10:30 P.M., Fri–Sun continuous service noon–10:30 P.M.

RESERVATIONS
Suggested for restaurant only

CREDIT CARDS
AE, DC, MC, V

PRICES
Pub: à la carte, £6–8;
restaurant: £10–20; minimum
charge: £8

SERVICE
Service discretionary in
restaurant, no service charged
or expected in pub

MISCELLANEOUS
Sherlock Holmes T-shirts and
memorabilia for sale

mainly English-based dishes are named after characters in the stories and reflect better cooking than you will find in most pubs. In the summer, tables and umbrellas are set up outside.

Tearooms/Pâtisseries

CAFÉ VALERIE–COVENT GARDEN (37)
8 Russell Street, Covent Garden, WC2

See Pâtisserie Valerie in W1, page 73, for full description. Café Valerie faces the Piazza at Covent Garden. It began as a bookstore and tearoom in 1725 and was a meeting place for London's literatti, including the diarist Mr. James Boswell, who met the famous Dr. Samuel Johnson here for tea in 1763. All other information is the same.

TELEPHONE: 020-7240-0064
TUBE: Covent Garden
OPEN: Daily
CLOSED: Christmas Day
HOURS: Mon–Sat 7:30 A.M.–11 P.M., Sun 9 A.M.–6 P.M., continuous service

---

Wine Bars

CORK & BOTTLE (53)
44–46 Cranbourn Street (off Leicester Square), Soho, WC2

TELEPHONE
020-7734-7807

TUBE
Leicester Square

OPEN
Daily

CLOSED
Christmas Day, New Year's
Day

HOURS
Mon–Sat 11 A.M.–midnight,
Sun noon–10:30 P.M.,
continuous service

New Zealander Don Hewitson was one of the first to introduce Londoners to the wine bar, and his has become a legend, attracting connoisseurs who appreciate reasonably priced and consistently good food and wine in pleasant surroundings. Please do not let the location, between a greasy spoon and a sex shop, deter you. Once down the stairs and in the basement, with its poster- and print-covered walls, you will rub elbows with an attractive crowd that always returns to this oasis of style just off Leicester Square.

One of the most popular dishes is a simple one: a layered ham and cheese pie, similar to a quiche, but don't tell Don I told you this . . . he has a fit when it is referred to as a quiche. Grilled garlic-infused prawns, hot spicy sausages, hot and cold specials, or Don's spicy chicken and apple salad satisfy the lunch and dinner crowd, while wines from all over the world keep the drinkers happy. On Sunday, turn up for the brunch, which offers bucks fizz, smoked salmon, scrambled eggs, green salad, and a selection of cheeses. Don even does dessert. I haven't been able to stray from the chocolate fudge pie, but the vanilla ice cream with honeycomb butterscotch sauce is always tempting.

RESERVATIONS
Accepted only before 12:45 P.M. for lunch and before 6 P.M. for dinner

CREDIT CARDS
AE, DC, MC, V

PRICES
À la carte, £10–15

SERVICE
Service discretionary

SW1

Belgravia, Pimlico, St. James's, Victoria, Westminster, and Whitehall

The second earl of Grosvenor owns two prime portions of London: Mayfair and Belgravia, both of which are vying for "most-expensive real estate" status. Belgravia was originally an area that housed servants of Buckingham Palace, but today it's a quiet, dignified neighborhood with ten acres of private gardens in its center. Warning: Belgrave Road leading away from Victoria Station is not a good address. It is full of sleazy B&Bs that, with a few exceptions (see *Cheap Sleeps in London*), should be avoided, no matter how slim your budget is.

The Mall is the beautiful processional leading up to the gates of Buckingham Palace, where tourists gather faithfully each day hoping to catch sight of one of the royals or to watch the changing of the guard. You will know if the queen is in residence if you see the royal standard flying. Nearby is St. James's Place, which was built by King Henry VII. All foreign ambassadors are accredited to "The Court of St. James's." The palace is not open to the public. St. James's Park has all anyone could wish for in a royal park, including pelicans descended from a pair given to Charles II.

Pimlico is far from tourist central, but it does have its admirers, especially those looking for a quiet area close to the River Thames and the Tate Gallery, as well as antique buffs who enjoy the shops along Pimlico Road where it meets Lower Sloane Street. By 2000, the Tate is scheduled to move its modern art collection to the former Bankside Power Station on the south side of the River Thames between Southwark and Blackfriars Bridges.

In the forecourt of Victoria Station is London's largest tourist information center. The area around the station is not known for its sights, fine restaurants, or entertainment value. There are many good, inexpensive B&B hotels around Victoria Station, notably on Ebury Street (see *Cheap Sleeps in London*).

Westminster is the small section of London containing the Houses of Parliament, Big Ben, and Westminster Abbey. Whitehall is bureaucratic, government London. The prime minister lives at 10 Downing Street and the chancellor of the exchequer at No. 11. New Scotland Yard is here and so are the Cabinet War Rooms, from which Churchill and his chiefs of staff directed the British efforts in World War II.

($) indicates a Big Splurge

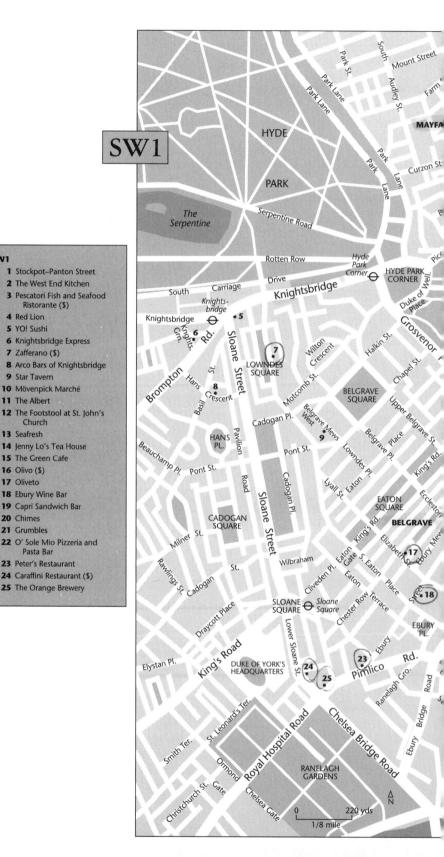

SW1

Restaurants

ARCO BARS OF KNIGHTSBRIDGE (8)
46 Hans Crescent, Knightsbridge, SW1

TELEPHONE
020-7585-6454

TUBE
Knightsbridge

OPEN
Mon–Sat

CLOSED
Sun, holidays

HOURS
Mon–Fri 7 A.M.–6 P.M., Sat
8 A.M.–6 P.M., continuous
service

RESERVATIONS
Not accepted

CREDIT CARDS
None

PRICES
À la carte, £4.50–9.50,
minimum charge: £4 from
noon–3 P.M.

SERVICE
Service discretionary

Arco Bars of Knightsbridge is right across the street from Harrods. It reminds me of an American chain of coffee shops with its low prices, plasticized menus, and food that is a step above fast-food joints. There is zero in the ambience department and no background music to soften the brightly lit room; seating is in Naugahyde-covered booths that you will probably share during the morning coffee rush. Along one wall is a deli case worked by a string of sandwich chefs and headed by George, the manager here for years. The food is predictable, from the egg and bacon breakfast to daily specials and sandwiches made to order. It is the type of place you can pop into anytime and get either a coffee and a piece of pie or a three-course meal with a glass of house wine. The best part is that you can be in and out in less than an hour and spend less than £10. In prime turf Knightsbridge, that is a Cheap Eat in London for sure.

NOTE: There is a smaller location in SW3 in the Brompton Arcade (see page 169).

CAPRI SANDWICH BAR (19)
16 Belgrave Road, Victoria, SW1

TELEPHONE
020-7834-1989

TUBE
Victoria

OPEN
Mon–Fri lunch only

CLOSED
Sat–Sun, holidays

HOURS
7 A.M.–3:30 P.M., continuous
service

RESERVATIONS
Not accepted

CREDIT CARDS
None

PRICES
À la carte, £2–6, minimum
charge: £2 from noon–2 P.M.

SERVICE
No service charged or expected

Escape the food sleaze in and around Victoria Station and walk down Belgrave Road, where you will find the Capri Sandwich Bar with the same family members working behind the counter since 1949. It doesn't look like much, with its four round tables, steamy windows, and assembly-line sandwich counter. A sandwich is a sandwich, you say, but at the Capri, you will bite into upmarket exceptions. I like the toasted mozzarella and ham with sun-dried tomatoes, artichokes, and a dash of Dijon mustard, or the mozzarella cheese number layered with tomatoes, olives, and fresh basil. Weekly sandwiches get top billing and so do their homemade soups: smoky bacon and mushroom, potato and leek, and spinach and nutmeg. Peanut butter fans can have their sandwich four ways: plain, with honey, dates, or bananas. All the meats are roasted here and the spreads made in their kitchen. If you don't want a sandwich, you can design your own filling for a jacketed potato, order a salad or an onion and cheddar cheese omelette, or eat a jelly doughnut. The usual coffees are served, as is Snapple.

MISCELLANEOUS
Takeaway available

CARAFFINI RESTAURANT (24, $)
61–63 Lower Sloane Street (corner of Holbein Mews), Sloane Square, SW1

If you are not pinching your pence too hard, Caraffini, a short stroll from Sloane Square, offers contemporary Italian cuisine prepared with imagination and a knowing hand. Despite the bare floors and crowded, noisy dinner atmosphere, the restaurant looks, feels, and is elegant, thanks to the tables, which are beautifully set with crisp linens, heavy cutlery, sparkling crystal, and fresh flowers. The service, by a waitstaff wearing black pants and blue shirts, is professional, yet friendly, and appreciated by the smartly dressed Chelsea patrons.

The menu offers tantalizing choices, such as tiger prawns in hot chili and olive oil, mixed wild mushrooms with polenta, and a beef carpaccio with spinach and fresh Parmesan for starters. Seasonally, the choices reflect the best of the market. In the spring, I love the fresh artichoke with garlic mayonnaise and the tuna with *borlotto* (kidney) beans and raw onions as out-of-the-ordinary starters. The grilled baby chicken with fresh rosemary or fresh salmon with ginger, spring onion, and soy sauce are both top sellers. So is the simply grilled calves' liver with sage and the rack of lamb with a crust of fresh herbs. There are plenty of pastas to try and a trio of risottos. If you like truffles, theirs will make you want to return often just for this dish. Don't overlook the desserts, which are all made here and perfectly balanced to end this special meal on a sweet note.

TELEPHONE
020-7259-0235

TUBE
Sloane Square

OPEN
Mon–Sat

CLOSED
Sun, holidays

HOURS
Lunch 12:15–3:30 P.M., dinner 6:30–11:30 P.M.

RESERVATIONS
Essential

CREDIT CARDS
AE, MC, V

PRICES
À la carte, £28–38

SERVICE
£1.25 cover charge, service discretionary

THE FOOTSTOOL AT ST. JOHN'S CHURCH (12)
Smith Square, Westminster, SW1

St. John's Church on Smith Square is considered one of the masterpieces of English Baroque architecture. Since its completion in the early 1700s, it has survived fires, lightning, bombs, and plans to tear it down. Now, thanks to the efforts of the Friends of St. John's, the church has been beautifully restored and is at the forefront of London's cultural and musical life. The church is the setting for a heavily subscribed concert series with afternoon and evening performances by noted artists.

TELEPHONE
020-7222-2779

TUBE
Westminster, St. James's Park

OPEN
Mon–Fri lunch only; dinner on concert evenings only

CLOSED
Sat–Sun

HOURS
Lunch 11:30–2:45 P.M.,
dinner on concert evenings only
6–10 P.M.

RESERVATIONS
Suggested for the à la carte
lunch, essential by noon for
concert evenings (by noon Fri
for weekend concerts)

CREDIT CARDS
AE, MC, V

PRICES
À la carte, lunch only,
restaurant £18–22, buffet £7–
12; set-price, concert dinners
only, £12, 2 courses including
coffee

SERVICE
Service discretionary,
12½ percent service charge for
6 or more

The Footstool restaurant is in the crypt of the church. Lunch caters to two different pocketbooks. You have the choice of going through a self-service buffet line and selecting from hot and cold dishes, salads, baked potatoes with assorted fillings, and a range of tempting desserts. Or you can sit at one of the formally set tables and order from the sophisticated, monthly changing menu. On concert evenings only, a preordered, set-price prepaid meal will be laid out for you at a table complete with flowers and candles. What better way to relax from the rigors of the day than to dine in one of the most beautiful churches in London, enjoy a nice meal with a glass of wine, and then listen to a beautiful concert?

THE GREEN CAFE (15)
16 Eccleston Street, Belgravia, SW1

TELEPHONE
020-7730-5304

TUBE
Victoria

OPEN
Mon–Fri; Sat breakfast only

CLOSED
Sun, holidays

HOURS
Mon–Fri 6 A.M.–6:30 P.M., Sat
6:30 A.M.–noon,
continuous service

RESERVATIONS
Not accepted

CREDIT CARDS
None

PRICES
À la carte, £3.50–6

SERVICE
No service charged or expected

MISCELLANEOUS
Takeaway available, no alcohol
allowed, unlicensed

A London cabbie told me he has been eating at the Green Cafe for almost forty years. That was all I needed to make it a top Cheap Eating priority for the day. For nostalgia buffs, you will be glad that I did. The Fioris family have been opening the door to their little hole-in-the-wall since 1955, treating everyone not just as paying customers but as members of their extended family. Brother Andrew has now retired, but John is still here, running the upstairs operation while his father's best friend and cousin hold down the fort in the kitchen downstairs.

Only seven tables are set in the green room, which is usually filled with beefy working-class regulars diving into a multitude of sandwiches, heartburn-inducing hot specials, and that Holy Grail of grease: the full English breakfast. If you order with wild abandon, you will probably have a hard time spending more than £5 or £6. Avoid any soup other than the homemade minestrone, as the rest are straight from Heinz. Do consider their specialty, spaghetti Bolognese, or any of the sandwiches, which are made on bread baked by the family. The puddings may not be worth an extra half hour on the treadmill, but I love their jam roll with custard or the slightly more sophisticated rhubarb crumble.

GRUMBLES (21)
35 Churton Street (off Belgrave Road), Pimlico, SW1

Smart Cheap Eaters pack the tables every lunch and dinner at Grumbles, which serves good food and wine at noninflationary prices. The pine-paneled walls and closely packed bare wood tables and chairs create an informal look that is softened in the evening by fresh flowers and candles on each table, even those in the almost-airless basement. The best part about eating in the basement is viewing the display of old photos of Grumbles employees on the stairway wall going down.

The food leans toward French provincial, with the odd English dish and Sunday roast lunch. Starters range from a simple soup of the day or grilled goat cheese on an herb crouton to sautéed garlic mushrooms on rocket (arugula) with fresh Parmesan. Carnivores have loads of choices, ranging from steak, chicken, lamb, and veal to roast duck. Vegetarians will have no worries with the roasted aubergine stuffed with tomatoes and peppers, and the Thai rice flavored with basil and coriander, or the spinach and Parmesan cheese pancakes with tomato sauce and cheese topping. Grumbles' fish pie and trout are constant favorites, and so are the desserts, which are all made here and loaded with guilty calories.

TELEPHONE
020-7834-0149

TUBE
Pimlico

OPEN
Daily

CLOSED
Holidays

HOURS
Lunch Mon–Sat noon– 2:30 P.M., Sun 12:30–3 P.M., dinner Mon–Sat 6–11:45 P.M., Sun 6–10:30 P.M.

RESERVATIONS
Advised for weekend evenings

CREDIT CARDS
AE, DC, MC, V

PRICES
À la carte, £15–20; set-price, lunch only, Mon–Sat £10, 2 courses, £14, 3 courses; Sun £14, 2 courses, £15, 3 courses

SERVICE
£1 cover charge, 10 percent service charge

JENNY LO'S TEA HOUSE (14)
14 Eccleston Street, Belgravia, SW1

Noodle houses are currently high on the list for healthy Cheap Eating in London. The daughter of the late Ken Lo has set up shop on her own, around the corner from what was once her father's famous restaurant. The action at Jenny's takes place in a bright room with red-and-purple-lacquered walls, black tables, and simple chairs, all offset by a tank of live fish. The placemat/menu is a simple listing of what they offer: either rice, noodle soup, or wok-fried noodles topped with combinations of duck, pork, chicken, vegetables, seafood, beef, curry, herbs, and seasonings. No MSG is used in the kitchen. There are ten side dishes—including spring rolls and pork or vegetable dumplings (better than the spring rolls)—and three desserts. To drink, you have a choice of green and red teas, including the Iron Goddess of Mercy Wulong tea, which has been blended by a qualified Chinese herbalist for cleansing and strengthening the liver and kidneys; freshly squeezed juice; and organic or regular wine and beer.

TELEPHONE
020-7259-0399

TUBE
Victoria

OPEN
Mon–Sat

CLOSED
Sun, holidays

HOURS
Lunch Mon–Fri 11:30 A.M.– 3 P.M., Sat noon–3 P.M., dinner 6–10 P.M.

RESERVATIONS
Not accepted

CREDIT CARDS
None

PRICES
À la carte, £7–10

SERVICE
Service discretionary

KNIGHTSBRIDGE EXPRESS (6)
17 Knightsbridge Green (off Brompton Road), Knightsbridge, SW1

TELEPHONE
020-7589-3039
TUBE
Knightsbridge
OPEN
Mon–Sat
CLOSED
Sun, holidays
HOURS
Mon–Sat 7 A.M.–5:30 P.M.,
continuous service
RESERVATIONS
Not accepted
CREDIT CARDS
None
PRICES
À la carte, £1.95–5
SERVICE
No service charged or expected
MISCELLANEOUS
Takeaway available

For Cheap Eaters who don't want to shell out big pounds for a sandwich, head across Brompton Road to Knightsbridge Green, a vehicle-free lane that runs between Brompton Road and Knightsbridge. The street is lined with sandwich bars, a restaurant or two, and takeout shops. Some have been cited for poor sanitation, others are known for stingy servings, but heartiness is the guiding principle at the Knightsbridge Express, where the lunch queue forms daily for one of George's handcrafted sandwiches made to order on substantial bread with good fillings and fresh trimmings. Look for daily hot dishes advertised on paper plates: jacket potatoes, soup, and a full English breakfast (served all day), which has the usual egg, bacon, sausage, tomato, mushrooms, beans, and fried bread, plus potatoes. If you can move after this one, let me know.

MÖVENPICK MARCHÉ (10)
Portland House, Bressenden Place, Victoria Station, SW1

TELEPHONE
020-7630-1733
TUBE
Victoria
OPEN
Daily
CLOSED
Christmas Day
HOURS
Mon–Sat 11 A.M.–11 P.M., Sun
11 A.M.–9 P.M.,
continuous service
RESERVATIONS
Accepted for large parties only
CREDIT CARDS
MC, V
PRICES
À la carte, £5–15
SERVICE
No service charged or expected
MISCELLANEOUS
Nonsmoking section, fresh
produce for sale

The Mövenpick Marché is housed in a modern glass structure known as the Portland House. You enter at the street level and go downstairs to what looks like a big, open food market with fresh fruit and produce displayed throughout. Each stand is a food-serving area. There is no set-price menu and no set time to eat. Just come as you please and have whatever turns on your taste buds. Once you have decided what to eat, your meal is cooked for you while you wait. You select your food from a huge variety of cheeses and cold meats, antipasti, salads, pastas and *rösti,* stir-fries, grilled meat and fish, pastries to die for, and the creamiest ice creams you can imagine. Guests record their food selections on a personal checkout ticket that becomes their bill.

A stylish bar designed as a sailing ship offers Happy Hour from 5 to 7 P.M. nightly. Next to it is the nonsmoking section with seaside murals gracing the walls. In addition, there is a fresh juice bar and a coffee station. Live music entertains patrons from 7–10 P.M. Wednesday through Saturday evenings.

Even if you do not eat at this Mövenpick, you positively must stop by and use the ladies' or men's toilets. I know this is odd, but I promise you they win the sweepstakes for the most fantasy-filled, amusing, and imaginative public loos in Great Britain. I will say no more, other than don't miss these WCs, please.

OLIVETO (17)
49 Elizabeth Street, Belgravia, SW1

At Oliveto—the pizza and the pasta spin-off of Olivo (see below)—the food is amazing for the price. It all happens in an uncomplicated yet chic room where only paper napkins, salt and pepper shakers, and a cruet of olive oil grace the bare tables. For the high-rent area, prices aren't outrageous. The locals flock here, and during prime feeding hours, the two waiters covering the twenty-five tables need track shoes and patience to withstand the high-density crunch. The all-Italian menu confines itself to a few well-chosen starters, a half dozen pastas, twice as many pizzas, and desserts guaranteed to keep cholesterol levels raised to the max.

TELEPHONE
020-7730-0074

TUBE
Victoria

OPEN
Daily

CLOSED
Christmas Day

HOURS
Lunch noon–3 P.M., dinner 7–11:30 P.M.

RESERVATIONS
Advised

CREDIT CARDS
AE, MC, V

PRICES
À la carte, £12–20

SERVICE
Service discretionary

OLIVO (16, $)
21 Eccleston Street, Belgravia, SW1

Olivo is a modern Italian restaurant that has been a success since the day it opened, thanks to its constantly changing, delicious menu. For the effort and ingredients put into every dish, it is an excellent value (especially at lunch), and you have to take your hat off to the imagination and ambition of the chef. The strikingly simple interior has bright royal blue and sand walls with a marigold-stenciled strip dividing the middle. Heavy cutlery and a small vase of fresh flowers rest atop paper-covered tables.

The lunch caters to office workers, offering a set-price menu geared toward faster and better meals for those with time and budget limits. But lunch can also be a madhouse with hungry patrons standing about and the frenzied staff trying to oblige. The pace is more leisurely at night when only an à la carte menu is available. As the evening wears on, however, a crescendo builds, and by 10 P.M., every table is taken and the restaurant is in full swing again.

The food has a Sardinian influence, making it appealing to those who like zing in their flavorings. Two good beginnings are the air-dried tuna tossed with green

TELEPHONE
020-7730-2505

TUBE
Victoria

OPEN
Mon–Fri; Sat–Sun dinner only

CLOSED
Sat–Sun lunch, holidays

HOURS
Lunch noon–2:30 P.M., dinner 7–11 P.M.

RESERVATIONS
Essential for both lunch and dinner

CREDIT CARDS
AE, MC, V

PRICES
À la carte, £20–30; set-price, lunch only, £16, 2 courses, £18, 3 courses

SERVICE
£1.80 cover charge, service discretionary

beans and sun-dried tomaotes or the marinated swordfish or tuna carpaccio with chives. Pasta portions are flexible; you can either order them as entrées or dine daintily on them as starters. In April and May, watch for *tagliatelle alle cozze e asparagi* (fresh tagliatelle with mussels and asparagus) or *linguine al granchio* (linguine with fresh crab, garlic, and chili). In the winter, you will find wild boar ravioli with fresh truffles. You can skip this course altogether and have only a substantial main course, perhaps chargrilled veal with sautéed spinach, or marinated lamb with rosemary, or the perennial Italian favorite, sautéed calves' liver with balsamic vinegar. To finish in style, Italian-style that is, order *sebada,* a traditional Sardinian pastry filled with sweet cheese and dressed with honey.

O' SOLE MIO PIZZERIA AND PASTA BAR (22)
39 Churton Street (off Belgrave Road), Pimlico, SW1

TELEPHONE
020-7976-6887

TUBE
Pimlico

OPEN
Mon–Fri; Sat dinner only

CLOSED
Sun, Sat lunch, holidays

HOURS
Lunch noon–2:30 P.M., dinner 6–11:30 P.M.

RESERVATIONS
Accepted for 6 or more

CREDIT CARDS
None

PRICES
À la carte, £12–18

SERVICE
Service discretionary, 10 percent service charge for parties of 6 or more

MISCELLANEOUS
Nonsmoking section

Whenever I am visiting the Tate Gallery and feel like a taste of Italian, O' Sole Mio gets my vote because the food and management is 100 percent *Italiano.* The menu is strictly thin-crust pizzas and pastas, many with homemade noodles all with their own sauces, preceded by a list of antipasti, each one sounding better than the last. For an out-of-the-ordinary Italian starter, sample the mozzarella in *carrozza* (mozzarella and anchovies dipped in batter, deep-fried, and served with a tomato-garlic sauce). Go for their signature pizza, *la pizza sole mio,* a messy and marvelous combination of tomato, mozzarella, ham, sausage, artichokes, black olives, mushrooms, peppers, asparagus, and a fried egg. *La pizza kiss* offers a lighter touch with its topping of tomato, mozzarella, oregano, and *rucola*. If you're going for pasta, the *gnocchi di ricotta e spinaci* (homemade ricotta and spinach dumplings in a tomato-basil sauce) is surefire, and so is the *rigatoni amatriciana* (pasta in tomato sauce flavored with chopped onions, crisp bacon, and pecorino cheese). For dessert, the best reason to splurge is *bomba al caffè*—hazelnut ice cream drowned in coffee liqueur.

PESCATORI FISH AND SEAFOOD RISTORANTE (3, $)
66 Haymarket Street, Piccadilly, SW1

This Pescatori is in the heart of London's theater district and therefore caters to a pre- and post-theater dinner audience with special set-price menus for these times. See Pescatori in W1, page 55, for full description. All other information is the same.

TELEPHONE: 020-7839-3641
TUBE: Piccadilly Circus
OPEN: Mon–Sat
CLOSED: Sun, holidays
HOURS: Lunch noon–3 P.M., dinner 5:30–11 P.M.
PRICES: Set-price, lunch £16, 2 courses and coffee; pre-theater 5:30–7:30 P.M., £17, 2 courses and coffee; post-theater 10–11 P.M., £20, 3 courses and coffee

PETER'S RESTAURANT (23)
59 Pimlico Road, Belgravia, Sloane Square, SW1

"Hey lady, anyone eating at Peter's should go into training, 'cause this ain't no sissy food!" barked the tattooed cabbie sharing my breakfast table the first time I ate here. He must have seen the look on my face as the waitress brought his breakfast platter overflowing with sausage, bacon, beans, fried eggs, fried bread, grilled tomatoes, and mushrooms accompanied by several cups of strong coffee and plenty of sugar. Lordy! Peter's has been feeding London cabbies for years and has become almost hallowed ground for the many regulars who brave their health to eat here. Salt, sugar, and caffeine are the holy trinity at this typical blue-collar café, where the artery-clogging grub is served in mountainous quantities. You can order less than the burly regulars do, but beware: this is not the home of tea, toast, and crumpets. Nor is it a bastion of service with a smile. Some of the staff need definite attitude adjustments and the sooner the better.

If you miss the breakfast grease-out, there is always lunch or dinner, when you can roll up your sleeves and dig into one of the daily Italian specials, one of their popular chicken dishes, which come with potatoes and three vegetables, or the shepherd's pie, served in a casserole that would serve eight easily. Orders are placed at the counter, and when they are ready, the waiter or waitress shouts over everyone, "Who gets the fried liver?" You'll want to leave your mother-in-law home for this one, but if you are hungry and have no cholesterol or waistline worries, but a few in the cash department, Peter's is an experience you should not miss.

TELEPHONE
020-7730-5991
TUBE
Sloane Square
OPEN
Daily
CLOSED
Holidays
HOURS
Mon–Sat 6 A.M.–10 P.M., Sun 8 A.M.–4 P.M., continuous service
RESERVATIONS
Not accepted
CREDIT CARDS
None
PRICES
À la carte, £3.75–7
SERVICE
Service included
MISCELLANEOUS
BYOB, no corkage fee, unlicensed

SEAFRESH (13)
80–81 Wilton Road, Victoria, SW1

TELEPHONE
020-7828-0747
TUBE
Victoria
OPEN
Mon–Sat
CLOSED
Sun, holidays
HOURS
Noon–10:30 A.M., continuous service
RESERVATIONS
Not necessary
CREDIT CARDS
AE, MC, V
PRICES
À la carte, £12–15
SERVICE
Service discretionary
MISCELLANEOUS
Takeaway available

Marios Leonidou is the sixth-generation family member to be at the helm of this popular fish-and-chips shop near Victoria Station. The fish is all fresh, the portions enormous, and the prices very much in the Cheap Eats in London category. Preparations of the usual standards are reliable and competent. One of the house specialties, the seafood plate, consists of cod, haddock, plaice, rock skate, salmon, king prawns, shrimp scampi, and calamari either fried in a light ground nut oil, or grilled. It is served all on one plate and all for one person. The homemade fresh-fish soup made with chunks of whitefish, prawns, and mussels, Dover sole, and deep-fried shrimp scampi are other specialties I can heartily recommend.

Hot dogs, Spam fritters, jacket potatoes slathered with beans, and sausage and southern-fried chicken are also on the menu . . . but for goodness sakes, not here! Fish should definitely be your order of the day at the Seafresh.

STOCKPOT–PANTON STREET (1)
38 Panton Street, Piccadilly Circus, SW1

See Stockpot–Soho in W1, page 62, for full description.

TELEPHONE: 020-7839-5142
TUBE: Piccadilly Circus
OPEN: Daily
CLOSED: Christmas Day
HOURS: Mon–Sat 7 A.M.–11:30 P.M., Sun noon–10 P.M., breakfast 7–11 A.M., lunch 11:30 A.M.–4:45 P.M., dinner 4:45–11:30 P.M.
RESERVATIONS: Not accepted
CREDIT CARDS: None
PRICES: À la carte, £5–9, minimum charge at peak times: £2.20; set-price, lunch and dinner £4, 2 courses, £6.50, 3 courses
SERVICE: Service discretionary

THE WEST END KITCHEN (2)
5 Panton Street, Piccadilly Circus, SW1

TELEPHONE
020-7839-4241
TUBE
Piccadilly Circus
OPEN
Daily

Every Cheap Eater on the planet who has been to London soon learns about the Stockpot restaurants. The West End Kitchen, on the same block as a Stockpot (see above), was opened by the original owner of the Stockpot chain . . . after he had sold them and retired. Obviously retirement did not suit him, and a new restaurant was the solution. The West End Kitchen follows the same penny-pinching formula with a twice-daily changing menu. The almost austere surroundings consist of pine booths with plastic seats (shared at crowded times) and white walls. Here a collection of the owner's Spy prints from 1911 and 1912 softens the antiseptic look to a degree. The no-surprise, basic food includes several three-course set-price meals from under £4 to around £5. The high-ticket meal includes a glass of wine and tea or coffee. There are at least three choices for each course— say, egg mayonnaise, a half of a grapefruit, or garlic bread to start; fish pie, grilled liver (check to see what animal it comes from), or tuna fish cake to follow; with custard, apple crumble, Jell-O, or fruit trifle to finish. If the kitchen is known for any dish, it is the Lancashire Hotpot, a boyhood favorite cooked by the owner's mother and the reason for the original name of the Stockpot. What is it? Basically a lamb stew with root vegetables and potatoes.

Considering the portion size and variety of food, prices are terrifically cheap, but for these prices, don't expect to eat for gourmet pleasure, rather for sustenance.

CLOSED
Christmas Day

HOURS
Breakfast 7–11:30 A.M., lunch 11:30–4:45 P.M., dinner 4:45–11:45 P.M.

RESERVATIONS
Not accepted

CREDIT CARDS
None

PRICES
À la carte, £3–8; set-price, £3.50, 2 courses, £5.70, 3 courses

SERVICE
Service discretionary

YO! SUSHI (5)
109–125 Knightsbridge, SW1

This YO! Sushi is on the fifth floor of Harvey Nichols, the famous Knightsbridge luxury store. See YO! Sushi in W1, page 69, for full description. All other information is the same.

TELEPHONE: 020-7235-5000
TUBE: Knightsbridge
HOURS: Mon–Sat noon–11 P.M., Sun noon–6 P.M.

ZAFFERANO (7, $)
15 Lowndes Street, Belgravia, SW1

I am often asked to name my favorite restaurant in a particular city. Here is my answer for London— Zafferano. If I had only one meal to eat in London, it would be here. In fact, writing about it now makes me wish I could pick up the phone and reserve my table. Because reservations are in such high demand, I will book my table at Zafferano at the same time I book my next flight to London.

Everyone who eats at Zafferano agrees that it serves some of the best food he or she will have in London, in

TELEPHONE
020-7235-5800

TUBE
Knightsbridge

OPEN
Mon–Sat

CLOSED
Sun, holidays

HOURS
Lunch noon–2:30 P.M., dinner 7–11 P.M.

RESERVATIONS
Essential as far in advance as possible

CREDIT CARDS
AE, DC, MC, V

PRICES
Set-price only, lunch £18.50, 2 courses, £21.50, 3 courses; dinner £28.50, 2 courses, £33.50, 3 courses, £40, 4 courses

SERVICE
Service discretionary

addition to offering top value for the dining pound. Owner/chef Giorgio Locatelli worked in Paris at the Michelin two-star Laurent, and it is this French influence that lifts his cooking far above the ordinary mainstream Italian fare. The set-price two- and three-course lunches and dinners, which change to reflect seasonal products, are bargains to behold, especially when you consider the high-caliber ingredients and preparation that go into each dish.

The rather small restaurant is beautifully decorated with massive, color-coordinated floral displays. Crisp linens, lovely table arrangements, nice paintings, and attentive service set the formal tone for the wonderful food to come. Just reading the menu is a pleasure. Depending on the season and your main course, you might begin with a salad of French beans with Jerusalem artichokes and Parmesan cheese, the unique sweet-and-sour skate salad, or one of my favorites . . . a deep-fried envelope of Swiss chard with fontina cheese. Sophisticated pastas include pheasant ravioli with rosemary, pumpkin parcels with Amaretto, or the unusual combination of buckwheat pasta ribbons tossed with savoy cabbage, leeks, and sage. If you like risotto, the creamy saffron and bone marrow risotto *allo Zafferano* is a must.

Meat-based entrées favor simplicity over complexity and star several chargrilled dishes. If you are feeling slightly adventurous, try the roast rabbit cooked with Parma ham and served with polenta. Less daring but delicious in their own right are the chargrilled chicken with spinach and the pan-fried plaice encrusted in basil. When it comes time for dessert, do not even consider leaving without tasting something, even if you only have room to share with your dining companion. The hot chocolate tart with nougat and hazelnut ice cream is one you might be willing to share, but frankly, the lemon and mascarpone (cream cheese) tart or the tiramisu served in its own biscuit cup surrounded by a heavenly sea of espresso sauce are two creations you will want all to yourself.

Pubs

THE ALBERT (11)
52 Victoria Street, Westminster, SW1

The Albert is a handsome pub positively bursting with atmosphere. Here you have it all: polished wood, original gas lamps, engraved glass windows that were removed and hidden during World War II, and a "division bell," which calls members of Parliament back to the House of Commons in time to vote. A set of old Victorian prints depicts the evils of drinking, and portraits of past and present prime ministers glare down at diners on the Victorian stairwell leading to the restaurant. This is one of the few pubs where reservations are necessary if you hope to get a table during busy lunch hours.

If you eat downstairs, you'll enjoy pub food while standing or sitting in very close proximity to your neighbor, who will probably be part of one of the endless tour groups who stream through. If you are more serious about your meal, reserve a table upstairs in the carvery, where you are served an appetizer and select your main course roast at the carving table, or order salmon, chicken kiev, lemon sole, or vegetable lasagna. All plates are garnished with vegetables or a salad. Desserts are brought to your table on a three-tier trolley loaded with cakes, fresh fruits, and a tray of English cheese and crackers. Freshly brewed coffee completes the substantial repast.

TELEPHONE
020-7222-5577, 020-7222-7606

TUBE
St. James's Park

OPEN
Daily

CLOSED
Christmas Day

HOURS
Pub: Mon–Sat 11 A.M.–10:30 P.M., Sun noon–10 P.M.; restaurant: noon–9:30 P.M.; continuous service

RESERVATIONS
Advised for restaurant

CREDIT CARDS
AE, DC, MC, V

PRICES
À la carte, £7–12; set-price, restaurant £16, 3 courses

SERVICE
No service charged or expected in the pub, service discretionary in the restaurant

THE ORANGE BREWERY (25)
37 Pimlico Road, Belgravia, SW1

Orange Square was developed in the nineteenth century and served as a main pleasure haunt. Today's remaining link to its rural past is the Orange Brewery, where six thousand pints of their own brews are made and consumed weekly. The pub is popular thanks to these specialty beers, which are geared toward party animals. Their most famous and award-winning beers, both bitters, are the SW1, named after the postal code, a classic bitter with a hoppy aroma and fruity, malty finish, and the SW2, a darker and more powerful version that has full flavor and an intense finish. The patrons are a mixed bag of Sloanies, Pimlico types, the odd batch of workers during the day, and those with fun on their

TELEPHONE
020-7730-5984

TUBE
Sloane Square

OPEN
Daily

CLOSED
Christmas Day

HOURS
Mon–Sat 11 A.M.–11 P.M., Sun noon–10:30 P.M.; food service noon–10 P.M.

RESERVATIONS
Not accepted

CREDIT CARDS
AE, MC, V

PRICES
À la carte, £5–8
SERVICE
No service charged or expected
MISCELLANEOUS
Brewery tours can be arranged in advance

mind and youth on their side after sundown. This is a place for serious drinkers looking to have a good time.

The blackboard menu displays a short list of pub food: beef and beer pie, a plate of Cumberland sausages with mash, peas, and beer gravy, baguette sandwiches, burgers, the usual ploughman's, bowls of chili con carne, and desserts no one pays any attention to.

RED LION (4)
2 Duke of York Street, St. James's, SW1

TELEPHONE
020-7930-2030
TUBE
Piccadilly Circus, Green Park
OPEN
Mon–Sat
CLOSED
Sun, holidays
HOURS
11 A.M.–11 P.M.
RESERVATIONS
Not accepted
CREDIT CARDS
None
PRICES
À la carte, £4–9.50
SERVICE
No service charged or expected

The tiny Red Lion pub just off Jermyn Street near Piccadilly Circus is a true jewel. It began as a gin palace. In the 1800s, William of Orange taxed beer, but not gin, making gin the "beer of that day." It has been said that this tax resulted in gin's killing more people at this time than all the wars William fought in Ireland. Today, much of the original pub remains intact. Look for the hand-etched, silver-leafed mirrors with each panel depicting a different English flower, the wraparound mahogany bar, which is a single piece of wood unjointed in the middle, and the gas rose ceiling lights. Outside by the entrance is a brass plaque with a polite notice: "Customers wearing dirty work clothes will not be served." This is a dignified and quiet pub,with no music or pinball machines to break the concentration and conversation of the sophisticated customers who stop by at their regular daily time. Sandwiches are served every day, and on Friday and Saturday, fresh fish-and-chips (cod or haddock in a special beer batter), and when the spirit moves the chef, hot meat pies.

STAR TAVERN (9)
6 Belgrave Mews West, Belgravia, SW1

TELEPHONE
020-7235-3019
TUBE
Knightsbridge
OPEN
Daily
CLOSED
Christmas Day
HOURS
Pub: Mon–Fri 11:30 A.M.–
11 P.M., Sat–Sun 11:30 A.M.–
3 P.M. and Sat 6:30–10:30 P.M.,
Sun 7–10:30 P.M.;
food service: lunch daily noon–
2:30 P.M., Mon–Sat dinner
6:30–9 P.M., Sun 7–9 P.M.

It takes some searching to locate the Star Tavern because it is off the beaten track for most casual visitors. There is no actual pub sign, just a large star suspended from a metal bracket above the entrance and prize-winning flowering baskets hanging outside from May to September. The pub is a friendly place that welcomes new faces. The main ground-floor room is similar to a gentlemen's club. There are tables, chairs, a carpeted floor, globe lights, and revolving fans suspended from the ceiling. A real fire adds a welcoming touch on cool days. The cozy upstairs lounge has an open fireplace, a small bar in one corner, and large windows overlooking the cobbled mews below. Every day the pub offers all the basic fare pub-goers know and love, from doorstop sandwiches filled with rib eye steak or ham and cheese to cod in parsley sauce and sandwiches made to measure.

RESERVATIONS
Not accepted

CREDIT CARDS
MC, V

PRICES
À la carte, lunch £4–8, dinner
£7–9

SERVICE
No service charged or expected

Wine Bars

CHIMES (20)
26 Churton Street, Pimlico, SW1

Over the years, English food has had a bad rap, and no wonder. Overdone meats swimming in gluey gravy, mushy peas, soggy chips, limp carrots—it was a cuisine that seemed as cold and gray as the London fog. But after one meal at Chimes, your faith will be rapidly restored, and your opinions are guaranteed to change. Every day locals arrive eager to dip into a memorable, delicious bite of their heritage and past.

The long menu makes for some interesting reading, mostly for its variety of individual meat pies. There is West Country, which is cidered cod and haddock with tomatoes, mushrooms, and parsley; chicken pie with celery and almonds cooked in a sherry and cream sauce with a puff pastry lid; fidget pie made with ham, potato, onion, and apple; or Gloucestershire lamb pie with fresh rosemary and apples served with a shortcrust top. These, plus a host of monthly specials based on old English recipes and a traditional Sunday roast lunch, have made Chimes a smart destination for those looking for the real thing in English food. Chimes also stocks a variety of draught ciders from major independent producers and many fruit wines, including elderflower, damson, plum, and raspberry. For dessert, the puddings are a must, especially the orange treacle tart served with dairy cream or hot custard.

A nice thing to remember about Chimes is that you can come here either for a full meal in the upstairs dining room or have only a glass or two of their unusual wines or ciders and eat a light meal at the bar in front.

TELEPHONE
020-7821-7456

TUBE
Pimlico

OPEN
Daily

CLOSED
2 to 3 days at Christmas

HOURS
Lunch noon–2:30 P.M., dinner
6–10:15 P.M.

RESERVATIONS
Suggested for dinner and for
Sunday lunch

CREDIT CARDS
AE, MC, V

PRICES
À la carte, £10–20; set-price,
dinner £11.95, 2 courses; lunch
roast Sunday, £9

SERVICE
Service discretionary,
10 percent service charge for
6 or more

MISCELLANEOUS
Downstairs dining room
usually used for private parties,
no beer served

EBURY WINE BAR (18)
139 Ebury Street, Belgravia, SW1

TELEPHONE
020-7730-5447
TUBE
Victoria
OPEN
Daily
CLOSED
2 days at Christmas
HOURS
Bar: 11 A.M.–11 P.M.,
continuous service; lunch noon–
3 P.M., dinner 6–10:30 P.M.
RESERVATIONS
Advised
CREDIT CARDS
AE, DC, MC, V
PRICES
À la carte, £17–24
SERVICE
12½ percent service charge

The Ebury Wine Bar has a well-deserved reputation as one of London's premier wine bars, serving consistently good food and excellent wines. The professionally dressed patrons are sophisticated and should be, considering that the neighborhood boasts some of the most expensive real estate in London. It is the sort of place to which these locals bring family, friends, and business colleagues from abroad so they will forget that old chestnut about the Brits being a stuffy lot who don't know how to mix, relax, and have fun. The narrow interior combines the look and feel of a Paris bistro, with metal-base tables, wooden chairs, and bare floors. The menu changes often, displaying international and British cooking. Appetizers might include spicy fish cakes with peanuts and a sweet chili cucumber on the side, sardines cooked in a Parmesan crust or a hefty Caesar salad . . . either plain or with roast chicken. Their main course special, Cumberland sausages with mashed potatoes, fried onions, and gravy, is always present. Meat loaf with bubble and squeak is in demand, and amazingly enough, so is the chargrilled, rare, kangaroo served with parsnip cakes. Vegetarians will be happy with the roasted root veggies and wild mushrooms under a spicy carrot dressing. Bar snacks, including a great BLT, are always available for those popping in for a special featured wine and a munchie or two. The service is efficiently friendly and knowledgeable.

SW3

Brompton and Chelsea

Brompton Road starts at the Knightsbridge tube stop by Harrods and cuts through this tony section of London. The area is chiefly expensive townhouses occupied by yuppies talking on their cell phones while driving their Range Rovers and Jeep Wranglers.

Chelsea is also home to London preppies known as Sloane Rangers and Hooray Henries. The main thoroughfare is King's Road, a private road until the nineteenth century, extending from Sloane Square. Hipsters, punks, and fashion weirdos still ply King's Road hoping to soak up some of its past history when it was the center of all things wild and strange in London. Today the street is filled with boutiques (both far out and far in), trendy cafés, restaurants, and pubs. The tube stop is Sloane Square and a very long walk to most destinations, unless you jump on buses 11 or 22, which go up and down the road. Along the Thames is a short street called Cheyne Walk (pronounced CHAIN-y). Over the years it has been home to George Eliot (No. 4), Dante Gabriel Rossetti (No. 16), and Mick Jagger (No. 48). Other noteworthy neighbors have been J. M. W. Turner, Thomas More, Thomas Carlyle (whose house is at 24 Cheyne Row), James Whistler (who painted his mother at No. 19), and Johnny Rotten and the Sex Pistols.

One of my favorite places in London is the Chelsea Physic Garden. The walls around the garden make it almost tropical, and flowers bloom year round. The garden was established in 1673 by the Society of Apothecaries and was used for studying the medicinal properties of herbs and other plants.

Sir Christopher Wren's Chelsea Royal Hospital is still the home of the Chelsea Pensioners, retired servicemen who wear their uniforms—a dark blue overcoat in winter, a bright red one in summer—as they walk along King's Road when not performing humanitarian good deeds like visiting the sick, marching in parades, and serving as Chelsea's official greeters. The Pensioners do these deeds with goodwill and a smile in exchange for room, board, clothing, and a daily portion of beer and tobacco.

HYDE PARK

Kensington Road

Kensington Gore

ROYAL ALBERT HALL

KNIGHTSBRIDGE

MONTPELIER SQ.

TREVOR SQ.

3

Queen's Gate

Prince Consort Road

Prince's

Ennismore

Gardens

Ennismore

Cheval Pl.

Brompton Road

Beaufort Gdns.

Hans R

Queen's Gate Ter.

Exhibition

Gardens

Garden Mews

Brompton Road

5

Beauchamp Pl.

6

Elvaston Place

Imperial College Road

SCIENCE MUSEUM

Road

VICTORIA AND ALBERT MUSEUM

7

8

E. Gdn.

Mews

OVINGTON SQ.

Yeoman's Row

Queen's Gate Pl.

NATURAL HISTORY MUSEUM

9

Egerton Terrace

10

Street

Egerton Gdns.

11

Ovington St.

Le

Gdns.

Cromwell Road

THURLOE SQUARE

Brompton Road

Hasker St.

First St.

12

Mil

Gloucester Road

Gardens

Stanhope

Queen's

Thurloe St.

South Ter.

Walton

13

14

Mossop St.

Rawlings

Harrington Road

South Kensington

Pelham Street

Denyer St.

15

Draycott

16

Avenue

Cadoga

Gate

Road

Lucan

Sloane

Avenue

SOUTH KENSINGTON

Rosary Gdns.

Old

Brompton

Cranley Pl.

Sumner

Place

ONSLOW SQUARE

Pelham Cr.

Road

17

Place

Elystan St.

SW3

Cranley Gdns.

Onslow Gdns.

Foulis Ter.

Fulham

20

Pond Place

Sydney

Ixworth Place

Elystan Place

Roland Gardens

Neville Ter.

South Parade

Street

Cale Street

St. Luke's St.

Godfrey St.

Jubilee Pl.

MARKHAM SQ.

Drayton

Evelyn Gardens

21

Elm Park

Old Church St.

CHELSEA SQ.

Dovehouse Street

Manresa Rd.

22

Britten St.

King's Road

Radnor Walk

Shawfield St.

23

Flood

Priory Wk.

Gilston Road

Cardens

Fulham Road

Elm Park Rd.

Mulberry Walk

CARLYLE SQ.

24

CHELSEA

Chelsea Manor

Margaretta Ter.

Oakley

Street

Redbu

Redcliffe Rd.

Seymour Walk

Park Walk

Beaufort St.

29

26

27

King's Road

28

25

Glebe Pl.

St.

Limerston St.

30

PAULTONS SQUARE

Old Church St.

Upper Cheyne Row

Street

Cheyne Walk

Edith Grove

Gertrude St.

Lamont Rd.

King's Road

Beaufort St.

Danvers St.

Cheyne Walk

Albert Bridge

31

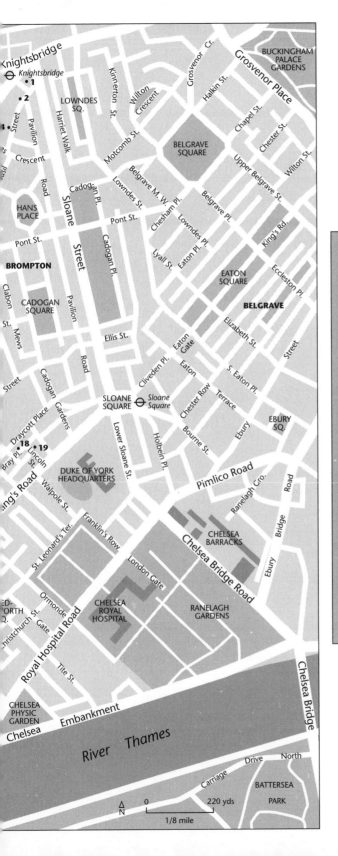

RESTAURANTS in SW3

PUBS

TEAROOMS/PÂTISSERIES

WINE BARS

($) indicates a Big Splurge

Restaurants

ARCO BARS OF KNIGHTSBRIDGE (1)
16 Brompton Arcade (on Brompton Road), Knightsbridge, SW3

See Arco Bars of Knightsbridge in SW1, page 150, for full description. All other information is the same.

TELEPHONE: 020-7584-3136
TUBE: Knightsbridge
OPEN: Mon–Sat
CLOSED: Sun, holidays

BECCOFINO (15)
100 Draycott Avenue, Chelsea, SW3

Warm sienna colors, velvet banquettes, walls crowded with oil paintings, and an Italian staff (including Louis and Pio from the former Au Bon Acceuil) create the mood of this restaurant in Chelsea. Tables set with heavy silver and starched linens underscore the formal tone. It all sounds expensive, but the food and atmosphere add up to an unbeatable dining combination that guarantees many repeat visits. In fact, every time I am in London, I make a special point of having at least one dinner here.

Trying to decide what to order is a problem, but a nice one. If you are here for lunch, you can have the Cheap Eat set-price menu, which might include the soup of the day or grilled sardines, rabbit stew or saltimbocca (chicken cooked with ham and sage in a wine sauce), and your choice of dessert. Otherwise you might want to start with the Beccofino salad made with spinach, mozzarella cheese, avocado, and warm bacon, or perhaps the grilled mushrooms with garlic and radicchio. The homemade pastas and sauces are some of the best in London. And the risotto, bursting with seafood, garlic, and chili peppers in a light tomato sauce, is, in a word, delicious. The veal *picatta* in lemon sauce, the roast lamb, or the roast chicken make good pasta alternatives, and so do any of the daily specials. It is hard to save room for dessert, but the temptation is strong when you see them displayed so seductively in the center of the room. The selections change every day, but the cloudlike custard is a must if it is there, and so are the fat spring strawberries or sliced mangoes. Lingering over an espresso is the perfect ending to your excellent meal. When reserving for dinner, please bear in mind that the

TELEPHONE
020-7584-3600, 020-7581-3387

TUBE
South Kensington

OPEN
Mon–Sat

CLOSED
Sun, holidays

HOURS
Lunch 12:30–2:30 P.M., dinner 7–11:30 P.M.

RESERVATIONS
Advised for dinner

CREDIT CARDS
AE, MC, V

PRICES
À la carte, £18–22; set-price, lunch only, £10, 3 courses

SERVICE
£1.30 cover charge, service discretionary

best time to arrive is around 9 P.M.; otherwise, you could be dining alone.

BIG EASY (26)
332–334 King's Road, Chelsea, SW3

TELEPHONE
020-7352-4071
TUBE
Sloane Square, then bus 11, 19, or 22
OPEN
Daily
CLOSED
Christmas Day
HOURS
Noon–midnight (Fri–Sat till 12:30 A.M.), continuous service
RESERVATIONS
Advised on weekends
CREDIT CARDS
AE, MC, V
PRICES
À la carte, £10–20, minimum charge at peak hours: £7.50; set-price, Mon–Fri noon–5 P.M., 2 courses and dessert £5.95
SERVICE
12½ percent service charge
MISCELLANEOUS
Nonsmoking section, takeaway available, 2-hour table limit at peak hours; Big Easy T-shirts (£6.95 children, £12.95 adults) and teddy bears (£4.95) for sale

Arrive starved and be prepared to party the night away at the Big Easy on King's Road, where the signs posted around the big room laughingly tell you what to expect: "Down home cookin' and uptown hoofin'," or "Emily Post fainted here," and "Duncan Hines never ate here . . . Betty Crocker wishes she hadn't." Heel-kicking live music every night, a buffed-bod staff, and wild drinks with names like Kickass Lemonade, Miami Whammy, and Tropical Itch keep the masses jazzed and pulsating. It all happens in a rough-hewn, big, barnlike building that serves a taste of American and almost-Cajun cooking. That's not all. The Big Easy is the home of the ultimate Scottish prime beef steaks, which range from eight to sixteen ounces each and come smothered with béarnaise sauce, creamy peppercorn, or a mushroom and onion sauce, a pile of fries, or a baked potato covered in sour cream or drenched in melted butter. Classic American burgers with whatever "fixins" you want on them, crab, shrimp, and lobster platters, or the Big Easy's "Big Bowl" mussel dinner featuring a kilo of mussels with garlic or hot and spicy sauce, salad, and french fries are just a few of the other belt-busting meals offered every day of the week. Monday night features all-you-can-eat barbecued ribs or chicken, coleslaw, and beans. There is a two-for-one happy hour all night on Monday and Tuesday and from 4 to 7:30 P.M. on Wednesday through Friday nights. Children always eat free if the adults order an entrée. And as the sign says "If you are in a hurry, we'll mail your lunch"—fast service is not a virtue here, but the mammoth portions are.

BRASSERIE ST. QUENTIN (9, $)
243 Brompton Road, Knightsbridge, SW3

TELEPHONE
020-7589-8005
TUBE
Knightsbridge
OPEN
Daily
CLOSED
Christmas Day

Expect a French brasserie atmosphere, French-accented waiters clad in black, and a dinner bill around £30 when you are dining at St. Quentin. In keeping with its French background, you can also expect your food, wine, and service to be taken seriously. The stylish and urbane crowd reflects this part of London, and to feel a part of it all, you will want to dress for success and make a dinner reservation for 8 or 8:30 P.M. The excellent value set-price meals change twice weekly, are available daily for both lunch and dinner, and in keeping with the times, also include vegetarian dishes for first and second courses. If I am not ordering the set-price menu, I like to start with the *salade St. Quentin,* which is made with baby hearts of romaine lettuce and sprinkled with cured black olives, red peppers, and slivers of pecorino cheese in a lemon and garlic dressing. I thought the risotto and truffles looked small, but it was so rich and filling that I had trouble finishing it all. The lamb shank served with parsley potato puree is delicious and so is the grilled veal chop, seasoned with rosemary and served with a mound of perfect french fries. Dessert is a deliberate attempt to destroy discipline, especially the lemon tart served with a dollop of crème fraîche and a sprinkling of candied lemon peel. Coffee is served with a piece of chocolate.

HOURS
Lunch noon–3 P.M., dinner 6:30–11 P.M.

RESERVATIONS
Advised

CREDIT CARDS
AE, DC, MC, V

PRICES
À la carte, £20–32; set-price, lunch daily, dinner 6:30–7:30 P.M., £14.50, 2 courses, vegetarian option £11, 2 courses

SERVICE
12½ percent service charge

CHEZ GÉRARD (7)
Yeoman's Row, Knightsbridge, SW3

Chez Gérard in Knightsbridge has a lunchtime café menu in addition to the regular restaurant menu found in all the others. After a few hours taking on Harrods or Harvey Niks, a light salad, baguette sandwich, or plate of cheese or charcuterie should hit the spot. See Chez Gérard in W1, page 39, for full description. All other information is the same.

TELEPHONE: 020-7581-8377

TUBE: Knightsbridge

OPEN: Tues–Sat; Sun–Mon lunch only

CLOSED: Sun–Mon dinner, holidays

HOURS: Lunch noon–2:30 P.M. (Sun until 3 P.M.), dinner 6:30–10:30 P.M. (Fri–Sat until 11:30 P.M.)

PRICES: Café: à la carte, £5–10; restaurant: £14, 2 courses, £16.50, 3 courses, £4.95 extra for 4 courses

DAN'S (22, $)
119 Sydney Street, Chelsea, SW3

If I am in the mood for a lovely meal after browsing through the shops at the lower end of King's Road, I walk down Sydney Street just past the Chelsea Market and enter the green door at Dan's. The airy interior is formally dressed in crisp linens, sparkling crystal, signature china, and a great collection of primitive animal prints, on loan from a friend of the owner who deals in them. The select tables are in the garden and conservatory,

TELEPHONE
020-7352-2718

TUBE
Sloane Square, then bus 11, 19, or 22

OPEN
Mon–Sat

CLOSED
Sun, holidays, Dec 24–Jan 2

HOURS
Lunch noon–2:30 P.M., dinner
7–10:30 P.M.
RESERVATIONS
Advised for the garden area,
especially in summer
CREDIT CARDS
AE, MC, V
PRICES
À la carte, £25–32; set-price,
lunch only £14, 2 courses, £18,
3 courses
SERVICE
12½ percent service charge

where the ceiling can be rolled open on pretty days. The clientele is aloof and rich, and the owners, who hold court behind the bar and at a table by the entrance, know them all.

The set-price lunch menu offers two courses plus dessert with several well-prepared, seasonally appropriate choices for each dish. The à la carte menu changes every month or so and is naturally more expensive, but the choices are wider. Starters might include a grilled prawn salad with sun-dried tomatoes, capers, basil, and toasted pine nuts, or a roulade of eggplant parmigiana dressed in an herb vinaigrette. The pan-fried ostrich steak is a novel, low-fat, interesting main course, but frankly I would order the breast of duck in a Madeira and red currant sauce, or the chargrilled rack of lamb served with roasted Provençal vegetables seasoned with rosemary instead. If the lusty chocolate truffle cake with coffee bean sauce is on . . . it makes a dramatic sweet finale.

ED'S EASY DINER (29)
362 King's Road, Chelsea, SW3

See Ed's Easy Diner in W1, page 45, for full description. All other information is the same.

TELEPHONE: 020-7352-1956
TUBE: Sloane Square, then bus 11, 19, or 22
OPEN: Daily
CLOSED: Christmas Day
HOURS: Mon–Thur 11:30 A.M.–11:30 P.M., Fri 11:30 A.M.–midnight, Sat 9 A.M.–1 A.M., Sun 9 A.M.–11:30 P.M., continuous service; deliveries 6–11:30 P.M.

ELISTANO (17)
25–27 Elystan Street, Chelsea, SW3

TELEPHONE
020-7584-5248
TUBE
South Kensington
OPEN
Mon–Sat
CLOSED
Sun, holidays
HOURS
Lunch 12:30–2:30 P.M., dinner
7:30–11 P.M.
RESERVATIONS
Essential
CREDIT CARDS
AE, DC, MC, V

Elistano is the most popular Italian restaurant in this corner of Chelsea, and for good reason. This is thanks to word of mouth, not the glitzy firestorm of publicity that many London restaurants seem to need to fill their tables. Here, the good food advertises itself. The restaurant is owned by two brothers, Marco and Carlo Morelli, who named it after the street. A picture of their grandfather, a former chef at the Excelsior Hotel in Naples, appears on the corner of the menu cover.

The two rooms are done in austere good taste with light sienna walls, marble-topped tables on stone slab floors, and a palm tree in an imported pot. Because it is always filled to capacity, it does get noisy, especially in the evening when diners can linger over another bottle of good red wine. The brothers are always present, tending bar, greeting guests, and escorting them out at the end of their stay. There are usually only two or three waiters, wearing jeans, speaking with heavy Italian accents, and working at their own slow pace.

The seasonal menu takes an Italian point of view, playing it safe yet very sound, with starters of minestrone soup, grilled vegetables, deep-fried mozzarella, salmon carpaccio, and a crisp spinach salad. Warm bowls carry the pastas anointed with their homemade sauces. Their signature pasta—fusilli loaded with tomato, mozzarella, and eggplant—had zip, but the green and white noodles topped with a fresh tomato and crabmeat dressing received the A+ of the evening. Of the five pizzas, the top vote getter is the Elistano, wearing the usual tomato and mozzarella but enlivened by thinly sliced filet steak. Veal and chicken dominate the *secondi piatti,* and most come nicely garnished. Practice has made perfect two of their dessert cakes filled with lemon or chocolate mousse. If there are two of you, order both and share.

THE ENGLISH GARDEN (19, $)
10 Lincoln Street, Chelsea, SW3

For a meal with someone special or simply to taste how fine British cooking really can be, reserve a table at either the English Garden or the English House (see below). Both are converted Chelsea townhouses with food to match their stylish settings and clientele, who agree with the owner, who states, "We should be proud of our English food. In my restaurants we use only the finest, freshest ingredients and devote much thought and care to creating imaginative menus." The English Garden is patterned after a comfortable country home. Dining in the garden room, surrounded by floral murals, topiary trees, and masses of potted plants and flowers, is a delightful experience. At the English House, the charm of dining in intimate rooms filled with chintz and impressive decorative furniture is pleasant, despite the close proximity of your dining neighbor.

The menus in both restaurants change seasonally and are always interesting and modern, with dishes presented in just the right portions. The à la carte meals can quickly become expensive, but ordering from the set-price lunch menu is a wiser option for many. Depending

PRICES
À la carte, £18–25

SERVICE
Service discretionary

MISCELLANEOUS
Nonsmoking section

TELEPHONE
020-7584-7272

TUBE
Sloane Square

OPEN
Daily

CLOSED
2 days at Christmas

HOURS
Lunch Mon–Sat 12:30–2:30 P.M., Sun 12:30–2 P.M., dinner Mon–Sat 7:30–11:15 P.M., Sun 7:30–10:30 P.M.

RESERVATIONS
Essential

CREDIT CARDS
AE, DC, MC, V

PRICES
À la carte, £30–35; set-price, lunch Mon–Sat £18.75, Sun £20

SERVICE
Service discretionary

MISCELLANEOUS
£3 cover charge per person for private rooms, which are available for parties of 6 to 25; menu can be arranged in advance

on the time of year you might start with a home-smoked chicken and asparagus salad served with a citrus dressing, a broccoli and Stilton tart with a warm tomato sauce, or the black fig, pear, and pine nut salad tossed with a blue cheese vinaigrette. Your main course could be the traditional roast beef and Yorkshire pudding, roast guinea fowl served on braised lentils with deep-fried parsnip crisps, or roast rump of lamb with a tomato and basil *tarte tatin*. Vegetarians will enjoy seasonal dishes of sautéed butternut squash and potato cakes served with a piquant red pepper sauce or the house fish cakes with a green pepper herb relish. Desserts are works of art, not only in taste but in looks. Perhaps you will have the dark chocolate terrine with a pear puree, a blueberry and apple crumble with vanilla custard, or the sinfully rich, sticky toffee pudding topped with hot fudge sauce and gilded with clotted cream. A platter of petits fours and chocolate served with coffee ends the meal. Yes, it will cost more than most, but it is worth the Big Splurge for the memories that will last long after you have left London.

THE ENGLISH HOUSE (12, $)
3 Milner Street, Chelsea, SW3

See the English Garden above for full description. All other information is the same

TELEPHONE: 020-7584-3002
TUBE: Sloane Square
OPEN: Daily
CLOSED: Christmas Day (for dinner), Dec 26

THE ENTERPRISE (11)
35 Walton Street, Brompton, SW3

TELEPHONE
020-7584-3148
TUBE
South Kensington
OPEN
Daily
CLOSED
2 days at Christmas, some holidays (call to check)
HOURS
Lunch Mon–Fri 12:30–2:30 P.M., Sat–Sun 12:30–3:30 P.M., dinner Sun–Thur 7–10:30 P.M., Fri–Sat 7–11:30 P.M.

The Enterprise began life as a gloomy pub serving gloomy food, and it basically stayed that way until it was resurrected from the ashes by Kit and Tim Kemp, the savvy owners of some of London's most recognized boutique hotels (see the Dorset Square, *Cheap Sleeps in London*). Drawing on their interior design talents, which epitomize good taste and style, they transformed the pub into a thirty-six-seat restaurant that is one of the area's most sought-after casual dining destinations. For proof, witness the wait during Sunday lunch, or try to get a dinner table after 9 or 9:30 P.M., when (inexplicably) no reservations are taken.

The substantial appetizers and salads can be ordered as starters or mains. The *maché* salad with lightly toasted pine nuts, anchovies, beets, and avocado is kept simple enough to let the flavors of each ingredient come through. If you are sharing, the quesadillas with salsa and guacamole or the new potato skins topped with caviar and sour cream are succulent choices. Follow these with a light-handed entrée such as their signature salmon fish cakes or the whole butterflied artichoke served with spinach gratin and warm vinaigrette. The roast duckling was tender, but the orange dumplings and plum sauce was heavy and cloying. How will you get through dessert? Very well if you the order the banoffee (banana and toffee) pie or the lemon tart.

RESERVATIONS
Accepted for lunch Mon–Fri only

CREDIT CARDS
MC, V

PRICES
À la carte, £20–28

SERVICE
£1 cover charge, 12½ percent service charge

LA BERSAGLIERA (30)
372 King's Road, Chelsea, SW3

Pasta partisans on modest budgets should not miss a visit to La Bersagliera. Stuck at the far end of King's Road from Sloane Square, it escapes most tourists, but not the neighborhood cognoscenti who have had it pegged for years. At midnight, every seat in the small room is still filled with people eating, drinking, and enjoying themselves. The closely placed marble-topped tables, along with the generally noisy, aggressive crowd standing in the aisles waiting for a table, make it uncomfortable for some. The service, by a mostly non-English-speaking Italian waitstaff, is continually rough around the edges and at times unprofessional—such as asking for the order before the menu is handed out, and presenting the bill before the meal has been served. Both of these faux pas have happened to me every time I have eaten here! With these drawbacks, why do I continue to recommend it? Because the food, especially the homemade pastas, sauces, and bread, is just too good to ignore, and the prices are definitely right for all Cheap Eaters in London.

Keeping in mind that the portions are huge, start with *carpaccio alla rucola* (sliced raw filet steak on a bed of bitter arugula and topped with Parmesan shavings) or the *insalata di mozzarella* (mozzarella cheese, tomato, and avocado served with homemade pizza bread). These two starters will leave plenty of room for one of the overflowing dishes of pastas and delicious sauces made in the tiny back kitchen by Lina Molino, the Italian mama who owns La Bersagliera. The pizza also wins top

TELEPHONE
020-7352-5993

TUBE
Sloane Square, then bus 11, 19, or 22

OPEN
Mon–Fri for dinner only; Sat lunch also

CLOSED
Sun, Christmas Day

HOURS
Mon–Fri 5:30 P.M.–midnight, Sat noon–midnight, continuous service

RESERVATIONS
Accepted for 6 or more

CREDIT CARDS
MC, V

PRICES
À la carte, £11–18, minimum charge: £8.50

SERVICE
Service discretionary

reviews . . . with eighteen choices ranging from a simple mozzarella and garlic to the Riccardo with olive paste, tomato sauce, zucchini, sun-dried tomatoes, mozzarella, and oregano. With the exception of the veal, the meat dishes do not quite live up to the standard set by the pasta. If you have dessert in mind, the crème caramel is the best.

MY OLD DUTCH PANCAKE HOUSE (25)
221 King's Road, Chelsea, SW3

See My Old Dutch Pancake House in WC1, page 115, for full description. All other information is the same. Note that it's a long walk from the Sloane Square tube stop, but since King's Road is great for shopping and browsing, the walk might turn out to be a good way to work up an appetite or to work off your meal afterward.

TELEPHONE: 020-7376-5650
TUBE: Sloane Square, then bus 11, 19, or 22
OPEN: Daily
CLOSED: Christmas Day
HOURS: Sun–Thurs noon–11:30 P.M., Fri, Sat until midnight, happy hour daily 6–7 P.M.

NEW CULTURE REVOLUTION (28)
305 King's Road, Chelsea, SW3

See New Culture Revolution in W2, page 84, for full description. All other information is the same.

TELEPHONE: 020-7352-9281
TUBE: Sloane Square, then a long walk or bus 11, 19, or 22

NIPPON TUK (16)
165 Draycott Avenue, Chelsea, SW3

TELEPHONE
020-7589-8464

TUBE
South Kensington

OPEN
Mon–Sat; Sun dinner only

CLOSED
Sun lunch, holidays

HOURS
Lunch noon–3 P.M., dinner 6–11 P.M.

RESERVATIONS
Not necessary

The name caught my eye as I took the shortcut from the tube stop to my Chelsea flat. I watched it for a few weeks, noting that the twelve hard-metal chairs (somewhat softened by a little cushion) were always full. Must be good, I thought, and it is . . . if you like sushi, sashimi, miso soup, and *udon* noodles. It seems to draw the locals, and I must admit, it is worthy of a pit stop if you are in the mood for something a bit different in this conservative neck of the woods.

Sushi novices can start with two pieces of floured rice topped with raw fresh salmon, king prawns, eel, or tuna. Seasoned rice seaweed rolls come with salmon and chives, cucumber and sesame, spicy tuna, or veggies. The Foundation Lunch Box is a twelve-piece selection of *nigiri, maki,* and *unari.* The latter is a mixture of fish and vegetable sushi with pickled ginger, fresh cucumber, daikon (radish) salad, green wasabi, and soy sauce on the side.

If raw fish sushi doesn't speak to you, perhaps the vegetarian lunch box or a big bowl of steaming *udon* noodles with vegetables and seafood might. For dessert, try the Japanese custard pancakes with chestnut ice cream on the side. As for drinks, you have a choice of Japanese or green tea, beer, saki, or water. Everything on the menu can be eaten here or packed to go.

CREDIT CARDS
AE, MC, V

PRICES
À la carte, £6–15

SERVICE
Service discretionary

MISCELLANEOUS
Takeaway available

RICCARDO'S (21)
126 Fulham Road, Chelsea, SW3

Calling all grazers who like to nosh on a variety of small dishes and not have a week's worth of food dumped in front of you . . . Riccardo's on Fulham Road is for you. Of course, you have to like Italian-inspired food to even think of Riccardo's, where the menu is long and most of the diners are regulars, many of them Italian. Another lure is the hours. Riccardo's is open daily from 9:30 A.M. to midnight, serving Italian-inspired breakfasts, lunches, afternoon teas, and dinners.

Successful eating here means you should hone in on the dishes everyone in your party would like to share, or at least taste. To start the day, one of you should order *La Toscana*—a complete Tuscan breakfast that includes a poached egg, sausage, Parma ham, grilled tomato, toast and homemade jam, fresh juice, and coffee or tea. Another might want the frittata (an Italian omelette) or *crespelle*—those wonderful Italian pancakes served with stewed apples and honey. For your midday or evening repast, get going with a bowl of raw vegetables dipped in an anchovy-garlic sauce and the antipasti *Toscani,* featuring prosciutto, salami, crostini, and frittata. Vegetarians have a multitude of options: grilled vegetables and Gorgonzola, pizza topped with fresh tomato and mozzarella (capers optional), a zucchini omelette, ravioli filled with spinach or aubergine (eggplant) and ricotta and tossed in butter and sage, or spaghetti sprinkled with sun-dried tomatoes, garlic, and olive oil. Fresh Scottish salmon and pesto; baby calamari stewed with Swiss chard, tomatoes, and chili; or prawns perfumed with garlic, lemon, rosemary, and chili should keep the

TELEPHONE
020-7370-6656

TUBE
South Kensington

OPEN
Daily

CLOSED
Never

HOURS
Breakfast 9:30 A.M.–noon, lunch noon–3 P.M., afternoon tea 3:30–6 P.M., dinner 6 P.M.–midnight

RESERVATIONS
Advised after 7:30 P.M.

CREDIT CARDS
AE, DC, MC, V

PRICES
À la carte, £10–20

SERVICE
12½ percent service charge

fish eaters happy. Italian sausage and lentils, skewered quail wound with peppers and zucchini, carpaccio, and Tuscan meatballs will please carnivores. If you are at Riccardo's between 3:30 and 6 P.M., order one of their *panini* (an Italian sandwich filled with chargrilled veggies, smoked salmon, or chicken with roasted peppers and zucchini). Other late afternoon possibilities include pastas and a salad. Desserts don't strike high notes, but the tiramisu is authentic, as is the *cantucci con vin santo*—a plate of crisp Italian nut cookies served with a glass of sweet wine for dipping.

ROTISSERIE JULES (27)
338 King's Road, Chelsea, SW3

See Rotisserie Jules in W11, page 105, for full description. All other information is the same.

TELEPHONE: Restaurant 020-7351-0041, delivery 020-7221-3331

TUBE: Sloane Square, then bus 11, 19, or 22

OPEN: Daily

CLOSED: Christmas Day

HOURS: Mon, Wed 5 P.M.–11:30 P.M., Tues, Thur– Sat noon–11:30 P.M., Sun noon–10 P.M., continuous service; delivery hours: Mon–Fri 6–10:30 P.M., Sat noon–3 P.M., Sun noon–10:30 P.M.

MISCELLANEOUS: Licensed only at this and the Notting Hill Gate (W11) location

SAN MARTINO (13, $)
103–105 Walton Street, Chelsea, SW3

A lovely formal setting, excellent service, attention to the smallest detail, and absolutely wonderful food are what you can expect, and will receive, when dining at San Martino, a Walton Street institution that has outlasted scores of competitors.

You could almost close your eyes and put your finger on anything on the menu and come up with a winner. In addition to its regular bill of fare, the restaurant is acclaimed for its rotating specials, many featuring produce from the owner's own garden, which allows the kitchen to take advantage of these products, using them with verve and style in everything that is prepared. Home-cured olives and a basket of fresh bread with butter starts the meal on a pleasing note. Fresh artichoke salad, risotto with wild mushrooms, stone crab claws, prawns lightly sautéed in garlic butter, baby octopus

TELEPHONE
020-7589-3833, 020-7589-1356, 020-7581-3718

TUBE
South Kensington

OPEN
Mon–Sat; Sun dinner only

CLOSED
Sun lunch, holidays

HOURS
Lunch noon–3 P.M., dinner 6–11:30 P.M. (Sun till 10 P.M.)

RESERVATIONS
Essential

CREDIT CARDS
AE, DC, MC, V

PRICES
À la carte, £22–32; set-price, lunch daily £14, 3 courses, beverage, and coffee

steamed in virgin olive oil and garlic, Dutch veal osso buco, Tuscan sausages, loin of venison, suckling pig, wild strawberries poured over rich ice cream, *torta della nonna* . . . it never ends. All I can say is that a meal at San Martino promises heaven on your plate, satisfaction in your mind, and vows to return to it as soon as possible.

S & P PATARA (6)
9 Beauchamp Place, Knightsbridge, SW3

The S & P story began on October 14, 1973, when five brothers and sisters opened a small ice cream store on the corner of Soi Prasanmitr in Bangkok. They called it S & P Ice Cream Corner. From that humble beginning, the shop grew into a chain of restaurants called S & P Patara with branches in Bangkok, Geneva, Taipei, Singapore, and London. Both London locations are bright and clean with adequate lighting and subtle Thai decorating touches. Service is polite and shyly accommodating.

Unless you are a Thai food connoisseur, put your full attention on the house specialties, which include deep-fried soft-shelled crab, prawn satay, and spring rolls with either pork or vegetable filling. The set-price lunches and any of the stir-fried rice and noodle dishes offer excellent value. The level of spices can be turned up or down in their coconut chicken, beef, or prawn curries and several stir-frys starring duck, pork, or beef sirloin. While their sweets will probably not become addictive, they are interesting to try, especially the steamed coconut custard in pumpkin or the baked banana with vanilla ice cream and toasted almonds.

TELEPHONE
020-7581-8820

TUBE
Knightsbridge

OPEN
Daily

CLOSED
Never

HOURS
Lunch noon–2:30 P.M., dinner 6:30–10:30 P.M.

RESERVATIONS
Advised

CREDIT CARDS
AE, DC, MC, V

PRICES
À la carte, £20–25; set-price, lunch £9.95 includes starter and main course; £3 extra includes combination of appetizers or soup, choice of 5 main courses, stir-fried mixed vegetables, side dish, and rice

SERVICE
12½ percent service charge

MISCELLANEOUS
Nonsmoking section

S & P PATARA (20)
181 Fulham Road (corner of Sydney Street), South Kensington, SW3

See S & P Patara above for full description. All other information is the same.

TELEPHONE: 020-7351-5692
TUBE: South Kensington

STOCKPOT–KING'S ROAD (24)
273 King's Road, Chelsea, SW3

See Stockpot–Soho in W1, page 62, for full description. All other information is the same.

TELEPHONE: 020-7823-3175
TUBE: Sloane Square, then bus 11, 19, or 22

OPEN: Daily

CLOSED: Christmas Day

HOURS: Mon–Sat 8 A.M.–11:30 P.M., Sun 11:30 A.M.–11 P.M., continuous service

RESERVATIONS: Not accepted

CREDIT CARDS: None

PRICES: À la carte, £5–10, minimum charge at peak hours: £2.50; set-price, breakfast £3.50–4.25, lunch and dinner £5.50

SERVICE: 10 percent service charge

STOCKPOT–KNIGHTSBRIDGE (2)
6 Basil Street, Knightsbridge, SW3

See the Stockpot–Soho in W1, page 62, for full description. All other information is the same.

TELEPHONE: 020-7589-8627

TUBE: Knightsbridge

HOURS: Mon–Sat 7:30 A.M.–11:30 P.M., Sun 11:30 A.M.–11 P.M. (no breakfast served on Sun), continuous service

VEG (8)
8 Egerton Gardens Mews, Knightsbridge, SW3

TELEPHONE
020-7584-7007

TUBE
Knightsbridge

OPEN
Daily

CLOSED
Christmas Day

HOURS
Lunch Mon–Fri noon–2:30 P.M., Sat–Sun 1–3 P.M., dinner 6:30–11 P.M.

RESERVATIONS
Advised

CREDIT CARDS
None

PRICES
À la carte, £15–18; set-price, lunch and dinner £13.50–18.50, minimum of 2 persons

SERVICE
10 percent service charge

Veg prides itself on being the only Chinese vegetarian restaurant in London serving both traditional Chinese and modern spicy vegetarian cuisine. They also offer an unusual range of simulated meat dishes in modern interpretations of *fozhaicia,* the traditional Buddhist vegetarian cooking. If you like hot and spicy, savor the splendor of Veg's delightful dishes by ordering one of their special set-price menus that offer a cross sampling. The most popular appetizer is the aromatic crispy veg-duck served with six pancakes, *hoi sin* sauce, shredded cucumber, and spring onions. Slightly more adventurous is the fiery, slow stir-fried Ma Po Tofu, made with diced tofu, Szechuan sauce, spring onions, ginger, and plenty of chilies. For a very sweet ending, try the deep-fried toffee banana with honey. There are the usual wines and beers to drink, plus a selection of freshly squeezed juices and herbal teas, including chrysanthemum, which is supposed to be good for your internal organs and eyes.

Pubs

ADMIRAL CODRINGTON (14)
17 Mossop Street, Brompton, SW3

The Admiral Cod, as it is called, has a reputation as one of the better-known pubs in this section of Chelsea. During the seventies and eighties, it was a happening place, frequented by Lady Diana, Prince Andrew, and Fergie. In the past decade, it suffered at the hands of a series of managers, which unfortunately led to its decline, especially in the food department. Now that it's back in the hands of Mel Barnett and his wife, Irene Dunford, let's hope the Admiral Cod is on the road to recovery.

The inside is very appealing, just what most people imagine a pub should be: wood paneling, old gas lamps, roaring fires in the winter, friendly bartenders, and knots of regulars sitting around swapping lies and war stories. There is an outside patio along one side and a pretty, covered conservatory garden in back that is heated in winter. The pub offers a selection of malt whiskeys in addition to beer. The menu changes often, offering somewhat more imaginative dishes than one usually sees in a pub. There is always a soup . . . perhaps cream of mushroom and garlic, and a dozen or so mains consisting of chargrilled chicken on ciabatta bread, wild boar sausages sitting on a bed of olive oil mash with a tomato and basil sauce, or boiled bacon with cabbage in a parsley cream sauce. Dessert is not part of the program.

TELEPHONE
020-7581-0005

TUBE
South Kensington

OPEN
Daily

CLOSED
Never

HOURS
Mon–Sat 11 A.M.–11 P.M., Sun noon–10:30 P.M.; lunch Mon–Fri 12:30–3 P.M., dinner Mon–Thur 6–9 P.M.

RESERVATIONS
Not accepted

CREDIT CARDS
MC, V

PRICES
À la carte, £7–10

SERVICE
No service charged or expected in the pub, appreciated in the restaurant

COOPERS OF FLOOD STREET (23)
87 Flood Street, Chelsea, SW3

The high cost of dining reduces many unknowing London visitors to pub grub consisting of greasy sausages, microwaved casseroles, or bowls of gassy chili con carne. You will have none of this unpleasant fare at Coopers of Flood Street, a smart pub that not only serves diverse food that is way better than most other pubs', but has had interesting regular patrons, both human and otherwise. Neighborhood regulars have included Vanessa Redgrave's mother, who lunched here daily, and a ninety-six-year-old man who stopped by every day for his beer and to tend to the plants. Presiding over the activities at the present time is a stuffed bear in one corner and a hat-wearing water buffalo who watches patrons from his position above the bar.

TELEPHONE
020-7376-3120

TUBE
Sloane Square

OPEN
Daily

CLOSED
Never

HOURS
Mon–Sat 11 A.M.–11 P.M., Sun noon–10:30 P.M., lunch 12:30–3 P.M.

RESERVATIONS
Advised for Sun lunch

CREDIT CARDS
AE, MC, V

PRICES
À la carte, £12–18

SERVICE
Service discretionary for table service, otherwise no service charged or expected

The yellowed walls are proof that pubs are one of the last refuges of tobacco addicts, but Coopers is big enough to absorb everyone and their smoke. I like it because it is quiet with no disruptive music or ringing pinball machines. The fireplace warms on a damp day, newspapers invite dallying, and eyeballing the Chelsea crowd sipping beer and recounting memories is a great pastime. If you go on Sunday, get there early. By early afternoon there is no place to stand or to sit.

The chalkboard menu (for lunch only) can be ordered at the bar or at a table for the same price. There are some definite winners here if you are a meat-and-potatoes eater: haunch of wild boar with apple and *calvados* (applejack) gravy, chargrilled rib-eye steak, and roast guinea fowl cooked with bacon, mushroom, and shallots. Vegetarians need not panic; there is always a dish for you. For dessert, order a fresh fruit crumble unashamedly covered with cream, soft custard, or ice cream or the sticky toffee pudding. In addition to the usual number of beers, wines from around the world are strongly featured.

KINGS HEAD AND EIGHT BELLS (31)
50 Cheyne Walk, Chelsea, SW3

TELEPHONE
020-7352-1820

TUBE
Sloane Square

OPEN
Daily

CLOSED
Christmas Day

HOURS
Mon–Sat 11 A.M.–11 P.M., Sun noon–10:30 P.M.; food service: Mon–Sat noon–10 P.M., Sun 12:30–4 P.M., 7–10 P.M.

RESERVATIONS
Advised for Sunday lunch

CREDIT CARDS
MC, V

PRICES
À la carte, £7–12

SERVICE
Service discretionary in restaurant, no service charged or expected in pub

MISCELLANEOUS
The bathrooms are very nice

The Kings Head and Eight Bells is a historic Chelsea pub dating from the late 1500s. Between 1524 and 1534 they had been part of the estate of Sir Thomas More, chancellor of England, who lived around the corner on Beaufort Street. In 1580 the two separate inns, the Kings Head and the Eight Bells, were merged into one. It is said that Henry VIII called here on his way up the Thames to Hampton Court, when the gentry would patronize the Kings Head and their entourage would use the Eight Bells. Located in the fashionable Cheyne Walk facing the River Thames, it has always been a favorite stop for the famous writers and artists who have lived in the neighborhood (see SW3 introduction). The comfortable pub is worth the hike from the Sloane Square tube stop. If you use a good map and the Michelin Green Guide as you go along, you will find all sorts of interesting tidbits about this part of London that will add to your visit. The pub kitchen offers the standard soups, chili, homemade meat pies, grills, fish-and-chips, sausages and mash, a list of sandwiches, and the usual Sunday roast lunch.

Tearooms/Pâtisseries

BEVERLY HILLS BAKERY (10)
3 Egerton Terrace, Knightsbridge, SW3

Oh, I can almost smell the muffins now. . . .

The Beverly Hills Bakery was often my early morning London treat as I walked from my flat to buy the morning papers. What delicious decisions I had as the hot-from-the-oven, preservative-free muffins were brought out. Should I have two minimuffins or one large dark chocolate, carrot, lemon, blueberry, or honey bran raisin muffin to go with my pot of brewed tea or hot chocolate? If I felt especially virtuous, I could still indulge in one of their fat-free muffins.

Muffins aren't the only stars. Look for their own quiches, soups (from noon on), salads, and ready-made sandwiches piled on assorted breads and rolls. May I tempt you further with their fat cookies, carrot cake made with pineapple, cheesecakes, and almost illegally rich chocolate cake or brownies?

"Remember us and your friends will remember you"—this is the motto for their gift baskets (starting at £25), which they can prepare and send anywhere in the U.K. and deliver free in London. Each basket has an assortment of their minimuffins, cookies, brownies, and Beverly Hills jam (which is marvelous, by the way). They will cater a kid's party and throw in the balloons, send a corporate basket, send a basket with a gingham bear to a new mom, guarantee true love with their Valentine basket, fill a festive Christmas basket, or pack your order in a tin for you to deliver yourself.

TELEPHONE
020-7584-4401

TUBE
Knightsbridge

OPEN
Daily

CLOSED
Christmas Day

HOURS
Mon–Sat 7:30 A.M.–6:30 P.M.,
Sun 8 A.M.–6 P.M.

RESERVATIONS
Not accepted

CREDIT CARDS
AE, MC, V

PRICES
À la carte, bakery £3–8; gift baskets from £25

SERVICE
No service charged or expected

MISCELLANEOUS
No toilets, no smoking allowed

PÂTISSERIE VALERIE (5)
215 Brompton Road, Knightsbridge, SW3

Please see Pâtisserie Valerie in W1, page 73, for full description. The Knightsbridge location, on Brompton Road just down the street from Harrods, is more relaxed and spacious. It has the added advantage of an expanded menu and a changing display of art, which is for sale. All other information is the same.

TELEPHONE: 020-7823-9971
TUBE: Knightsbridge
OPEN: Daily
CLOSED: Holidays

HOURS: Mon–Fri 7 A.M.–7:30 P.M., Sat 7:30 A.M.–7 P.M., Sun 8:30 A.M.–6 P.M.

RESERVATIONS: Not necessary

CREDIT CARDS: AE, DC, MC, V

PRICES: À la carte, £5–20, minimum charge at peak times: £7.50

SERVICE: Service discretionary, 10 percent service charge for 5 or more

MISCELLANEOUS: All the artwork is for sale.

RICHOUX–KNIGHTSBRIDGE (3)
86 Brompton Road, Knightsbridge, SW3

See Richoux–Mayfair in W1, page 75, for full description. All other information is the same.

TELEPHONE: 020-7584-8300

TUBE: Knightsbridge

OPEN: Daily

CLOSED: Christmas Day

HOURS: 8 A.M.–9 P.M., breakfast served all day

SERVICE: Service discretionary, 10 percent service charge for 6 or more

---

Wine Bars

CHARCO'S (18)
1 Bray Place, Chelsea, SW3

TELEPHONE
020-7584-0765

TUBE
Sloane Square

OPEN
Mon–Sat

CLOSED
Sun

HOURS
Lunch noon–2:30 P.M. (Sat until 3 P.M.), dinner 6–10:30 P.M., pre-theater 6–7:30 P.M.

RESERVATIONS
Essential on weekends or after 8:30 P.M. weekdays

CREDIT CARDS
AE, MC, V

PRICES
À la carte, £22–28; set-price, lunch and pre-theater £10.50, 2 courses

Charco's, with its upstairs wine bar and downstairs dining room, puts the T in trendy. In the evening, the upstairs bar is a sea of successful, black-clad trendsetters, secret lovers, and singles who come to schmooze, flirt, brag, drink, and maybe work up a business deal. Around 9:30 or 10 P.M., they sit down to eat. At lunch, the scene is professional and businesslike with the patrons wearing designer-label power outfits and checking their office messages on their cell phones. Food? Did someone mention food in all of this? Yes, and it is very good modern British fare prepared with imagination, attractively served, and reasonably priced.

The menu changes monthly to keep the flock returning and reflects a hint of Oriental influence. I like the spicy corn fritters served with chargrilled pickled bacon. The Parmesan and sage risotto drizzled with olive oil is a combination that is like feasting on cheesy clouds. Who wouldn't want to try the duck breast served with a tomato and herb fondue or the unusual pan-fried mullet with *udon* noodles, Green Lip mussels, and a Japanese dipping sauce? I could quickly become a glutton on any of their desserts, especially the warm cornbread pudding with a boozy bourbon caramel sauce or the citrus tart with crème fraîche.

LE METRO (4)
28 Basil Street, Knightsbridge, SW3

Le Metro wine bar is around the corner from Harrods, a handy location if you and your shopping companion or tagalong need sustenance or a drop to drink while combing the shops in Knightsbridge. Le Metro tries to be all things to all people and generally succeeds, though it rarely excels in any one area. You can start your day with croissants and a glass of fresh orange juice or a cup of cappuccino. Later on, stop by for one of the daily specials or a light salad. In the afternoon they serve light teas, and in the evening the menu is structured so that you can order a bowl of soup and another appetizer or go for every course. It is a wine bar, and in this area it is impressive. At any time there are at least fifty wines available by the glass, allowing you to sample not only French and California wines, but those from Chile, New Zealand, Australia, and Italy.

SERVICE
Service discretionary

TELEPHONE
020-7589-6286

TUBE
Knightsbridge

OPEN
Mon–Sat

CLOSED
Sun, holidays

HOURS
7:30 A.M.–10:30 P.M., continuous service

RESERVATIONS
Not necessary

CREDIT CARDS
AE, MC, V

PRICES
À la carte, £8–16

SERVICE
10 percent service charge

SW5

Earl's Court

Earl's Court is often called "Kangaroo Court" because it serves as the unofficial headquarters of London's large Australian community. It is also a backpacker's haven and hangout, thanks to the many low-priced (and very low quality, in most cases) hostels and B&Bs. Around the tube stop is a fertile ground for druggies and their hangers-on. The whole area is dicey at night. There is a saving grace, and that is the huge convention and exhibition center, but unless you are doing business there, this is not a top-choice location for most tourists, unless economy is your sole and primary issue. However, the Cheap Eats listings for this area are on the edge of the district and absolutely safe anytime.

Restaurants

BENJY'S (14)
157 Earl's Court Road, Earl's Court, SW5

Benjy's claim to fame is breakfast, served until late afternoon in a utilitarian coffee shop with plastic ketchup and A.1. sauce dispensers gracing its tables, which are filled with a colorful clientele of poor and cash-strapped international Cheap Eaters. If you want to send your cholesterol level into overdrive and max out your fat-gram allowance for the next two months, eat one of Benjy's breakfasts. More specifically, gorge on the Builder Breakfast. For about £4, you will be served a platter overflowing with bacon, two sausages, eggs, baked beans, toast, and all the coffee and tea you can consume. For the same price, you can dive into a sirloin steak, eggs, beans, peas, chips, and, again, all the coffee and tea you want. Lesser mortals can order smaller versions or à la carte. The menu also lists sandwiches, specials, and other dishes cooked according to the chicken-fried-steak school of culinary excellence. But remember, the only thing to consider at Benjy's is breakfast. The statements on the menu say it all in terms of the management's attitude and service: "This is not the Ritz, so be prepared to share a table, you might make a friend," and "When there is a queue at the door, vacate your table promptly," and "The only thing served small is the bill."

TELEPHONE
020-7373-0245

TUBE
Earl's Court

OPEN
Daily

CLOSED
Holidays

HOURS
7:30 A.M.–10:30 P.M., breakfast served until 4:30 P.M., continuous service

RESERVATIONS
Not accepted

CREDIT CARDS
None

PRICES
À la carte, £5–9, minimum charge: £3

SERVICE
Service discretionary

LA PAPPARDELLA (17)
253 Old Brompton Road, Earl's Court, SW5

Readers continue to write to me about La Pappardella. If other restaurants knew about these rave notices, they would dispatch spies to La Pappardella to take serious notes. One woman admitted that she ate here every night during her London stay and had the Pappardella Surprise three times! Others have loved the creamy cauliflower soup with fresh Parmesan and the *gamberoni all'aglio*—butterflied prawns with butter, wine, and garlic sauce, served on a bed of rice—saying it was one dish they never wanted to end.

These readers and I definitely agree that La Pappardella is one of London's best roll-up-your-sleeves Italian restaurants. Many nights, by 9 P.M., there's a line waiting to get into this noisy trattoria along Old Brompton Road. Once inside, seating is sardine-style on

TELEPHONE
020-7373-7777, 020-7259-2933

TUBE
Earl's Court

OPEN
Daily

CLOSED
Holidays

HOURS
Noon–midnight, continuous service

RESERVATIONS
Advised for dinner

CREDIT CARDS
AE, DC, MC, V

PRICES
À la carte, £12–20

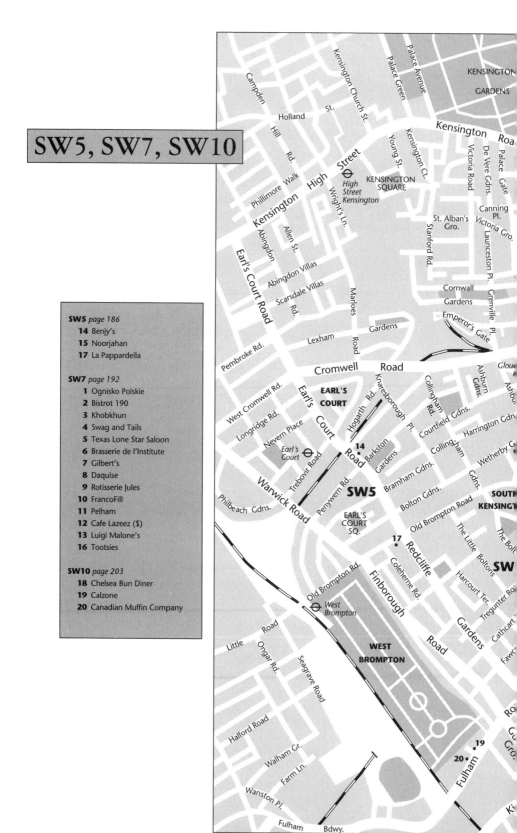

SW5, SW7, SW10

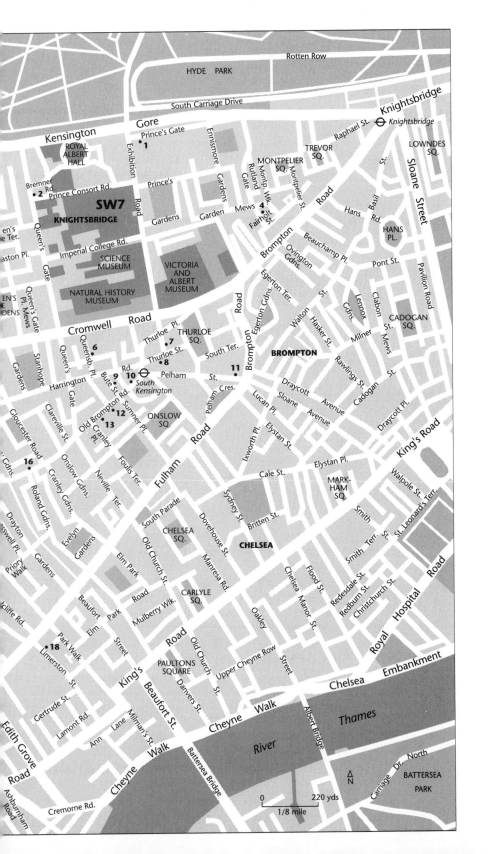

SERVICE
Service discretionary

red seats squeezed around little marble-topped tables. In the summer, the best tables are outside in the back garden, where there is more space and the noise from the banter between the diners and the young waitstaff is less strident. Actually, this bright and colorful repartee only adds to the enjoyment of the inexpensive food, which is good from the first bite to the last and all of it is made here—from the bread to the pasta and the sauces that cover them.

It is important to go easy on the appetizers and not fill up on the homemade pizza bread before anything else arrives. Begin with a light choice: the grilled sardines with a splash of fresh lemon or the carpaccio—raw, thinly sliced beef filet served with Parmesan shavings. All the familiar pastas are here, including spaghetti with pesto and lasagna. Two to remember are the *all'avocado,* a delicious combination of homemade, thin green and yellow noodles covered in a rich, fresh avocado sauce, and the *pappardelle della casa,* wide noodles with ricotta cheese and tomato sauce. Pizza lovers have eighteen choices, and the more than twenty preparations of veal, beef, and chicken will appeal to meat eaters. Portions are all oversize to begin with, but if you are feeling Herculean, larger helpings are always available. By the time you get to dessert, a scoop of ice cream or sorbet may be all you will be able to fit in. That is too bad, because the Pappardella Surprise, a mountain of whipped cream with fresh strawberries, almonds, macaroons, and liqueur, is something else for sure.

NOORJAHAN (15)
2a Bina Gardens (off Old Brompton Road), South Kensington, SW5

TELEPHONE
020-7373-6522
TUBE
Gloucester Road, South Kensington (both long walks)
OPEN
Daily
CLOSED
2 days at Christmas
HOURS
Lunch noon–2:30 P.M., dinner 6–11:45 P.M.
RESERVATIONS
Advised
CREDIT CARDS
AE, DC, MC, V

Where to go for some reliable Indian food? One choice is Noorjahan, the local favorite in an area of South Kensington that has several restaurants serving food from the subcontinent. Tandoori chicken and lamb, plus a wide variety of curries, headline the menu. If you are a beginner with Indian food, order the chicken *tikka masala,* one of the chef's specialties. Tandoori, or tikka, is a staple of northern Indian cooking. The meat, usually lamb or chicken, has been marinated in herbs and cooked in a tandoor—an Indian clay oven—which cooks the meat quickly, sealing in the juices and leaving the outside crisp. Noorjahan's version is cooked with ground almonds and cashews, fresh cream, yogurt, and mild spices. Add a vegetable, rice, and nan—the puffy, chewy Indian bread also cooked in the tandoor—and you will be all set. Old India hands will want to try one of the fourteen curries ranging from mild to explosive or one of the sweet-and-sour prawn dishes, and the unusual grated coconut chutney mixed with a variety of spices. For dessert, I suggest *kulfi,* the Indian ice cream flavored with cardamom and pistachios.

The service is always polite and helpful at explaining each dish, the food is dependable time after time, the kitchen is up to cleanliness standards (which is not the case at most Indian restaurants in London), and the simple dining room with fresh flowers on each table is attractive. It all adds up to a nice Indian meal.

PRICES
À la carte, £20–25; set-price, lunch or dinner £19.50, 3 courses and dessert

SERVICE
10 percent service charge

MISCELLANEOUS
Takeaway available, special dishes can be prepared if requested in advance

SW7

South Kensington and Knightsbridge

Knightsbridge is the well-heeled shopper's paradise, anchored by Harvey Nichols and Harrods, where extravagance is the top commodity. Chauffeured limousines are stacked three deep and taxies wait for tourists, Middle Eastern potentates, and dowagers intent on shopping sprees while dragging their poodles behind. Smart designer boutiques line Sloane Street, and very expensive shops make window-shopping along Beauchamp (pronounced BEE-chum) Place about all most of us can afford.

South Kensington is an appealing residential area with many nice hotels and restaurants. It is also known for its museums—the Victoria and Albert (decorative arts), Natural History (dinosaurs), and the Science and Technology Museum (with interactive exhibits). The Royal Albert Concert Hall is also here.

Restaurants

BISTROT 190 (2)
190 Queen's Gate, Kensington, SW7

Bistrot 190 is the upstairs offspring of the more expensive Queensgate 190, located in the basement of the Gore Hotel next door (see *Cheap Sleeps in London* for a description of this fabulous hotel). At Bistrot 190, bare floors dotted with tables scattered in a room bedecked with great prints and paintings, old mirrors, and garlands set the stage for this bustling, ever-popular spot overflowing with a classy crowd who come for weekday breakfasts, weekend brunches, and lunch and dinner daily.

Starting with breakfast, provided you are a sumo wrestler in training, you can tuck into the 190 full English breakfast: streaky back bacon, Cumberland sausages, grilled mushrooms and tomatoes, two eggs cooked to order, toast with honey and preserves, fresh orange juice, coffee, tea, or hot chocolate. The less daring can order any combination of these, or delight in the Heinz baked beans on toast, oak-smoked salmon and scrambled eggs, or grilled Loch Fyne kippers in butter. Homemade muesli, old-fashioned oatmeal with maple syrup, Greek yogurt with honey and wheat germ, baskets of warm breads, pastries, and freshly squeezed juices also ensure that you will start your London day without any hunger pangs. The Sunday brunch includes everything on the daily breakfast, plus steak and eggs, salmon and codfish cakes with a spinach and sorrel sauce, eggs Benedict, wonderful pastas, and on Sunday beginning at noon, the traditional roast lunch with all the trimmings.

The seasonally conceived lunch and dinner menu, which is the same and served from noon until closing, displays a fondness for unusual combinations that truly work. Start by ordering a basket of bread that comes with *tapenade* to dip into. For a wintry appetizer, I love the salad made with chicory, feta, and roasted figs. For those with a taste for the Orient, the platter of sashimi (raw fish), Thai king prawn salad, sushi, marinated scallops, and pickled cucumber and ginger would serve as a meal in itself. For a different main course, look for the venison and wild mushroom or pheasant and pear sausages, both accompanied by herb mash and onion gravy. Chorizo and butter bean cassoulet with roasted tomatoes

TELEPHONE
020-7581-5666

TUBE
Gloucester Road

OPEN
Daily

CLOSED
Christmas Day

HOURS
Mon–Fri 7 A.M.–midnight, Sat–Sun, holidays 7:30 A.M.–midnight; breakfast Mon–Fri 7–11 A.M., Sat–Sun, holidays 7:30–11 A.M., continental breakfast available daily until noon; brunch Sat–Sun noon–4:30 P.M.

RESERVATIONS
Not accepted unless you are a guest at the Gore Hotel

CREDIT CARDS
AE, DC, MC, V

PRICES
À la carte, breakfast/brunch £6–16, lunch and dinner £15–25

SERVICE
12½ percent service charge

MISCELLANEOUS
Management's policy: "Smokers and users of mobile phones are asked to be considerate of others."

and an herb crust is a filling choice, as is the rib-eye steak served with marinated field mushrooms and a béarnaise sauce. If you have had the whole citrus cake with tangy lemon curd for dessert once, you will have it every time you eat here, which, if you are in London for any length of time, you will do more than once.

You cannot make reservations unless you are staying in the Gore Hotel, so arrive early or be prepared to wait up to an hour. When you are seated, try to avoid the central tables on the main flight path of the waitstaff, who despite their busy appearance, provide lackluster service if the rush is really on.

BRASSERIE DE L'INSTITUTE (6)
17 Queensberry Place, South Kensington, SW7

TELEPHONE
020-7589-5433
TUBE
South Kensington
OPEN
Daily
CLOSED
Holidays (call to check in August)
HOURS
Mon–Sat 10 A.M.–9 P.M., Sun 2–8 P.M.
RESERVATIONS
Not necessary
CREDIT CARDS
MC, V
PRICES
À la carte, £5–15; set-price, £7.95–12.95, 4 two-course menus available
SERVICE
10 percent service charge

The French presence in London is large, and nowhere is it more evident than in this corner of South Kensington. All around the neighborhood you will find French-run businesses and shops, boulangeries, butchers, a greengrocer, several bookstores, and the Institute Française, which has over one thousand pupils pursuing their French academic studies while living in London. Knowing the French never compromise on their food, it is not surprising to find this brasserie located just inside the side entrance to the Institute Française. The large, rather faceless dining room overlooks the school playground. Seating is on hard wooden chairs, thus lingering too long is probably not going to be a comfortable option. Starting at the civilized hour of 10 A.M., you are invited to stop by, catch up on your French periodical browsing, and enjoy a café au lait and a *pain aux raisins*. During the lunch hour, there are several set-price meals, the simplest being a choice of quiche or pizza followed by *poulet Basquaise*. To pull out all the stops, you can order the most expensive meal and dine on six oysters or foie gras served with grapes, pepper steak in a brandy sauce, or salmon with hollandaise, topped off with one of their pastries or a dish of sorbet. For a lighter meal, consider one of the seven salads, six escargots, a bowl of *soupe à l'oignon au gratin,* or *l'assiette de charcuterie* (plate of assorted cold cuts). Other French standbys include *andouillette grillée* (chitlins, no matter how you try to dress them up), *magret de canard* (duck), and a cassoulet . . . all waiting for you every day of the week.

CAFE LAZEEZ (12, $)
93–95 Old Brompton Road, South Kensington, SW7

The two Lazeez restaurants in London exemplify the defintion of the word *lazeez*: delicate and aromatic; pleasing to the senses; delicious to taste. Indian food still holds the most-favored nation status among ethnic food lovers in London, right up there with pizzas and Big Macs, but Americans often consider this unfamiliar food to be strangely exotic, complicated, and mysterious. A visit to either of the Lazeez restaurants is the perfect place to change your attitude about this multifaceted cuisine. Historically, Indian fare has been perceived as hot, spicy, and saturated in *ghee* (clarified butter). At Lazeez, the use of chili as a hot spice is moderated, and sunflower oil is substituted for the ghee, which does not compromise either your health or your palate. The menu presents the diner with a choice of either traditional dishes using authentic recipes or evolved dishes representing a style and taste that has grown in Britain over the last thirty years. None of the food will be masked with curry, a word that does not even appear on the lengthy menu. "Curry" is an English derivative of the Tamil word for sauce, *karhi,* and as such has been used as a catchword for all Indian cuisine.

When booking at Cafe Lazeez on Old Brompton Road, be specific and request a table in the café downstairs for lunch, and in the more formal room upstairs for dinner. On Friday and Saturday nights, there is live jazz, with no cover charge if you are dining here. From Monday to Saturday, between 4–7 P.M., the Happy Hour offers special prices for all cocktails (except champagne). One of the best deals in the café is the Sunday buffet, in which you have a sampling of their best dishes. The next best Cheap Eats are the set-price menus (one each for vegetarians and nonvegetarians) and the two-course set-price lunch. For a wider range, à la carte is another option, and the one I recommend (though it's something of a Big Splurge). If there are more than two of you, start with the House Feast appetizer—a large selection of marinated pieces of chicken *tikka,* chicken and lamb kebabs, spring lamb chops, and jumbo prawns cooked in a tandoor oven over charcoal. This feast is served with a small salad, lemon, and mint. If you love lamb chops, the Officers Chops—spring lamb chops marinated in a honey-soy sauce with garlic and baked in the oven and

TELEPHONE
020-7581-9993

TUBE
South Kensington

OPEN
Daily

CLOSED
Never

HOURS
11 A.M.–1 A.M., continuous service; set-price lunch menu and Sun buffet 11 A.M.–3:30 P.M.

RESERVATIONS
Advised

CREDIT CARDS
AE, DC, MC, V

PRICES
À la carte, £15–32; set-price, lunch Mon–Fri £7.50, 2 courses; Sunday buffet, £12, 10 dishes and dessert; set-price menus £12.95–15.50 for one, £32 for two, available lunch and dinner

SERVICE
£1 cover charge, 12½ percent service charge

MISCELLANEOUS
Happy Hour Mon–Sat 5–7 P.M., live jazz Fri–Sat 9 P.M.–1 A.M., no cover charge if eating

served with spinach, potatoes, and mushrooms—is good. Vegetarians have a score of choices, and dessert eaters a dozen or more.

NOTE: The second restaurant, City Lazeez, is in Clerkenwell in EC1 (page 219).

DAQUISE (8)
20 Thurloe Street, South Kensington, SW7

If you have been to Eastern Europe, you will recognize Daquise immediately for its front window crowded with green plants and the well-worn corn path down the center aisle of the front room, which is lined with booths and Formica-topped tables. During the morning and at teatime, this popular Polish gathering place operates as a café and attracts a cross section of families with small children, toothless pensioners, and dignified Polish émigrés sharing memories over glasses of steaming tea. If you arrive for lunch or dinner, chances are you will be seated downstairs, where the more appealing atmosphere resembles a Polish country cottage with bright table coverings and painted handicrafts scattered around the room. Order a shot or two of 100 proof vodka or a Polish beer while waiting for the robust specialties of beetroot soup, salted raw herring, boiled beef, or the house specialty: potato pancakes served with sour cream, stuffed cabbage, *pierozoki* (pasta shells filled with seasoned ground meat), buttery pastries, and dessert pancakes slathered in ice cream, orange caramel sauce, and almonds. Daquise is only a few doors away from the South Kensington tube station and handy to the museums in Kensington.

TELEPHONE
020-7589-6117
TUBE
South Kensington
OPEN
Daily
CLOSED
Christmas Day, New Year's Eve, some holidays (call to check)
HOURS
Mon–Fri 11:30 A.M.–11 P.M., Sat–Sun 10 A.M.–11 P.M., continuous service; set-price lunch served Mon–Fri noon–3 P.M.
RESERVATIONS
Not necessary
CREDIT CARDS
MC, V
PRICES
À la carte, £8–18; set-price, lunch only £8, noon–3 P.M., 2 courses, wine, and coffee
SERVICE
Service discretionary
MISCELLANEOUS
Nonsmoking area

FRANCOFILL (10)
1 Old Brompton Road, South Kensington, SW7

Fast food à la française in London? *Mais oui* . . . at FrancoFill, a *très bon* Cheap Eat done up in the colors of the French flag. The bright interior features red, white, and blue with wide plank floors, paper table dressings, and a flotilla of French-speaking waiters and waitresses nattily attired in denim shirts and red bandannas. The signature dish is FrancoFill, a country loaf filled with your choice of cooked-to-order chargrilled meats, engagingly sauced with either *moutard* (mustard), *Provençale* (tomato-based), *herbes et ail* (fresh herbs and garlic butter), *champignon et estragon* (mushroom and tarragon), or *poivre vert* (green peppercorns). Sandwiches are accompa-

TELEPHONE
020-7584-0087
TUBE
South Kensington
OPEN
Daily
CLOSED
Christmas Day
HOURS
11 A.M.–11 P.M., continuous service
RESERVATIONS
Accepted and preferred for 6 or more

nied by *les frites* (french fries) or *une salade*. Other dishes on the French-accented menu include a bold ragout, ratatouille, steak *frites, croque monsieur* (grilled ham and cheese), *canard à l'orange, moules frites* (steamed mussels served with fries and bread and butter), the plat du jour, and several salads. The last thing to watch for is their version of *tarte tatin* (the famous French upside-down apple pie), with the British addition of caramel sauce and cream. The bar, with streetside window viewing, is a pleasant place for a relaxing beer, a glass of traditional Breton cider, or an afternoon snack ordered from the small bar menu.

GILBERT'S (7)
2 Exhibition Road, South Kensington, SW7

Gilbert's has a new owner, a new menu, and new prices, but not necessarily a new look. The small, formal dining room is set with linens, tablecloths, and napkins, none of which suggests for a minute that this is a place where diners are encouraged to order as much or as little as they want. The new owner and chef, Anne Butler, has devised a seasonal Cheap Eater–friendly menu composed of light meals based on homemade soup and five varieties of bread, designer salads, fresh crab cakes, quiches, and several chicken dishes. Desserts, all made by Anne, play a major role. I like her hot caramelized apple tart covered in vanilla ice cream or her banana, walnut, and cinnamon cake. The wine list is more extensive than the food offered, so with a glass of good French Pouilly-Fuissé or Sancerre to go with your crab cake . . . you will be Cheap Eating and drinking in style.

KHOBKHUN (3)
9a Gloucester Road, Kensington, SW7

If you like different food and are not afraid to experiment, consider Khobkhun. I was first attracted to this narrow Thai restaurant because it looked so fresh and clean, with flowers in the window box outside and pretty blue-and-white dishes on linen-covered tables inside. The best sign of all was the lunch crowd: all Thais. They obviously were on to something that I needed to know more about. Those of us who like Thai food know that it can be hot and spicy, sometimes too much, if caution and common sense are not exercised. The food here manages to capture the tastes, aromas, and subtleties of

CREDIT CARDS
AE, MC, V

PRICES
Restaurant: à la carte, £9–16; bar: £4–6; set-price, daily specials from £11

SERVICE
12½ percent service charge

TELEPHONE
020-7589-8947

TUBE
South Kensington

OPEN
Tues–Sat

CLOSED
Mon, Sun, holidays, 2 weeks each at Christmas and Easter

HOURS
Noon–10 P.M., continuous service

RESERVATIONS
Not necessary

CREDIT CARDS
None

PRICES
À la carte, £4–12

SERVICE
Service discretionary

MISCELLANEOUS
Nonsmoking section

TELEPHONE
020-7584-9514

TUBE
Gloucester Road

OPEN
Mon–Sat; Sun dinner only

CLOSED
Sun lunch, holidays

HOURS
Lunch noon–3 P.M., dinner 6–11 P.M.

RESERVATIONS
Not necessary

CREDIT CARDS
MC, V

PRICES
À la carte, £10–18; set-price, £15–18, 6–9 dishes, 2-person minimum

SERVICE
10 percent service charge

MISCELLANEOUS
Takeaway available

Thai food without sacrificing Western digestion at the same time. Please remember, when ordering you can ask to have the spiciness adjusted, but you must ask or it could be turned on full force.

The menu, with over sixty selections, makes for tantalizing reading. Those with cast-iron stomachs can order the stir-fried squid with garlic and chilies or the *pomfret* (whitefish) with a fiery sauce. The most popular dish, and certainly one of the best, is surprisingly mild and almost soothing. It is No. 72, fried noodles "Siam Style." It comes beautifully arranged on a tray with side dishes of prawns, eggs, bean sprouts, peanuts, and fried noodles. It is not only pleasing to look at, but pleasing to eat as well. There are two set-price menus, but the best way to go here is to order individually according to your own taste and heat tolerance.

LUIGI MALONE'S (13)
73 Old Brompton Road, South Kensington, SW7

TELEPHONE
020-7584-4323

TUBE
South Kensington

OPEN
Daily

CLOSED
2 days at Christmas

HOURS
Mon–Thur noon–11 P.M., Fri–Sat noon–11:30 P.M., Sun noon–10:30 P.M., continuous service; Happy Hour Mon 5–11 P.M., Tues–Sat 5–7 P.M.

RESERVATIONS
Not necessary

CREDIT CARDS
AE, DC, MC, V

PRICES
À la carte, £8–18; set-price, Mon–Fri noon–5 P.M., £6.95, order any main course and receive a complimentary cocktail, beer, or carafe of wine

SERVICE
Service discretionary

Luigi Malone's is a great haunt for those seeking a vivacious and occasionally hectic atmosphere. Old gas lamps, ceiling fans, yellowed walls, wooden tables and chairs, and an assortment of semi-antique curiosities provide the decor for this American mall-style restaurant and bar. The far-reaching menu offers plenty to please everyone, from vegetarians to Mexican-food lovers suffering the pangs of salsa withdrawal. Nachos, chargrilled twelve-ounce Aberdeen Angus hamburgers with all the trimmings, deep-fried garlic chicken, pizzas, pastas, sandwiches, fajitas, salads, and fattening desserts keep diners definitely well fed. From Monday to Friday between noon and 5 P.M., select one of Luigi's specials or any main course meal and get a complimentary cocktail, beer, or carafe of wine for less than £7. Happy Hour on Monday from 5 to 11 P.M. and Tuesday through Saturday between 5 and 7:30 P.M. overflows with self-proclaimed professionals in to check out the action and lap up the cheap beer, wine, and crazy cocktails. Whenever you go, you are bound to have a good time and eat well in the bargain.

OGNISKO POLSKIE (1)
55 Prince's Gate (at 55 Exhibition Road), Knightsbridge, SW7

Ognisko Polskie (Polish Heart Club) was founded more than fifty years ago by the Polish aristocracy displaced in London after World War II. Princess Alexandra of Britain is the patroness, and the many photos hung throughout the faded but elegant rooms tell you that this was once *the* gathering place for Polish expatriates. Today you will see aging Poles who come to eat, drink, and reminisce about home and families left behind or lost during the world wars. Many of these patrons have been fixtures on this scene long before most Cheap Eat readers were born. The time-warped setting rambles through several high-ceilinged rooms, creating the impression that nothing much has changed in the minds of its members, who perhaps find yesterday's memories preferable to the harsh realities of today.

The club is open to visitors and is a good place for tea and cakes after a visit to the trio of nearby museums (Victoria and Albert, Natural History, and Science and Technology). If you need something a bit more bracing, stop by the bar and order the Polish national drink: *Slivovice*—a potent fruit brandy that will definitely make your head spin. Or, order a Cheap Eat set-price lunch for under £9, featuring a good selection of native dishes. Watch for the platter of Polish sausages and ham, stuffed dumplings, pork knuckle, pheasant with red cabbage and cranberry sauce, and pancakes rolled with sweet cheese and jam. In the winter you will be served in the formal dining room and seated on a little gold chair. In the summer, service is on the terrace overlooking the garden. The music is classical, the waiters Polish, and the experience nostalgic if you have any ties to this part of Europe.

TELEPHONE
020-7589-4635

TUBE
South Kensington, Knightsbridge

OPEN
Daily

CLOSED
3 days at Christmas and Easter

HOURS
Lunch 12:30–3 P.M., dinner 6:30–11 P.M.

RESERVATIONS
Accepted and preferred for 4 or more

CREDIT CARDS
AE, DC, MC, V

PRICES
À la carte, £20–25; set-price, lunch £8.50, 3 courses

SERVICE
Service discretionary

PELHAM (11)
93 Pelham Street, South Kensington, SW7

Pelham Street is a smart modern European dining choice at the intersection of Brompton and Fulham Roads and Sloane Avenue. Within a two-block radius, there are at least ten major London dining addresses, including the forever popular and wildly overpriced Bibendum, owned by Sir Terence Conran. At Pelham, the small, light-filled dining room is a delight, and the weekly and seasonal menus offer a choice of creative

TELEPHONE
020-7584-4788

TUBE
South Kensington

OPEN
Daily

CLOSED
Mon lunch, Christmas Day, holidays (call to check)

HOURS
Noon–11:30 P.M., continuous
service; lunch noon–3 P.M.,
dinner 7–11 P.M.; set-price
menus available at lunchtime
and from 7–8 P.M. and
10–11 P.M.

RESERVATIONS
Advised on weekends

CREDIT CARDS
AE, DC, MC, V

PRICES
À la carte, £25; set-price,
lunch, 7–8 P.M., and 10–11 P.M.
£14, 2 courses, £17, 3 courses

SERVICE
12½ percent service charge

dishes of a good standard that are always well prepared and attractively served. The Cheap Eat value here is the set-price menu, offered at lunch and before and after the theater. In the winter, look forward to starting with a rich roast parsnip and onion soup, followed by a carrot and saffron risotto topped with toasted pine kernels or a panache of fish and shellfish highlighted by a tomato and chervil sauce. For dessert, the chocolate *marquise* served with a *crème anglaise* forces you to throw calorie counting to the winds. On the à la carte portion of the menu, look for the Swiss cheese soufflé spiked with a garlic cream sauce or the seared scallop salad tossed with tomato, olives, and herbs. The linguine of wild mushrooms accented with green beans, snow peas, and truffle oil is definitely too heavy as a starter and should only be ordered as a main course. Scottish beef served with seared foie gras, a duck confit with a thyme potato puree, or the breast of corn-fed chicken served with Thai-spiced noodles are only three of the interesting second plates. For dessert . . . again, order the chocolate *marquise,* or the pistachio crème brûlée with a dollop of dark chocolate sorbet on the side.

ROTISSERIE JULES (9)
6–8 Bute Street, South Kensington, SW7

See Rotisserie Jules in W11, page 105, for full description. All other information is the same.

TELEPHONE: 020-7584-0600, for free delivery 020-7221-3331

TUBE: South Kensington

OPEN: Daily

CLOSED: Christmas Day

HOURS: 11:30 A.M.–11:30 P.M., continuous service

MISCELLANEOUS: Unlicensed

TEXAS LONE STAR SALOON (5)
54 Gloucester Road, South Kensington, SW7

TELEPHONE
020-7370-5625

TUBE
Gloucester Road

OPEN
Daily

CLOSED
Christmas Day

For a taste of home—Texas style—grab your boots and Stetson and head for the Texas Lone Star Saloon. While hardly the spot for a first date, it is a great place to go with your pals any day of the year (except Christmas). Close your eyes and imagine a Texas honky-tonk with wagon-wheel lights and pine booths in which you are served by a waitress named Sally Sue, wearing tight jeans and an even tighter T-shirt, and you will have this one down pat. Country music straight from KJ97 FM in San

Antonio, Texas, keeps everyone happy and humming along with Loretta Lynn, Conway Twitty, and Dolly Parton.

The rib-sticking chow is as real as the atmosphere, and it naturally comes in Texas-size portions. Slabs of barbecued ribs with coleslaw, three-alarm chili, T-bone steaks with mounds of fries, meat and vegetable fajitas, burritos, tacos, and assorted burgers are guaranteed to keep everyone off a diet. In addition, there are between twelve and fifteen choices, ranging from a Mexican platter to vegetarian chimichangas, grilled fajita plates dubbed "a sizzling fiesta," and potato skins served with sour cream, chives, or blue cheese. Libations include buckets of beer, Michelob and Dos Equis by the bottle, assorted margaritas, and wines. There is a kids' menu, along with coloring books (BYO crayons), and from Tuesday through Thursday and Sunday from 9:30 to 11:30 P.M., live toe-tapping music.

HOURS
Sun–Wed noon–11:30 P.M., Thur–Sat noon–12:30 A.M., continuous service

RESERVATIONS
Not accepted

CREDIT CARDS
AE, MC, V

PRICES
À la carte, £8–15

SERVICE
12½ percent service charge

MISCELLANEOUS
Takeaway available, sweatshirts and T-shirts for sale

TOOTSIES (16)
107 Old Brompton Road, Kensington, SW7

See Tootsies in W1, page 63, for full description. All other information is the same.

TELEPHONE: 020-7581-8942
TUBE: South Kensington
OPEN: Daily
CLOSED: Christmas Day

Pubs

SWAG AND TAILS (4)
10–11 Fairholt Street, Knightsbridge, SW7

Annemaria Boomer-Davies has a twelve-year-old success on her hands, and she has worked very hard to achieve it. The Swag and Tails is in one of London's prettiest and most exclusive neighborhoods, the type we would all live in if we could afford it. It is worth a visit if only to admire the mews houses with their brightly painted doors and pretty postage-stamp front gardens, which look straight from the pages of *Town & Country*. It is only a few minutes by foot to Harrods and the bustle of Knightsbridge shopping, but this attractive pub/restaurant seems miles away. If you are a nonsmoker, you will want to sit at one of the wooden tables in

TELEPHONE
020-7584-6926

TUBE
Knightsbridge

OPEN
Mon–Fri

CLOSED
Sat–Sun, holidays

HOURS
11 A.M.–11 P.M., lunch noon–3 P.M., dinner 6–10 P.M.

RESERVATIONS
Suggested for lunch

CREDIT CARDS
AE, MC, V

PRICES
À la carte, £9–18
SERVICE
10 percent service charge

the middle. Otherwise, the glass conservatory in back, decorated with a flowering plant on each table and framed Chinese textiles, is appealing on a sunny day. If it is cold and blustery, relax in a high wingback chair in front by the tile-framed fireplace and sip your imported wine or beer. There will be no pinball machines, no rowdies, and no invasive music to disturb your reverie.

The menu roams the globe, and I honestly wondered how the kitchen could turn out the United Nations–inspired fare. With only a few exceptions, everything I tried was good and something I would order again. The smoked duck, spiced Asian pear, and rocket (arugula) salad with a lime and sesame dressing was delicately seasoned and not overpowering. Other preludes included homemade soup, eggs Benedict, chargrilled pork ribs with a sweet *hoi sin* sauce, and seared tuna and salmon cakes with a sweet chili and lime dressing. Main plates are not left behind, especially the soul-satisfying beef, tarragon, and oyster mushroom casserole crowned with spring onion mash. If it's a snack you want, the American triple-decker club sandwich served on ciabatta bread with a side of sweet potato chips or the smoked salmon with cream cheese and chives should tide you over. No one should dismiss the lead item for the sandwiches: a homemade burger in a sesame bap (bun) served with a salad and shoestring french fries. When Annemaria tried to remove this, her regulars threatened to form a lynching party. Finally, there are the desserts, which are not something you see much of in pubs; here you have an interesting if unusual choice between passion fruit brûlée, coconut and apricot gratin with a cool mango sorbet on the side, or spiced pear and Amaretto tart served with crème fraîche.

SW10

South Kensington and West Brompton

South Kensington flows from SW7 into SW10 and, along with West Brompton, is mainly a residential area.

RESTAURANTS in SW10 (see map page 188)

Restaurants

CALZONE (19)
335 Fulham Road, South Kensington, SW10

See Calzone in W11, page 102, for full description. All other information is the same.

TELEPHONE: 020-7352-9797
TUBE: South Kensington (a long walk)
OPEN: Daily
CLOSED: 4 days at Christmas

CANADIAN MUFFIN COMPANY (20)
353 Fulham Road, West Brompton, SW10

TELEPHONE
020-7351-0015
TUBE
South Kensington (a long walk)
OPEN
Daily
CLOSED
2 days at Christmas and New Year's Day
HOURS
8 A.M.–8 P.M., continuous service

What's a muffin? The Canadian Muffin Company has the answer: muffin, noun. 1. *Brit.* A thick, round, baked yeast roll, usually toasted and served with butter. 2. *U.S. and Canada.* A small cup-shaped sweet bread roll, usually eaten hot with butter. 3. *Canadian Muffin Co.* A large, delicious, handmade, freshly baked oat bran vegetarian variety; low in fat and sugar, made from organic flour, buttermilk, fresh fruits, nuts, and vegetables.

Like its sister locations, this Canadian Muffin Company branch focuses its attention on muffins. On a rotating basis, they turn out seventy-one sweet varieties, fourteen savory choices, and thirty-four fat-free temptations. That is not all. Stuffed baked potatoes, sandwiches piled on baguettes or bagels, soup, frozen yogurt (yes, also fat-free for you health hippies), and good coffee in three sizes: regular, large, and serious. Because it is far from the usual tourist trail, it is filled with upbeat locals who stop by with their children on their way to school, sit and gossip with their friends, or sink into one of the cushioned wicker armchairs and scan the daily papers.

NOTE: See the Canadian Muffin Company in W1, page 38, for a complete description. All other information is the same.

CHELSEA BUN DINER (18)
9a Limerston Street, South Kensington, SW10

TELEPHONE
020-7352-3635
TUBE
Sloane Square, then bus 11, 19, or 22 down King's Road; from Earl's Court tube, take bus 31 to last stop

Calling all Cheap Eaters: the Chelsea Bun Diner is the place to go! It attracts hordes of bargain munchers from eighteen to eighty with its good-humored, casual ambience, its low, low prices, and its wide-ranging menu. It has been here since the days of Jonathan Swift, who is reported to have bought a bun here for a penny.

When you arrive, don't expect much in the way of decor or gracious service; do expect good food geared to big-league appetites, with portions that seem almost out of control. Breakfast is served until 6 P.M., during which time marathon eaters should consider the Ultimate Breakfast, which the restaurant bets you can't finish, and I agree. For under £8 you get three eggs, hash browns, three Scotch pancakes with maple syrup and clotted cream, bacon, country sausage, mushrooms, a beef burger, and French toast plus a large mug of tea or coffee. They don't mention needing a wheelchair to get out after this feeding frenzy. The Chelsea Bun Mega Omelette has four eggs and is filled with ham, salami, cheddar cheese, tomato, mushrooms, mozzarella cheese, peppers, and onions. It could feed three! The burgers range from regular to "all the way," which is topped with ham, egg, cheese, lettuce, and a tomato on a 100 percent beef patty. This comes with fries or country-style potatoes, a mixed salad, and a relish tray.

Other dishes definitely worth the Cheap Eater's attention include potatoes stuffed, baked, fried, or mashed; pasta eight ways; homemade meat pies; super sandwiches that come "overfilled" (or with triple the filling mix); mega desserts including a banana split and home-made apple crumble with custard; and the famed Chelsea Buns (sticky cinnamon rolls packed with raisins and topped with cinnamon sugar, available daily except Sunday). These dishes keep the hard chairs filled from dawn until almost midnight. Don't have time to sit down and eat? Don't worry; they also prepare everything to go.

NOTE: The Chelsea Bun Diner has another location in SW11, an area not covered by *Cheap Eats in London.* It's at 70 Battersea Bridge Road (tel: 020-7738-9009).

OPEN
Daily

CLOSED
2 days at Christmas

HOURS
Mon–Sat 7 A.M.–midnight, Sun 8 A.M.–7 P.M., continuous service

RESERVATIONS
Not necessary

CREDIT CARDS
MC, V

PRICES
À la carte, £5–10, minimum charge at lunch: £4, £6 at dinner

SERVICE
Service discretionary

MISCELLANEOUS
Takeaway available, unlicensed, BYOB, £.50 corkage fee, and they call the cab if you do not have a designated driver; daytime limit on tables 1 hour and 15 minutes, evening 2-hour limit

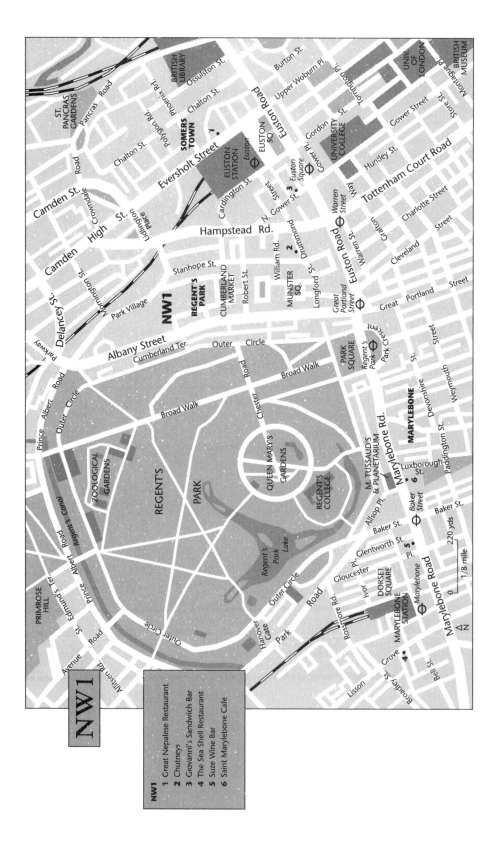

NW1

St. Pancras Gardens
St. Pancras Road
Pancras Road
Camden St.
Camden High St.
Camden High
Crowndale Road
Lidlington Place
Delancey St.
Mornington St.
Parkway

Phoenix Rd.
Polygon Rd.
Chalton St.
Chalton St.
BRITISH LIBRARY
Ossulston St.
SOMERS TOWN
Eversholt Street
Cardington St.
EUSTON STATION
Euston
EUSTON SQ.
N. Gower St.

Burton St.
Euston Road
Upper Woburn Pl.
Euston Road
Euston Road
Gordon St.
Gower Pl.
Gower Pl.
Euston Square
Warren Street
UNIVERSITY COLLEGE
Gower Street
Torrington Pl.
Huntley St.
Tottenham Court Road
UNIV. OF LONDON
Montague St.
Store St.
Gower St.
BRITISH MUSEUM

Hampstead Rd.
Stanhope St.
CUMBERLAND MARKET
Robert St.
William Rd.
MUNSTER SQ.
Longford St.
Drummond St.
Warren St.
Great Portland Street
Euston Road
Great Portland Street
Charlotte Street
Cleveland Street

NW1
REGENT'S PARK
Park Village
Albany Street
Cumberland Ter.
Outer Circle
Chester Road
Broad Walk
PARK SQUARE
Regent's Park
Park Crescent
MARYLEBONE
Devonshire St.
Weymouth St.
Portland St.

Prince Albert Road
Outer Circle
Broad Walk
REGENT'S PARK
QUEEN MARY'S GARDENS
REGENT'S COLLEGE
ZOOLOGICAL GARDENS
Regent's Canal
Regent's Park Lake
M. TUSSAUD'S & PLANETARIUM
Marylebone Rd.
MARYLEBONE
Luxborough St.
6
Baker Street
Baker St.

PRIMROSE HILL
Avenue Rd.
Prince Albert Road
St. Edmund's Ter.
Outer Circle
Hanover Gate
Park Road
Outer Circle
Rossmore Rd.
Ivor Pl.
Gloucester Pl.
Glentworth St.
5
DORSET SQUARE
MARYLEBONE STATION
Marylebone
Allsop Pl.
Baker St.

Artisan Rd.
Lisson Grove
Broadley St.
Bell St.
Marylebone Road
4
220 yds
1/8 mile
N

NW1
1 Great Nepalese Restaurant
2 Chutneys
3 Giovanni's Sandwich Bar
4 The Sea Shell Restaurant
5 Suze Wine Bar
6 Saint Marylebone Cafe

NW1

Regent's Park

The five-hundred-acre Regent's Park was once Henry VIII's hunting forest and later provided London with hay and dairy products. Today there is a boating lake, Queen Mary's Gardens, the London Central Mosque on the west side, and the London Zoo on the north. Close by is Madame Tussaud's wax museum, one of the top tourist attractions in the country—despite the fact that it is overrated and packed, resulting in snaked lines lasting two to three hours during peak tourist time. Next door is the London Planetarium.

The area's most famous resident was Sherlock Holmes, who, even though fictitious, still receives letters addressed to him at "221b Baker Street."

Since the 1400s, a church has stood on the site where the present St. Marylebone Church is now. This church was built by Thomas Hardwick and was where Robert Browning married Elizabeth Barrett.

Restaurants

CHUTNEYS (2)
124 Drummond Street, Regent's Park, NW1

TELEPHONE
020-7388-0604
TUBE
Euston Square, Euston
OPEN
Daily
CLOSED
4–7 days at Christmas
HOURS
Mon–Sat buffet lunch noon–
2:45 P.M., dinner 6–11:30 P.M.,
Sun buffet only noon–
10:30 P.M., continuous service
RESERVATIONS
Not necessary
CREDIT CARDS
MC, V
PRICES
À la carte, dinner only
Mon–Sat £10–15; set-price,
daily all-you-can-eat buffet
lunch £5.95; dinner £9.95,
multiple dishes
SERVICE
No service charge for the buffet,
10 percent service charge added
for dinner

Tired of sandwiches? Had it with burgers and chips? Burned out on pub grub? Looking for a Cheap Eat that is different, tastes good, and is not a heart attack on a plate? Head for London's "Little India" and try Chutneys—home of some of the best vegetarian food in the area. Card-carrying Cheap Eaters in London will get their ticket punched at the buffet lunch, which is served Monday to Saturday from noon until 2:45 P.M., and all day Sunday for the almost giveaway price of £5.95 for as much as you can pile on your plate. The fare varies daily, but it always includes a sampling of their homemade chutneys and other dishes covering the gastronomic diversity of the subcontinent. There are hot starters from Farsan, cold appetizers from Bombay's Chowpaty, *thali* from Gujarat, and southern Indian dishes from Madras. Everything is neatly labeled and prepared fresh daily. If you are not familiar with the variety Indian food offers, Chutneys is the place to change that.

NOTE: On Sunday, only the buffet is served, no à la carte.

GIOVANNI'S SANDWICH BAR (3)
152 North Gower Street (at Euston Road), Euston, NW1

TELEPHONE
020-7383-0531
TUBE
Euston Square, Euston
OPEN
Mon–Fri breakfast and lunch
only
CLOSED
Sat–Sun, holidays (sometimes
open if there is business)
HOURS
Mon–Fri 7 A.M.–3:30 P.M., Sat
8 A.M.–2 P.M., continuous
service
RESERVATIONS
Not accepted
CREDIT CARDS
None
PRICES
À la carte, £3–7

Giovanni's Sandwich Bar has hundreds of clones all over London, all doing about the same thing: dispensing filling food, coffee, talk, opinions, and good cheer to the friends and neighbors who check in daily to keep up with the local goings-on. If you are around Euston and need a quick bite, pop in here and pull up a chair at one of the four shared tables inside. In the morning, the drill includes variations on the full English breakfast: eggs, bacon, sausage, beans, tomato, toast, chips, and strong coffee or tea. Around noon, sandwiches, filled spuds, or a hot dish are on the plates. This is the time to watch for the lasagna and shepherd's pie, lovingly made by Giovanni's mother. In between times, you can order peanut butter or Marmite (the Australian national spread) on toast, a cappuccino, or a bottle of Snapple. Decor, well, there isn't much of that here, but Giovanni does have an interesting collection of black-and-white photos of old London, and the blackboard lettering was done by a pal in Phoenix, Arizona.

GREAT NEPALESE RESTAURANT (1)
48 Eversholt Street, Euston, NW1

The Great Nepalese Restaurant gets my vote as one of the best Indian/Nepalese dining experiences in London. The outside is unremarkable. The inside, however, is pleasant and comfortable with hand-carved wooden screens, a teak ceiling, and Nepalese masks and painted baskets on the walls.

A first visit usually means many returns to this friendly place, run by Gopal Manandhar and his three sons. Their service is professional, courteous, and always helpful. They will suggest a menu for the uninitiated, selecting for taste, interest, and price. Nepalese cooking uses fresh herbs and more spices than most Indian-inspired food, but there are many mild dishes available, and the kitchen will always adjust seasonings to suit a customer's wishes. House specialties include Nepalese starters *masco-bara* (two black lentil pancakes with curry) and the *haku choyala* (barbecued diced mutton with hot spices, ginger, and garlic). You will need a bottle or two of the Kathmandu Nepalese beer to temper the flames of this one. Main-course standouts are the tandoori dishes and the curries made with chicken, lamb, mutton, or pork. Vegetarians have more than twenty-five dishes from which to choose, including *aloo kerau ko achar* (a cold dish of potatoes, peas, green chili, and sesame seeds) and *mutter panir* (their homemade cheese and peas in curry). For dessert, try the house rice pudding, flavored with bay leaves, cardamom, and cinnamon and flecked with raisins. To finalize your culinary tour of Nepal, order a glass of Nepalese Coronation rum made in 1975.

SAINT MARYLEBONE CAFE (6)
17 Marylebone Road (in the church crypt), St. Marylebone, NW1

The Georgian Saint Marylebone Church was consecrated in 1817 as the fourth church in the parish. By church standards, it is not old or extremely historic, but it does have an interesting background. The focal point in the Holy Family Chapel is a painting by the same name, done by American-born artist Benjamin West.

SERVICE
No service charged or expected

MISCELLANEOUS
Takeaway available

TELEPHONE
020-7388-6737, 020-7388-5935

TUBE
Euston

OPEN
Daily

CLOSED
Christmas Day

HOURS
Lunch Mon–Sat noon–2:45 P.M., Sun noon–2:30 P.M., dinner Mon–Sat 6–11:30 P.M., Sun 6–11:15 P.M.

RESERVATIONS
Accepted and preferred

CREDIT CARDS
AE, DC, MC, V

PRICES
À la carte, £10–18; set-price, £13.50, 3 courses

SERVICE
10 percent service charge, minimum charge: £5.75

MISCELLANEOUS
10 percent discount for takeaway

TELEPHONE
020-7935-6374

TUBE
Baker Street

OPEN
Mon–Fri breakfast and lunch only

CLOSED
Sat–Sun, holidays

HOURS
8:30 A.M.–3 P.M., continuous
service
RESERVATIONS
Not accepted
CREDIT CARDS
None
PRICES
À la carte, £3.50–9
SERVICE
No service charged or expected
MISCELLANEOUS
Takeaway available, BYOB, no
corkage fee, unlicensed

On September 12, 1846, Robert Browning and Elizabeth Barrett were married in the church, and their marriage certificate is preserved in the archives. Charles Dickens lived nearby on Devonshire Terrace, and his son was baptized in the church, which he described in his novel *Dombey and Son*. He also based many characters in *David Copperfield* on his well-known Marylebone neighbors. Today, most visitors to this part of London come to see Madame Tussaud's famous wax museum and the Planetarium down the street.

The church café is a welcome oasis for light breakfasts and canteen lunches, and it offers a variety of vegetarian and vegan dishes cooked with just enough flair to keep them from being mundane. Tea, coffee, toast, croissants, scrambled eggs, muesli, and fresh fruit start off the morning at 8:30 A.M. By lunchtime the counter showcases salads, soups, filled potatoes, quiche, several hot dishes, and a few high-calorie desserts, all made in the kitchen behind the food counter. The café is downstairs in a white, arched room with shared tables and rotating art displays for sale by local artists.

THE SEA SHELL RESTAURANT (4)
49–51 Lisson Grove (at Shroton Street), Marylebone, NW1

Ask anyone around Marylebone where to go for the best fish and the response will be unanimous: The Sea Shell Restaurant, on the corner of Lisson Grove and Shroton Street. There are two parts to it: an open kitchen and counter entrance for the fish-and-chips takeaway crowd and an attractive two-level dining area punctuated by a spiral stairway, on which the aquatic theme is carried out by seashell murals, ceramic fish platters hung about, and a series of humorous prints depicting roly-poly fish eaters frolicking at the beach.

If you are dining in, treat yourself to an order of their perfect flaky, nongreasy fish cakes, delicately seasoned and parsleyed. Prices for everything are very Cheap Eater–friendly, considering the sizes of the dishes (ranging from huge to unbelievable) and the quality of the fresh fish (150 tons per year, to be exact), which arrives before dawn and by 4 A.M. is being cut and fileted by the fish cutters. They serve halibut, sole, salmon, plaice, cod, rainbow and sea trout, and haddock fixed any way you please, including grilled. Your choices of fried, creamed, or boiled new potatoes comes with your order (and just

TELEPHONE
020-7724-1063, 020-7723-
8703
TUBE
Marylebone
OPEN
Mon–Sat; Sun lunch only
CLOSED
Sun dinner, holidays
HOURS
Mon–Fri lunch noon–2:30 P.M.,
dinner 5–10:30 P.M.,
Sat continuous service noon–
10:30 P.M., Sun noon–2:45 P.M.
RESERVATIONS
Accepted for large parties only
CREDIT CARDS
AE, DC, MC, V
PRICES
À la carte, takeaway side
(fish-and-chips) £4–10,
restaurant £10–18;
set-price, lunch only £11,
3 courses; senior citizens, daily
lunch and dinner, £7.50,
3 courses

to keep the statistics even, over 200 tons of potatoes are peeled here per year). You will never miss the desserts, which take you from sorbet and apple pie to treacle sponge or spotted dick puddings.

NOTE: Antique buffs will want to walk farther up Lisson Grove to Church Street, which is lined on both sides with antique shops and also has an antique mall of sorts. Prices here are some of the best in London (See *Cheap Sleeps in London*, Cheap Chic).

SERVICE
Service discretionary

MISCELLANEOUS
Takeaway available, nonsmoking section, children's menu

Wine Bars

SUZE WINE BAR (5)
1 Glentworth Street, Marylebone, NW1

Tom and Susan Glynn's Suze Wine Bar is a quiet wine bar and restaurant celebrating the food, drink, and hospitality of their native New Zealand. In addition to the daily specials, look for seared New Zealand lamb filet with a balsamic and red peppercorn glaze, homemade lamb and rosemary sausages served on roasted garlic and cheddar mash with a red wine sauce, and their specialty, shelled green mussels in a creamy wine sauce, all accompanied by an interesting vintage of New Zealand red or white wine. Equal care is invested in their desserts, especially the New Zealand/Australian favorite, pavlova, a meringue filled with cream, fruit, and calories. Seating is either upstairs on a sidewalk terrace or downstairs in a light room displaying artwork for sale.

TELEPHONE
020-7486-8216

TUBE
Baker Street, Marylebone

OPEN
Mon–Fri

CLOSED
Sat–Sun, holidays

HOURS
11 A.M.–11 P.M.; lunch noon–3 P.M., snacks 3–5:30 P.M., dinner 5:30–10:30 P.M.

RESERVATIONS
Not necessary

CREDIT CARDS
AE, DC, MC, V

PRICES
À la carte, £10–18

SERVICE
Service discretionary

MISCELLANEOUS
Catering available

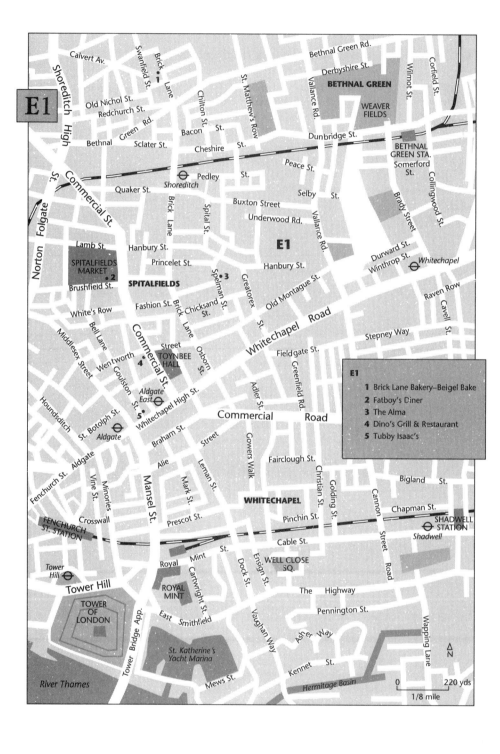

E1

E1

1 Brick Lane Bakery–Beigel Bake
2 Fatboy's Diner
3 The Alma
4 Dino's Grill & Restaurant
5 Tubby Isaac's

E1

Spitalfields and Whitechapel

In the Spitalfields and Whitechapel areas of London's East End, you can buy a bagel, eat at a cheap Asian or Indian restaurant, worship at a synagogue, visit the Spitalfields Heritage Center, which displays the history of the area's immigrants, buy organic fruit and produce at the Spitalfields Market on Sunday mornings, and see the latest in London's modern art movement at the Whitechapel Art Gallery. This is an area far removed in mind and spirit from the West End, but a vital and vibrant part of London's far-reaching makeup.

Restaurants

BRICK LANE BAKERY–BEIGEL BAKE (1)
159 Brick Lane, East End, E2

TELEPHONE
020-7729-0616
TUBE
Aldgate East
OPEN
Daily
CLOSED
Never
HOURS
24 hours a day, 7 days a week
RESERVATIONS
None
CREDIT CARDS
None
PRICES
Bagels 12 pence each, £21 for
14 dozen, £.85–2.50 filled
SERVICE
No service charged or expected

Twelve pence buys you one plain bagel, 72 pence a half dozen, and £21 will bag you fourteen dozen of the best, most authentic bagels in London. No matter how you spell it (bagels, beigels, or baigels), these are the real thing: a round roll with a hole in the middle, first boiled, then baked so they will be just crispy enough on the outside and slightly chewy inside. This East End institution is open twenty-four hours a day, seven days a week, 365 days a year, and dispenses over eight million bagels (four thousand on Sundays), which are consumed plain, buttered, piled high with smoked salmon and cream cheese, or stacked with slices of their own salt beef (twenty-five of these are cooked per day). Don't look for blueberry, poppyseed, or the "everything" bagel. There are only two choices: "ordinary," which are sold daily, and "salty," which are added on the weekends.

The trip from the tube stop to 159 Brick Lane is a fifteen- to twenty-minute hike through a marginal Indian neighborhood lined with more than forty cheap food dives and trashy clothing outlets. It is probably most interesting on Sunday mornings around 11 A.M. when families are shopping along here and at the Petticoat Lane Market. It looks a whole lot worse than it really is. You are okay in the daytime, but at night don't make the trek alone; go as a group for added safety.

Directions: From the tube stop, walk east on Whitechapel High Street and turn left on Osborn Street, which becomes Brick Lane. You will know you are close when you see the line outside at the counter.

DINO'S GRILL & RESTAURANT (4)
76 Commercial Street, Spitalfields Market, E1

TELEPHONE
020-7247-6097
TUBE
Aldgate East
OPEN
Mon–Fri; Sun breakfast and
lunch only
CLOSED
Sun dinner, Sat, holidays

Dino Bragoli and his right-hand helper and mom, Peggy, have been running this Cheap Eats outpost since the early sixties. It is a good, clean bet in an eyebrow-raising area around the Spitalfields fruit and vegetable market and the sleazy garment district surrounding Petticoat Lane. The emphasis is on back-to-basics food for breakfast and lunch, the stuff we all loved before sun-dried tomatoes, chèvre, and arugula took over the menus of more stylish eateries.

Truckers and market workers arrive at Dino's Grill around 6 A.M. for fry-ups of eggs, beans, bacon, sausage, chips, and slabs of fried bread. If you want just a cup of java and a pastry, order one of their famous homemade and well-named Rock Cakes, which are similar to heavy-duty scones, studded with raisins. By 11:30 A.M., regulars stream in for steak and mushroom pie, overflowing plates of pasta and grilled meats, bangers and mash (sausage and mashed potatoes), roast meat served with two vegetables, and fried fish. The special of the house is *pasta al Dino,* spaghetti with a choice of sauces, topped with ham and/or a fried egg with a Parmesan cheese topping and run under the broiler. Let's just say it is different. Desserts? This is a meat-and-potatoes place, so desserts are not part of the main attraction unless you have room for a slab of the homemade apple pie.

In an effort to attract a wider clientele, the downstairs red-brick basement was turned into a separate restaurant with its own entrance. The good Italian grub on the menu is almost the same as the food served upstairs, but if you eat down here, you will miss all the fun and local color that comes with your meal upstairs.

HOURS
Grill: Mon–Fri 6 A.M.–4:30 P.M., Sun 6 A.M.–2 P.M.; restaurant: Mon–Fri noon–3 P.M.

RESERVATIONS
Not necessary

CREDIT CARDS
AE, DC, MC, V

PRICES
À la carte, £5–10 for the grill or restaurant

SERVICE
Service discretionary

FATBOY'S DINER (2)
Inside Spitalfields Market (off Commercial Street), Spitalfields, E1

The Fatboy's Diner in London was built in Worcester, Massachusetts, by the Worcester Lunch Car Company and shipped in 1955 to Georgetown, Mass., where truckers, high-school students, businessmen, local cops, and tourists flocked to the diner over the years. Relocated to London about twenty years ago and restored to its fifties splendor, Fatboy's Diner is still serving the same food, in the same rock 'n' roll atmosphere. Long live Fatboy's Diner!

The Fatboy's Diner in London is located inside the Spitalfields Market. As Fatboy says, "For a mighty fine dine, where every bite is a delight, and the food is cooked as you like it, eat at Fatboy's." It has lots of chrome, stools, fry cooks behind the counter, and loud fifties and sixties American music booming nonstop. Don't stand on dining ceremony here. Your food order is shouted to the cooks and served on paper plates by fast-working waitresses. You can eat breakfast anytime, or stuff yourself with the Hillbilly Fatburger, a double burger with cheese, bacon, barbecue sauce, and topped with chili.

TELEPHONE
020-7375-2763

TUBE
Liverpool Street, Aldgate East

OPEN
Daily

CLOSED
Christmas

HOURS
Mon–Sat 10:30 A.M.–4 P.M., Sun 9:30 A.M.–6 P.M., continuous service

RESERVATIONS
Not accepted

CREDIT CARDS
None

PRICES
À la carte, £6–10

SERVICE
Service discretionary, "Don't be a nickel squeezer: if you enjoyed your meal, leave a tip."

Look for the A.B.C. burger, a giant Fatburger covered with avocado, bacon, and cheese, and there's a veggie cheeseburger for the health-minded. Hot dogs get fair exposure, and you will, too, if you indulge in the Hotbreath, with chili, Swiss or American cheese, and raw onions. To complete the meal, add a thick chocolate malt, a flamingo (a cream soda float with strawberry ice cream), or the "burn it and let it swim," a.k.a., a Pepsi-Cola float with chocolate ice cream. Slabs of apple or blueberry pie, and double chocolate brownies (all à la mode, of course) will take you further down memory lane. No, it isn't the stuff gastronomic thrills are made of, but for a Cheap Eat that will take you back—way back—it is fun.

TUBBY ISAAC'S (5)
Goulston Street (near Aldgate East tube station), Spitalfields, E1

TELEPHONE
None

TUBE
Aldgate East

OPEN
Daily

CLOSED
Christmas Day

HOURS
11 A.M.–11 P.M., continuous service

RESERVATIONS
Not accepted

CREDIT CARDS
None

PRICES
À la carte, £1.80–5

SERVICE
No service charged or expected

MISCELLANEOUS
This is a pushcart for takeaway only; catering available

Since 1889, the Isaac family has been selling jellied eels, rollmops (rolled-up pickled herring), mussels, oysters, fresh boiled crabs, prawns, cockles, and sea snails from a red-and-white cart near the Aldgate East tube station. The founder, Isaac Brenner, was fat and little, so everyone called him Tubby Isaac and the name has stayed with this well-loved East End institution. The man standing in front of me waiting for his eels told me, "I'm 82, and I remember this stand as a boy. . . . I have always loved it." Their fast-food stand-up specialty is jellied eels, which is an acquired taste that takes a great deal of determination and practice. It is included here as a very British Cheap Eat appealing only to those eager to collect cuisine experiences they can talk about once they return home. How do you eat a jellied eel, which is boiled, then cut up and served in its own gelatinous consommé in a Styrofoam cup? Very carefully. As anyone at Tubby Isaac's will tell you, the proper way to eat a jellied eel is to put a whole piece into your mouth, taking care to chew around the bone in the center. The lemon-colored jellied consommé in which the eels are served is helped by heavy doses of chili vinegar and chunks of bread from the bread bin. The best days to hit Tubby's are Thursday through Sunday, when he offers his biggest selection . . . just in case you didn't come for the eels.

Can't decide what to serve at your next party? Impress your friends with a spread from Tubby's—they cater!

Pubs

THE ALMA (3)
41 Spelman Street, Spitalfields, E1

Who do you think was Jack the Ripper? What happened to him? Did he commit suicide after his last grisly murder of another prostitute? No one will ever know for sure. Want to find out more? Then take one of the most chilling city walks of London, "The Jack the Ripper Walk" led by Steve Kane, a former actor and now the affable owner of the Alma. To arrange a walk (for a nominal fee), call ahead; they begin a little before 8 P.M. at the Aldgate East tube station, where Steve will meet you. After your walk through the neighborhood, many suspects will have been suggested, and you will have evidence for both the defense and prosecution of Jack the Ripper. At the close of the walk, you will arrive at the Alma, where you can have a beer or two and second-guess decades of other minor and major sleuths. Aside from its fame as being one of the pubs frequented by Annie Chapman, one of the Ripper's most brutalized victims, the pub dates back to 1854 when it was built to commemorate the only allied (French, Turkish, and English) victory in the Crimean War to stop the Russian expansion through India.

Today, this part of Jack the Ripper territory is otherwise a tourist wasteland surrounded by government flats. Aside from its infamy, the area is interesting because it gives a look at a blue-collar, working neighborhood where life is an uphill climb. However, if you find yourself here around lunchtime, stop in for one of Steve's Cheap Eat lunches and down a pint with the locals (dinner is not served except to groups by prior arrangement). Notice the hats around the bar belonging to past and present customers, and the collection of police badges from around the world. The mugs are presents from the CIA and FBI.

Directions: Spelman Street is not on most tourist maps of London. To locate the Alma, get off at the Aldgate East tube station and exit the station to Whitechapel Road. Take a left onto Osborn Street, which becomes Brick Lane. Take a right onto Princelet Street, then a right onto Spelman Street, and the Alma will be on your left. The neighborhood is not recommended at night if you are alone.

TELEPHONE
020-7247-5604

TUBE
Aldgate East

OPEN
Daily

CLOSED
Christmas Day

HOURS
Mon–Sat 11 A.M.–11 P.M., Sun 11 A.M.–10:30 P.M., lunch noon–2:30 P.M.

RESERVATIONS
Not necessary

CREDIT CARDS
AE

PRICES
À la carte, £3–7

SERVICE
No service charged or expected

EC1

Clerkenwell and Farringdon

Other than some exceptionally good restaurants, Clerkenwell and Farringdon hold little interest for most tourists. Smithfield Market off Farringdon Road has been in operation since the twelfth century. It is London's main wholesale meat market, and its annual turnover of more than two hundred thousand tons of goods makes it one of the largest meat and poultry markets in the world.

Leather Lane is a busy street market selling goods ranging from fruits and vegetables to sweaters and Levi's. Hatton Garden, the center of London's diamond trade, is here, and so are the London Silver Vaults, several ancient pubs, and the oldest Catholic church in London—St. Etheldreda's.

($) indicates a Big Splurge

Restaurants

CHEZ GÉRARD (4)
84–86 Farringdon Road, Clerkenwell, EC1

See Chez Gérard in W1, page 39, for a complete description. All other information is the same.

TELEPHONE: 020-7833-1515
TUBE: Farringdon

CITY LAZEEZ (5, $)
88 St. John Street, Clerkenwell, EC1

City Lazeez is a unique bar and restaurant in an architecturally listed building with an open modern style. The restaurant, which has kept its industrial overtones and character, has been transformed into a uniquely minimal space with exposed air ducts and pipes and an open kitchen providing diners with a direct view of the chefs creating their meals. Seating is either at the casual bar in front or in the conservatory, which is bright and well lit during the day and has a warm and intimate feel in the evening through the use of candles and soft lighting. The exposed brick wall along the side dates from the 1400s. The cuisine here is as light, delicious, and appealing as it is at Cafe Lazeez (page 195) in South Kensington, SW7.

TELEPHONE
020-7253-2224
TUBE
Farringdon
OPEN
Mon–Sat
CLOSED
Sun, holidays
HOURS
11 A.M.–10:30 P.M.
RESERVATIONS
Advised
CREDIT CARDS
AE, MC, V
PRICES
À la carte, £20–30; set-price, lunch only £8.50, 3 courses
SERVICE
12½ percent service charge

G. GAZZANO & SONS (2)
167–169 Farringdon Road, Clerkenwell, EC1

G. Gazzano & Sons, across the street from the Quality Chop House (see page 223), is considered the oldest Italian deli in London. It has been in the same family since 1901, providing Italians and would-be Italians with the best deli supplies this side of Milan. If you are nearby, it is worth a stop if only to buy a little bucket of their home-cured olives, which are sold every way, from plain, with the pit, to fancy-pitted green olives stuffed with sun-dried tomatoes. Salami, Parma ham, roast beef, prosciutto, smoked cheese, tomatoes, and artichokes can be mixed, matched, and piled high on your choice of ciabatta or focaccia bread, crusty rolls, or buns. Assorted Italian wines, packaged sweets, and other cooking staples will add to any Italian meal or picnic you plan. However, everything is for takeaway; there is no seating.

TELEPHONE
020-7837-1586
TUBE
Farringdon
OPEN
Daily
CLOSED
Holidays
HOURS
Mon, Sat 8 A.M.–5 P.M., Tues–Fri 8 A.M.–6 P.M., Sun 10:30 A.M.–2 P.M.
RESERVATIONS
Not accepted
CREDIT CARDS
None
PRICES
£2 and up
SERVICE
No service charged or expected

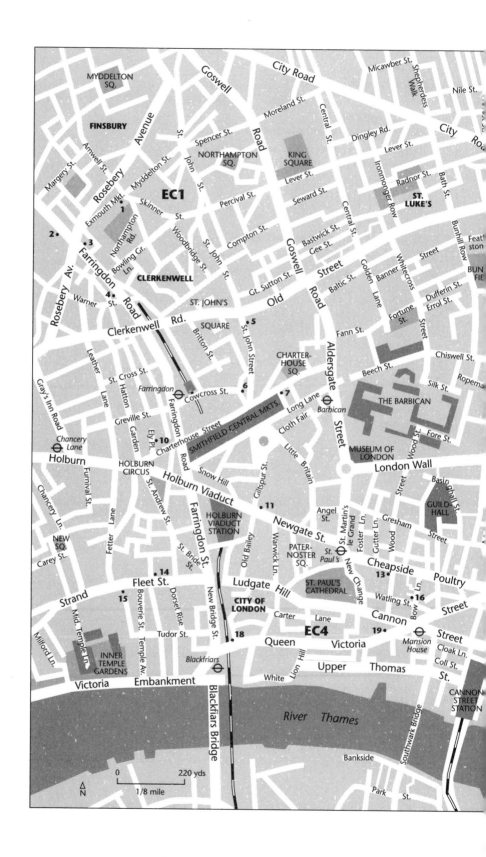

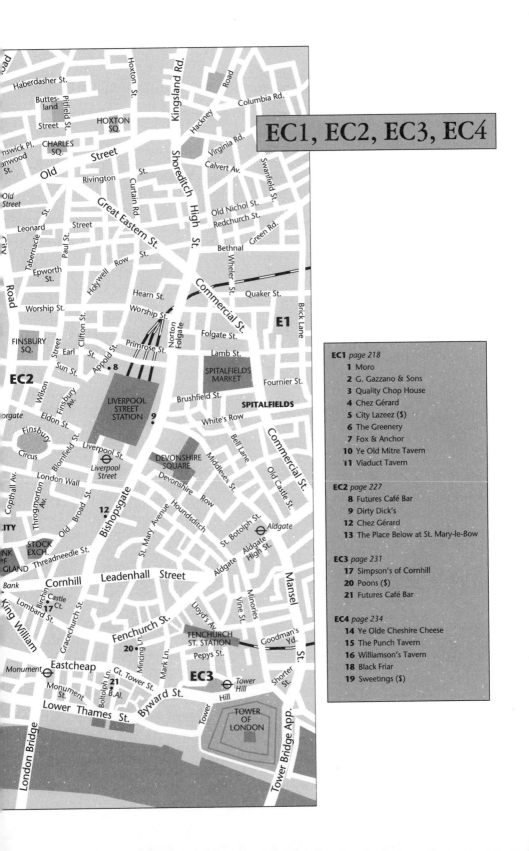

EC1, EC2, EC3, EC4

THE GREENERY (6)
5 Cowcross Street (at Peter's Lane), Clerkenwell, EC1

TELEPHONE
020-7490-4870

TUBE
Farringdon

OPEN
Mon–Fri breakfast and lunch only

CLOSED
Sat–Sun, holidays

HOURS
7 A.M.–5 P.M., continuous service

RESERVATIONS
Not accepted

CREDIT CARDS
None

PRICES
À la carte, £2.50–8; set-price, lunch "platter" £4.50

SERVICE
No service charged or expected

MISCELLANEOUS
Takeaway available

It pays to be a smart shopper at the Greenery, a vegetarian eatery/takeaway in Clerkenwell that is strictly a local landing spot. While the homemade pies, salads, and daily specials are almost always treasures, not every item on the menu is a gem. The pasty quiche was a dud and so were the heavy date and apricot vegan dessert slices. The steady customers stop by on their way to work for coffee and a bowl of muesli or a croissant, then they come back for the lunch "platters," which translate into the blue-plate special, and assorted salads. Sandwiches are all veggie and filled with eggs, cream cheese and chives, cottage cheese, or cheese and carrots. Seating is around a window bar, utensils are plastic, the owner, Alan, is friendly, and the prices are firmly in the Cheap Eater in London's budget. Plans are under way to expand the operation next door, which would mean more seating and a juice bar.

MORO (1)
34–36 Exmouth Market, Clerkenwell, EC1

TELEPHONE
020-7833-8336

TUBE
Farringdon

OPEN
Mon–Fri

CLOSED
Sat–Sun, holidays

HOURS
Bar: noon–10:30 P.M. for tapas; lunch 12:30–2:30 P.M., dinner 7–10:30 P.M.

RESERVATIONS
Essential for dinner

CREDIT CARDS
AE, MC, V

PRICES
À la carte, £22–28

SERVICE
Service discretionary, 12½ percent service charge for 7 or more

The stripped-down surroundings are sleek, the service functional, and the food first-rate at Moro, one of the new restaurants to open in this gourmet eating corridor in Clerkenwell. It is destination dining at its best if you enjoy modern Spanish/Mediterranean cooking with Moorish overtones. The imaginative food packs in the crowds ranging from uptight pin-striped executives to babes with body piercing, all of whom enjoy themselves in a big way. The all–à la carte menu changes twice monthly. The first course grazing starts with a Spanish-inspired oak-smoked beef served with braised artichokes and mint, or tuna roe with chickpeas, flavored with saffron and parsley, or a richly baked egg in yogurt with caramelized butter. Slow-cooked squid with potatoes and dry sherry, Morrocan wood-roasted chicken, and lamb *tangia*, which is cooked overnight and served with preserved lemon, flat bread, and herb salad, keep the regulars always intrigued. The sourdough bread is made here, cooked in a wood-burning oven. Desserts to complement the main courses are light and refreshing, especially the Seville orange tart, Malaga raisin ice cream served with Pedro Ximenez dessert wine, or the rosewater and cardamom ice cream. A wide range of sherry is served, and often special ones are recommended to go with specific dishes.

QUALITY CHOP HOUSE (3)
94 Farringdon Road, Clerkenwell, EC1

The Quality Chop House is a destination restaurant far afield from the basic tourist path. When you go, be sure to book a table and arrive by taxi. Otherwise, especially after dark, you will find yourself with a long hike from the tube through a sketchy part of London. The clock stopped ticking on the premises in 1869, when it first opened as a laborer's café. The old motto "Progressive Working Class Caterer" is still etched on the front window. The interior is also unchanged, from the original tilted bench seats you will undoubtedly have to share to the yellowing walls and black-and-white-tiled floor. In 1989, it was bought by Charles Fontaine, a former chef at La Caprice. Since then he has won praise for the quality of his fresh and simple preparations of old standards.

It is important that you arrive starved and prepared to indulge in a meat-lover's fantasy of grilled lamb chops, corned beef hash with a fried egg, Toulouse sausages with mash and onion gravy, or grilled Dutch calves' liver with bacon. For other appetites, there is always an omelette or fresh fish. The line is long for the Sunday brunch, which includes a jug of bucks fizzes or Bloody Marys, eggs Benedict, or waffles dressed in maple syrup. Not planning ahead for dessert would be a serious mistake, since everything is made here, from the caramel cheesecake and creamed rice pudding to the comforting bread and butter pudding and spotted dick.

TELEPHONE
020-7837-5093

TUBE
Farringdon

OPEN
Mon–Fri, Sun; Sat dinner only

CLOSED
Sat lunch, holidays

HOURS
Lunch noon–3 P.M. (Sun till 4 P.M.), dinner 7–11:30 P.M.

RESERVATIONS
Essential

CREDIT CARDS
MC, V

PRICES
À la carte, £20–25

SERVICE
Service discretionary, 10 percent service charge for 5 or more

Pubs

FOX & ANCHOR (7)
115 Charterhouse Street, Smithfield Market, EC1

The food served at the Fox & Anchor is a carnivore's dream and a heart specialist's nightmare. The record for London's most gigantic breakfast stands unbroken at this pub, less than a block from the Smithfield Market (the world's largest wholesale meat market). While the

TELEPHONE
020-7253-4838

TUBE
Farringdon, Barbican

OPEN
Mon–Fri

price tag on breakfast may seem high, you will actually save money because you won't need to eat for the rest of the day, and possibly the next.

As you can imagine, the butchers and pitchers (men who unload the trucks) demand the best quality meat, and the Fox & Anchor serves it to them in abundance every weekday. The pub opens at 7 A.M. for workers to have an eye-opening pint or two before tackling the morning meal, which is served until 3 P.M. Insiders generally ignore the menu and order the house favorite, which is not listed: the Mixed Grill. (If you want this, you must call ahead to order it.) Only hard-core meat lovers need apply for this gargantuan feast, which includes sausage, kidneys, steak, liver, black pudding, eggs, mushrooms, tomatoes, chips (french fries), and endless cups of coffee. Another blowout is the full English breakfast with an extra sausage and a pint of Guinness. If you feel you are not up to the Mixed Grill or the full English breakfast, consider lambs' liver and kidneys, or steak and eggs. For the prissy, they do have oatmeal or a meatless breakfast . . . but here? Please. If you can't bring yourself to down one of the heavy-hitting breakfasts, go for lunch and order another specialty: steak and kidney pie, a thick steak, or a large ham, cheese, tomato, or mushroom omelette. Don't pay attention to the salads, cold plates, or sandwiches—they do not measure up. This is a place where the protein-rich food is the only thing to order.

In 1992 the pub was restored to its original Victorian splendor. There is a back room, but you will have the most fun sitting in the front part, where the chef stands at the end of the bar in an open kitchen grilling the meats, which are served by waitresses who know everyone and their business to boot.

CLOSED
Sat–Sun, holidays

HOURS
Pub: 7 A.M.–11 P.M., breakfast until 3 P.M., lunch noon–3 P.M., bar snacks in the evening

RESERVATIONS
For breakfast before 9 A.M., or to order the Mixed Grill

CREDIT CARDS
AE, DC, MC, V

PRICES
À la carte, £8–18

SERVICE
Service discretionary

VIADUCT TAVERN (11)
126 Newgate Street (across from Old Bailey), EC1

The first public building in London to have electricity now functions as the Viaduct Tavern. Originally standing just outside the city walls, it was a debtors' prison linked to Newgate Prison, which is now Old Bailey. Some of the original twelve-by-six cells still exist beneath the bar and make up the Viaduct's cellars and are said to be inhabited by Fred, the ghost of a prisoner, who is blamed for all the noises and mishaps that have

TELEPHONE
020-7606-8476

TUBE
St. Paul's

OPEN
Daily

CLOSED
Christmas Day

inexplicably happened here over the years. The small, dark cells make it easy to imagine the horrible conditions in which prisoners existed, being stacked twenty deep in these airless cubicles with holes in the ceiling as the only ventilation. On request, the staff will conduct tours. Behind the Viaduct is St. Bartholomew's Hospital, which was founded in 1123 and is the oldest hospital in England standing on its original site. Inside are paintings by Hogarth. To learn more about this fascinating part of London, I recommend joining one of the London walking tours that give in-depth insight into the history and lore of the area.

As a pub, the Viaduct was a fashionable drinking spot for the upper classes of London society. The stone reliefs around the walls represent the heads of the sixteen hanging judges of Old Bailey. In the back, you can see an original etched-glass booth from which the landlady issued tokens that were exchanged at the bar for drinks because the bartenders could not be trusted with money.

History and ghosts aside, the Viaduct Tavern serves predictable pub food, concentrating on sandwiches, Cumberland sausage with mash and onion gravy, and a trio of ploughman's with either Stilton, baked ham, or cheddar cheese.

HOURS
Pub: Mon–Fri 11 A.M–11 P.M., Sat noon–11 P.M., Sun noon–10:30 P.M.; food service: noon–3 P.M.

RESERVATIONS
Not accepted

CREDIT CARDS
AE, MC, V

PRICES
£4–6

SERVICE
No service charged or expected

YE OLD MITRE TAVERN (10)
1 Ely Place, Holborn, EC1

Look for the old street lamp that marks the entrance to Ely Court, a narrow passageway linking Ely Place and Hatton Garden, which is a street lined with London's jewelry traders. In 1546, when the bishops of Ely lorded over this part of London, the Mitre Tavern was built for their palace servants. Rebuilt in the late eighteenth century, its oak-paneled rooms are filled with original antiques and relics dating back to the origins of the pub. In the corner of the bar is the preserved trunk of a cherry tree that grew on the boundary between the bishop of Ely's land, which was leased to Sir Christopher Hatton, who was a great favorite of Queen Elizabeth I. In fact, she once danced the "maypole" around this tree. During the English Civil War, the tavern was used as a prison and a hospital, but judging from its size, it could only have held a handful of prisoners and patients.

Today, the pub is popular with local office workers, who treat it as their private club and enjoy sitting and

TELEPHONE
020-7405-4751

TUBE
Chancery Lane

OPEN
Mon–Fri

CLOSED
Sat–Sun, holidays

HOURS
11 A.M.–11 P.M., food service until 9:45 P.M., continuous service

RESERVATIONS
Not accepted

CREDIT CARDS
None

PRICES
À la carte, £1–2

SERVICE
No service charged or expected

relaxing in a quiet atmosphere free from loud music or pinball machines. There is no hot food served, but it is a worthwhile stop for a freshly made sandwich and a pint of ale to savor one of London's most charming and authentic pubs. The sandwiches, which cost a whopping £1 to £2, are served Monday to Friday from 11 A.M. to 9:45 P.M. The choice is not large: four made with cheese and two with sausage.

EC2

The Barbican

The Barbican opened in 1984 and covers sixty acres. It is one of the most impressive and controversial buildings in London. It was built around the remaining portion of the old Roman wall as an ambitious scheme to promote the area as a residential quarter rather than only as a place to work. It contains high-rise flats, shops, offices, pubs, the City of London School for Girls, the sixteenth-century church of St. Giles Cripplegate, the Museum of London, the London Symphony Orchestra, and the Guildhall School of Music. The Bank of England and the Stock Exchange make this the financial hub of the country.

Restaurants

CHEZ GÉRARD (12)
64 Bishopsgate, The City, EC2

You will need reservations a week in advance at this Chez Gérard, which is open Monday through Friday only. See Chez Gérard in W1, page 39, for a complete description. All other information is the same.

TELEPHONE: 020-7588-1200

TUBE: Liverpool Street

OPEN: Mon–Fri

CLOSED: Sat–Sun, holidays

RESERVATIONS: Essential as far in advance as possible

FUTURES CAFÉ BAR (8)
2 Exchange Square, Broadgate Complex, Spitalfields, EC2

TELEPHONE
020-7638-6341

TUBE
Liverpool Street

OPEN
Mon–Fri

CLOSED
Sat–Sun, holidays

HOURS
7:30 A.M.–10 P.M., continuous service

RESERVATIONS
Suggested for lunch

CREDIT CARDS
AE, MC, V, minimum charge: £10

PRICES
À la carte, breakfast £4–8, lunch or dinner £8–15; set-price, lunch £9, 2 courses, £12.50, 3 courses

SERVICE
Service discretionary

MISCELLANEOUS
Nonsmoking at lunchtime

The Futures Café Bar on Exchange Square is a bold, bright, classy vegetarian grazing ground for the buttoned-down office workers, junior executives, and fashionable cute-young-things that populate this renovated section of London (see EC3, page 232, for second location). The decor and atmosphere of the contemporary, glass-enclosed dining room make it more reminiscent of California than of London, and so does the beautifully ex-ecuted and presented food, which is geared toward a breakfast and lunchtime feeding blitz, followed by a more subdued afternoon of tea and pastries, and closing with the BPs (beautiful people) back for cocktails and evening snacks.

It is always a good sign when you feel you could eat anything on the menu, and at Futures you can expect to do that. Breakfast stays the same day in and day out with omelettes, poached eggs on English muffins, homemade cereals, seasonal fruits, and freshly squeezed juices, plus the usual retinue of coffees and teas. The lunch choices change every two weeks and feature a short list of appe-tizers, beautifully sculpted salads, pastas, stir-frys, and desserts destined to wreak havoc with dieting willpower. My lunch starter of pine nuts and sun-dried tomato polenta served with a rich olive paste was the perfect support for the Oriental vegetables tossed in a light balti sauce served with basmati rice. For dessert, the chocolate and Amaretto terrine served with a cold chocolate sauce was the perfect finale.

The bustle and buzz of lunch comes back after 6 P.M., when the bar is filled with a black-clad fashionable crowd sipping cocktails and nibbling on orders of munchies called "evening bites," which can be platters of small pizzas or quiches, or indulgent potato skins dipped into a sour cream and chive sauce.

Directions: Finding Futures Café Bar requires the latest detailed street map of London available, as the area is undergoing massive renovation. The best approach is to enter Exchange Square opposite Earl Street, walk up the stairs, and look for the huge bronze statue of Venus of Broadgate. Futures will be on one corner of the square. Another approach is to exit the Liverpool tube station on Bishopsgate and turn left. Walk to Primrose Street and turn left. Exchange Square with Venus of Broadgate will be in front of you. Still lost? Probably. Ask any of the security men wearing white navy officer's hats, and they will direct you.

THE PLACE BELOW AT ST. MARY-LE-BOW (13)
St. Mary-le-Bow Crypt, Cheapside, The City, EC2

The St. Mary-le-Bow church serves as a religious and cultural landmark in the City. It has long been known that those born within earshot of her famous bells are considered to be the true Cockneys of London. The church, one of Sir Christopher Wren's masterpieces, houses another masterpiece in its eleventh-century crypt: Bill Sewell's the Place Below, a brilliant example of just how delicious vegetarian cooking can be in the hands of an imaginative and creative chef. Since opening day, he has received awards and rave reviews for his meatless cuisine. The two-room space, with a garden area for summer tables, is positively packed for lunch.

Naturally, everything is made here, from the moist olive and garlic bread to the old-fashioned lemonade. Breakfast and lunch are self-service and emphasize quiches, breads, soups, salads, wonderful hot dishes, and tempting desserts. The hot food selection changes daily, the salads weekly. When I was there, highlights included a mushroom bisque soup, roast pepper and goat cheese quiche, and fresh asparagus and spicy roast tofu tossed with noodles and dressed with a soy vinaigrette. The chocolate zucchini cake was dense and rich, and the banana cake just sweet enough.

You absolutely must arrive early for the best table selection—no reservations are taken. If you arrive between

TELEPHONE
020-7329-0789

TUBE
Mansion House, St. Paul's, Bank

OPEN
Mon–Fri breakfast and lunch only

CLOSED
Sat–Sun, holidays

HOURS
7:30 A.M.–2:30 P.M., continuous service

RESERVATIONS
Not accepted

CREDIT CARDS
MC, V

PRICES
À la carte, £7–12, 11:30 A.M.–noon all prices £2 less

SERVICE
Service discretionary

MISCELLANEOUS
Takeaway available

11:30 A.M. and noon, all prices are £2 less, but you might have to contend with the mop brigade I endured as they swooped through with their overpoweringly odorous disinfectant-infused mop buckets. As I left, I found their mopping gear stowed in the ladies' room!

If you want to bring some of Bill's magic cooking home with you, purchase a copy of his cookbook, *Food from the Place Below,* available here for around £10.

Pubs

DIRTY DICK'S (9)
202 Bishopsgate, The City, EC2

TELEPHONE
020-7283-5888

TUBE
Liverpool Street

OPEN
Mon–Fri, Sun

CLOSED
Sat, holidays

HOURS
Mon–Fri 11 A.M.–10:30 P.M.,
lunch noon–2:30 P.M., dinner
6–10:30 P.M.; Sun 12:30–
3 P.M. bar food only, no food
service

RESERVATIONS
Accepted for the restaurant only

CREDIT CARDS
AE, DC, MC, V

PRICES
Pub: £5–7; restaurant: £8–15

SERVICE
No service charged or expected
in pub, service discretionary in
restaurant

The story of Dirty Dick's is written on the walls around the upstairs rooms of the pub: "In a dirty old house lived a dirty old man. Soap, towels or brushes were not in his plan; for forty long years as his neighbors declared, his house never once had been cleaned or repaired. 'Twas a scandal and shame to the business-like street, and a terrible blot on a lodger so neat; the old shop with its glasses, black bottles and vats, and the rest of the mansion a run for the rats." As historic London pubs go, Dirty Dick's is hard to beat. It is named after one of the most famous characters in the City of London who inherited the property, a bonded warehouse for port and sherry, in the early 1700s from his father. Dick was a messy person, with a scruffy reputation he did not care about changing. At one point he was engaged to be married, but the bride-to-be died the day before the wedding. Dirty Dick was so emotionally bereft that he locked up the wedding table he had prepared for his wedding night, and it was not seen again until someone found it after his death.

Today the pub consists of three distinct eating and drinking areas with a different menu in each. Upstairs, there is a quiet restaurant with a full menu, on the ground floor a menu of finger food designed to be eaten while standing and drinking your pint of beer at the bar, and in the vault bar below, a smaller restaurant menu geared to a lively crowd who pack it on Friday nights.

EC3

Lloyd's of London and Tower of London

The world's most famous insurance company, Lloyd's of London, occupies a futuristic building with an observation deck that's open to the public only by written request.

Perhaps the most famous castle in the world, the Tower of London was the largest fortress in medieval Europe and the palace and prison of English monarchs for five hundred years. It was first built by William the Conqueror to both protect and control the City. Over time it has also served as the nation's storehouse for weapons and public records, kept the Crown Jewels, and housed the Royal Mint and the Royal Menagerie.

RESTAURANTS in EC3 (see map page 220)

($) indicates a Big Splurge

Restaurants

FUTURES CAFÉ BAR (21)
8 Boltolph Alley, The City, EC3

TELEPHONE
020-7623-4529

TUBE
Monument

OPEN
Mon–Fri breakfast and lunch only

CLOSED
Sat–Sun, holidays

HOURS
Breakfast 7:30 A.M.–10:30 A.M., lunch 11:30 A.M.–3 P.M.

RESERVATIONS
Not accepted

CREDIT CARDS
None

PRICES
À la carte, £3–9

SERVICE
No service charged or expected

MISCELLANEOUS
Takeaway only

If you are considering your breakfast or lunch options, there are two Futures markets for you. Both are tough to locate without a compass and steely determination (see EC2, page 228, for the other site). At this Futures, the vegan and vegetarian fare is strictly cash-and-carry takeaway or delivery. The food choices are brief, yet imaginative, and prepared below in a huge underground kitchen almost the size of a London city square block. In addition to a brisk takeaway, Futures faxes its menus to surrounding offices and delivers daily to a lunch crowd of eight hundred people.

Kick off your day on a healthy note with the breakfast special, a bowl of toasted oats covered in natural yogurt and fresh fruit. Add one of their own muffins, a glass of fresh orange or apple juice, and you will be set for the day. Real porridge cooked with milk and honey is another healthy bet. The lunch menu is never the same two days in a row, but it always lists unusual soups, a pasta or two, stir-frys, homemade rolls (plain or cheese and basil), and fresh desserts.

Directions: Exit the Monument tube stop on the Eastcheap side, walk east to Lovat Lane, turn right, and the first little street will be Botolph Alley.

POONS (20, $)
Minster Pavement (lower ground level), Minster Court, Mincing Lane, The City, EC3

At this location of Poons, it is important that Cheap Eaters eat in the fast-food café or in the dim sum wine garden, otherwise the bill will be in the Big Splurge category. In all dishes, MSG can be omitted on request. See Poons in W2, page 85, for full description.

TELEPHONE: 020-7626-0126
TUBE: Tower Hill, Monument
OPEN: Mon–Fri
CLOSED: Sat–Sun, holidays
HOURS: 11:30 A.M.–10:30 P.M., continuous service
RESERVATIONS: Advised for lunch in the restaurant
CREDIT CARDS: AE, DC, MC, V
PRICES: Café: à la carte, £10–20; restaurant: £20–30; set-price, £15–18, 2-person minimum; daily lunch special £6

SERVICE: £1.75 cover charge in restaurant, service discretionary, 10 percent service charge suggested

MISCELLANEOUS: No delivery, 10 percent discount on takeaway orders

SIMPSON'S OF CORNHILL (17)
38½ Castle Court (at Ball Court), The City, EC3

Finding Simpson's of Cornhill (not to be confused with the touristy and overpriced Simpson's-in-the-Strand) is not easy: walk along Cornhill, turn right on St. Michael's Alley, then right on Castle Court, walk until you come to Ball Court, and turn right again. To say it is a hidden find is the understatement of the year! But the search for the old-fashioned English food with old-fashioned prices to match is definitely worthwhile. For my lunching pound, this is the best food value in the City, as this part of London is known.

The restaurant was founded in 1757, and for decades the traditions and customs of male-dominated London eating houses were strictly maintained. Not until 1916 were women admitted to this conservative male bastion. Today, women are welcomed in both the upstairs restaurant and in the downstairs grill room. The food is heavy and hearty, so skip the starters and concentrate on a main course of grilled meat or the daily hot joint (roast meat). Liver and bacon, steak and kidney pie, poached or cold Scottish salmon, and a stew of some sort are always on board. Once a week their popular Simpson's fish cakes are equally recommended. For an after-meal savory, everyone orders the stewed cheese. This is a crock of melted cheddar cheese mixed with Worcestershire sauce and seasonings to spread on toast. You must try one. It is the house specialty, and the kitchen cannot turn them out fast enough.

NOTE: You can't call for reservations because they don't take them. By 12:30 P.M., it is completely full, so for assured seating, plan to arrive at noon sharp.

TELEPHONE
020-7626-9985

TUBE
Bank

OPEN
Mon–Fri lunch only

CLOSED
Sat–Sun, holidays

HOURS
11:30 A.M.–3 P.M.

RESERVATIONS
Not accepted

CREDIT CARDS
AE, DC, MC, V

PRICES
À la carte, £10–15

SERVICE
Service discretionary

EC4

The City, Fleet Street, and St. Paul's Cathedral

The City is an almost perfect square mile in the heart of London. During the week, the City teems with executives, office workers, and a constant rush of people on the go. On the weekends and at night it becomes silent, populated only by pigeons and the stray sightseer. It owes its appearance to Sir Christopher Wren, who was the chief architect after the Great Fire of 1666. He designed fifty-one churches to replace the eighty-nine that were destroyed.

Fleet Street used to be the newspaper and journalist headquarters of London. All major British daily papers had their offices here, and the pubs were full of journalists. No more. The offices have moved to the suburbs, but many still refer to Fleet Street as the home of the British Press.

Old Bailey, the Central Criminal Court, is open to the public, and it is a show worth seeing. You can visit an actual case in progress by participating in one of the daily walking tours in London. Consult your hotel for brochures.

St. Paul's Cathedral was built by Sir Christopher Wren between 1675 and 1710 on the site of the medieval cathedral destroyed in the fire of 1666. It serves as the bishopric of London and the "Parish Church of the British Commonwealth." Today, it retains its great dignity and grandeur even though it is overwhelmed by the huge tower blocks surrounding it.

($) indicates a Big Splurge

Restaurants

SWEETINGS (19, $)
39 Queen Victoria Street, The City, EC4

"We don't take reservations, accept credit cards, or serve coffee—we do serve the best fish you will eat in London," states owner Pat Needham. Generations of loyalists and I agree with her, and now patrons arrive with their children and grandchildren on a regular basis. Sweetings has been serving lunch on the same corner in London's financial district for over one hundred years, and it is required eating. The only change seems to have been the prices. The yellowed walls, a front window loaded with tubs of wine, and longtime customers milling around one of the long mahogany bars waiting for their favorite table set the tone. The fish is fresh daily from the Billingsgate fish market, and the oysters are supplied directly from West Mersea in Essex.

Every regular has his or her own favorite dish—whether it's the Dover sole, salmon, smoked haddock, halibut, or crab salad—and they would never consider experimenting. Familiar desserts like bread-and-butter pudding, baked jam roll, and steamed syrup pudding, along with excellent wines sold by the glass or bottle, complement the meal.

TELEPHONE
020-7248-3062

TUBE
Mansion House

OPEN
Mon–Fri lunch only

CLOSED
Sat–Sun, holidays

HOURS
11:30 A.M.–3 P.M.

RESERVATIONS
Not accepted

CREDIT CARDS
None

PRICES
À la carte, £25–35

SERVICE
Service discretionary

MISCELLANEOUS
Seating at the front counter if you are in a hurry

YE OLDE CHESHIRE CHEESE (14)
145 Fleet Street (off Wine Office Court), The City, EC4

Seventeenth-century chop houses were the forerunners of today's wine bars, and this centuries-old bar and restaurant is one of the most famous. It is almost impossible to pick up a guide to London restaurants without reading something about Ye Olde Cheshire Cheese. Even though this notoriety brings flocks of international tourists to the door, the restaurant has managed to remain true to its heritage. In the thirteenth century, the site formed part of a Carmelite monastery, and since 1538, a pub has been in business here. Rebuilt in 1667, the year after the Great Fire, the Cheshire Cheese has preserved the atmosphere of the intervening centuries, spanning the reigns of sixteen kings and queens. In the Chop Room, you can still see the long table at which Dr. Samuel Johnson, Oliver Goldsmith, and Charles Dickens dined. Pictures and artifacts adorn the multiroomed

TELEPHONE
020-7353-6170

TUBE
Blackfriars

OPEN
Mon–Sat; Sun lunch only

CLOSED
Sun dinner, holidays

HOURS
The Chop Room: Mon–Fri noon–9:30 P.M., continuous service; Sat noon–3:30 P.M., 5:30–9:30 P.M., Sun noon–3 P.M.; Johnson Restaurant: Mon–Fri noon–2:30 P.M., 6–9:30 P.M.; bar: Mon–Fri lunch only noon–2:30 P.M.

RESERVATIONS
Accepted for the Chop Room and Johnson Restaurant

CREDIT CARDS
AE, DC, MC, V
PRICES
Bar: £5–9; Chop Room: à la
carte, £10–18; Johnson
Restaurant: à la carte, £18–28
SERVICE
Service discretionary
MISCELLANEOUS
Available for private parties

pub, giving an account of the people and events that have left their mark. Today, little has changed: the original wooden floors are sprinkled with sawdust each day, the hard benches are worn smooth, and the same rickety staircase leads to the upstairs rooms.

Prices lean on the high side in the Johnson Restaurant, so Cheap Eaters will want to dine in the bar (lunch only) or the Chop Room. The food is predictably English, but for the historical value it is worth a visit, if only to step up to the bar and order a drink.

Pubs

BLACK FRIAR (18)
174 Queen Victoria Street, The City, EC4

TELEPHONE
020-7236-5650
TUBE
Blackfriars
OPEN
Mon–Fri; Sat lunch only
CLOSED
Sun, Sat dinner, holidays
HOURS
Mon–Fri 11:30 A.M.–11 P.M.,
Sat noon–5 P.M., lunch noon–
2:30 P.M., bar snacks until
closing
RESERVATIONS
Not accepted
CREDIT CARDS
AE, MC, V
PRICES
À la carte, £4–7
SERVICE
No service charged or expected

The best reason to visit the Black Friar is to see one of the richest and strangest pub interiors in London. This Art Nouveau fantasy, built in 1903 from designs by H. Fuller Clarke and sculptor Henry Poole, pays homage to the Dominicans, or black friars, who had a monastery on this site many years ago. The friars were known for being more interested in drinking than divinity, and their devotion to the bottle sets the theme for this amazing building. Outside over the door stands a figure of a good-natured friar, hands folded across his impressive beer belly. Mosaics on either side show other friars eating, drinking, laughing, and having fun. The remarkable interior is replete with polished stone, colored marble columns, and bronze bas-reliefs. The room in back, known as the Side Chapel, has a vaulted black, white, and gold ceiling and reflecting mirrors encircled by friezes of inebriated friars. They are accompanied by crouching demons, fairies, and carved alabaster animals. All around the room are mottoes of the friars: "Tell a gossip," "Finery is foolery," and "Haste is slow."

The main bar area has an enormous bronze-canopied fireplace and a small horseshoe bar. The tiny wedge-shaped front part of the pub is where hot and cold lunches are served. The food is not as spectacular as the surroundings, but it is basic pub fare at decent prices.

THE PUNCH TAVERN (15)
99 Fleet Street, The City, EC4

In its early days, prisoners were brought here for their "last one for the road," as they were taken to Newgate Prison (now Old Bailey) to be hanged. Later it served as the watering hole for employees of *Punch* magazine. Now, the magnificently restored Punch Tavern is a living museum and memorial to that famous London periodical, and is the quarterly meeting place for the Punch Appreciation Society. The original plans for the pub were used in detail when it was recently restored to its former glory, keeping the original prints, etched-glass mirrors, and fireplaces in place. A glass display case houses an interesting collection of *Punch* memorabilia. The pub is a mob scene at lunch with office workers ordering freshly cut sandwiches to have with their pints of beer.

While you are here, don't miss a visit to St Bride's Church next door, which has the highest spire designed by Sir Christopher Wren and was the inspiration for the first tiered wedding cakes. The first printing press with movable type was brought to the church in 1500, and that is the reason St. Bride's is referred to as the Printer's Cathedral and the Journalist's Church. Milton lived in the churchyard at one time, Samuel Pepys was baptized here, Samuel Johnson lived across the street and Dickens up the road, and in 1587, Virginia Dare's parents were married here. Virginia Dare was the first child of European descent born in Colonial America.

TELEPHONE
020-7353-6658

TUBE
Blackfriars, Temple

OPEN
Mon–Fri; Sat–Sun afternoon only

CLOSED
Sat–Sun evening, Christmas Day

HOURS
Mon–Fri 11 A.M.–11 P.M., Sat noon–5 P.M., Sun noon–6 P.M., lunch daily noon–2:30 P.M., bar snacks until 5 P.M. except Sat; shorter hours on holidays

RESERVATIONS
Not accepted

CREDIT CARDS
None

PRICES
À la carte, £3–5

SERVICE
No service charged or expected

WILLIAMSON'S TAVERN (16)
1–3 Groveland Court, Bow Lane, The City, EC4

Williamson's Tavern is appealing for its historic background, warm atmosphere, and better-than-usual food. Like many pubs in the City, it claims to be the oldest, a fact that is obviously determined in several creative ways. It does, however, mark the exact center of the City of London. Built after the Great Fire of 1666, it was a former Mansion House and the residence of London's lord mayors until 1753. The wrought-iron gates guarding the entrance of the alley that leads to the pub were presented by William III and Queen Mary to the lord mayor of London. Before its transition into a pub in the eighteenth century, it was Sir John Falstaff's home, and long before that the site of a Roman villa. The tiles used around the fireplace on the first floor were found ten feet

TELEPHONE
020-7248-6280

TUBE
Mansion House

OPEN
Mon–Fri

CLOSED
Sat–Sun, holidays

HOURS
Pub: 11:30 A.M.–11 P.M.; Tavern Bar food service: noon–9 P.M.; Martha's Bar food service: noon–2:30 P.M. and 5–9 P.M.

RESERVATIONS
Not accepted

CREDIT CARDS
AE, DC, MC, V

PRICES
À la carte, £6–9
SERVICE
No service charged or expected
in pub, service discretionary in
restaurant

below ground level during the most recent renovation one hundred years ago.

There are three parts to the pub: the Tavern Bar, a typical pub complete with loud music and pinball machines; the Williamson's Bar, a quiet sanctuary on the ground level; and Martha's Bar downstairs, where a large variety of interesting wines are served. What's to eat? The hands-down favorite is the house special: a four-ounce sirloin steak sandwich, chargrilled and served with parsley or garlic butter, and a small salad, all for less than £6.

SE1

South Bank and Waterloo

The South Bank of the Thames was bombed flat during World War II, but since then, it has risen from the ashes and become a hub for the arts in London. Included here is the Royal Festival Hall, the National Film Theatre, the Royal National Theatre, and the Museum of the Moving Image. The importance of the area is reflected in the number of visitors, which is expected to nearly double by 2000, from seven to twelve million, aided by the opening of a new Southwark tube station and the monolithic Millennium Dome. The magnificent views of the City from Waterloo Bridge have inspired generations of painters, including J. M. W. Turner, whose works are at the Tate Gallery.

Across the Tower Bridge from the City is Southwark (pronounced SUTH-uk), an area associated with entertainment from Elizabethan days. The Tate Gallery has its modern art collection displayed in the former Bankside Power Station. Directly fronting the river is the Design Museum, which is surrounded by a growing area of expensive restaurants and shops. Shakespeare's plays were performed at the Rose Theatre, and his Globe Theatre nearby has been renovated using the same construction materials and techniques as the craftsmen who built it in the sixteenth century. The Southwark Cathedral, a fine example of Gothic architecture, contains the Harvard Chapel, dedicated to the founder of Harvard University, who was baptized in the church in 1607.

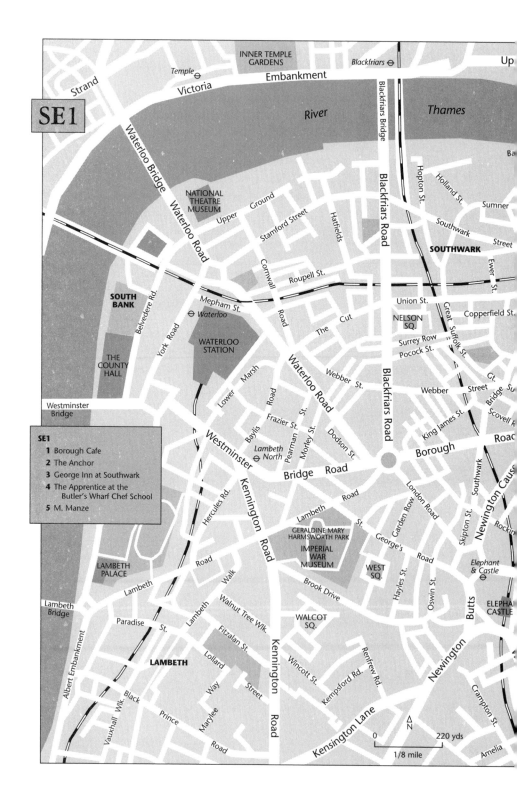

SE1

INNER TEMPLE GARDENS

Temple ⊖

Blackfriars ⊖

Up

Strand

Victoria

Embankment

River

Thames

Ba

Blackfriars Bridge

Waterloo Bridge

NATIONAL THEATRE MUSEUM

Upper

Ground

Stamford Street

Hatfields

Hopton St.

Holland St.

Sumner

Southwark

Street

SOUTHWARK

Cornwall

Roupell St.

Blackfriars Road

Ewer St.

SOUTH BANK

Belvedere Rd.

Waterloo Road

Mepham St.

⊖ Waterloo

Road

The Cut

Union St.

NELSON SQ.

Great Suffolk St.

Copperfield St.

York Road

WATERLOO STATION

Surrey Row

Pocock St.

THE COUNTY HALL

Marsh

Webber St.

Webber

Street

Gt. Su

Bridge S

Scovell R

Westminster Bridge

Lower

Road

Frazier St.

Baylis

Waterloo Road

Dodson St.

Blackfriars Road

King James St.

Borough

Road

SE1

1 Borough Cafe
2 The Anchor
3 George Inn at Southwark
4 The Apprentice at the
   Butler's Wharf Chef School
5 M. Manze

Westminster

Pearman

Morley St.

Lambeth North ⊖

Bridge

Road

Road

London Road

Southwark

Newington Caus

Rockin

Hercules Rd.

Kennington Road

Lambeth

St.

GERALDINE MARY HARMSWORTH PARK

IMPERIAL WAR MUSEUM

George's

Garden Row

Road

Skipton St.

Elephant & Castle ⊖

Road

LAMBETH PALACE

Road

Walk

WEST SQ.

Hayles St.

Oswin St.

Butts

ELEPHA CASTLE

Lambeth

Walnut Tree Wlk.

Brook Drive

WALCOT SQ.

Lambeth Bridge

Paradise

St.

Lambeth

Fitzalan St.

Newington

Albert Embankment

Lollard

Kennington

Wincott St.

Kempsford Rd.

Renfrew Rd.

Crampton St.

LAMBETH

Way

Street

Road

Vauxhall Wlk.

Black

Prince

Marylee

Road

Kensington Lane

N

0   220 yds

1/8 mile

Amelia

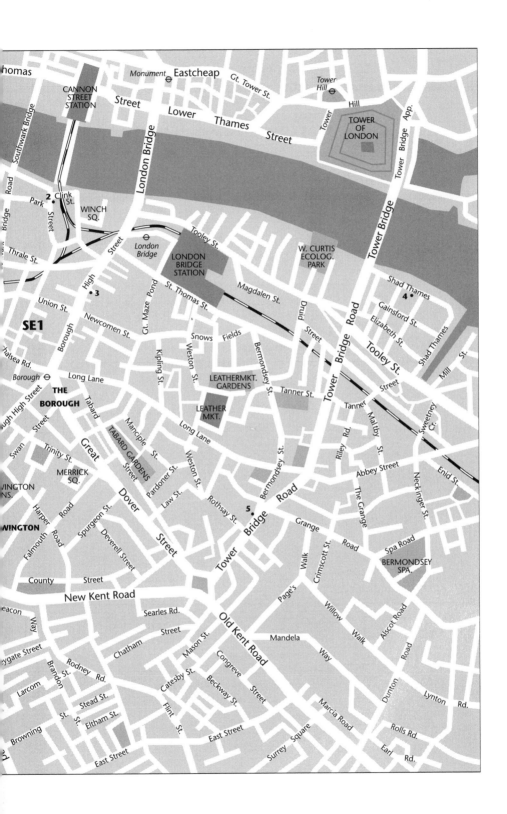

Restaurants

THE APPRENTICE AT THE BUTLER'S WHARF CHEF SCHOOL (4)
The Cardamom Building, 31 Shad Thames, SE1

TELEPHONE
020-7357-8842
TUBE
London Bridge, Tower Hill
(both a 15- to 20-minute walk)
OPEN
Mon–Fri
CLOSED
Sat–Sun, holidays
HOURS
Lunch noon–1:30 P.M., dinner
6:30–8:30 P.M.
RESERVATIONS
Essential, sometimes one week
in advance
CREDIT CARDS
AE, DC, MC, V
PRICES
À la carte, £18–26; set-price,
lunch £10.50, 2 courses, £14, 3
courses; dinner £19, 3 courses
SERVICE
Service discretionary

At this training institute for chefs and other restaurant personnel, you can taste gourmet cooking for a pittance compared to what a regular restaurant would charge to have it prepared by a fancy, name-brand chef undoubtedly represented by an agent and a public relations firm.

At the Apprentice, students practice what they have been taught on willing guinea pigs, i.e., us. Prices are at least half of what you will pay across the street at the cluster of expensive Conran restaurants—and the food is nearly the same. The Apprentice has a policy of not charging for service, but gratuities are welcome and will be used to support student training. Still, putting theory into practice doesn't always turn out the way it was planned, so you must allow for certain gaffes occasionally in both cooking and service.

The constantly changing menu is devised by the students and rotates through a roll call of current, fashionable modern British dishes, most of which pass muster. I was happy to start with the roasted tomatoes and field mushrooms served on toast, which is nothing new on the culinary scene, but nicely presented anyway, on a bed of designer greens lightly dressed with vinaigrette. Their roast duck breast and duck sausage were rich and smooth-tasting. The grilled mackerel, black pudding, and savoy cabbage had too many odd flavors going on and needs to be reworked . . . it was too fishy and strong. Main courses of loin of lamb, lemon sole, roast veal, and an interesting blue cheese spinach lasagne, were tops in their class. Wearing the dunce cap was the dry, overcooked stuffed chicken leg served with a gluey parsnip *dauphinoise.* Top honors in the dessert class went to the zippy lemon tart and simple brandy snap-cookie basket filled with mixed sorbets and a pear and honey tart with sharp ginger ice cream.

The interior of the restaurant is devoid of charm and character, and it needs some acoustical engineering, but you are not here to admire the decor. You are here to eat, and you will do that quite well.

BOROUGH CAFE (1)
11 Park Street, Southwark, SE1

For a taste of something pure and simple in the rapidly vanishing village life of Southeast Londoners, a meal at the Borough Cafe is required eating. Even though it is a small place on a backstreet, life here is never boring. It has been run by Mamma Amelia and her daughter Maria, who for forty years have been feeding everyone from the police and market people to lawyers and film stars who happily share the five tables squeezed into a tiled room with cafe curtains hanging at the steamy windows. The open kitchen allows Maria and Amelia to banter back and forth with everyone who eats here, taking a personal interest in them all by keeping close tabs on the ups and downs of their business and love lives. Their homemade turkey, ham, and steak pies, and proper vegetable soups are always popular . . . and for less than a U.S. dollar, they should be! However, the big sellers are their bubble and squeak, and their signature dish, which they call Bacon and Stuffing. This is homemade stuffing made with vegetables, plenty of garlic, herbs, and cheese, wrapped in lean bacon and fried until the bacon is crispy on the outside. "It is a work of art you can either climb or eat," claims Maria. They don't do much in the dessert department, other than a homemade bread pudding served in a portion I defy you to finish.

NOTE: If you are here on the third Saturday of the month, be sure to have a look at the organic and home-grown fruit and produce market that operates near Southwark Cathedral. Maria will give you directions.

TELEPHONE
020-7407-5048

TUBE
London Bridge

OPEN
Mon–Sat

CLOSED
Sun, Christmas Day

HOURS
Mon–Fri 4 A.M.–3 P.M., Sat 4 A.M.–11 A.M.

RESERVATIONS
Not accepted

CREDIT CARDS
None

PRICES
À la carte, £1.20–4

SERVICE
Service discretionary

MISCELLANEOUS
BYOB, no corkage fee, unlicensed

M. MANZE (5)
87 Tower Bridge Road (near Bermondsey and Caledonia Markets), SE1

"My grandfather, father, and now I have been eating at Manze's for over a hundred years total, and we are all well and healthy," said the man standing ahead of me in the ten-deep queue to get to the counter for an order of pie and mash. Judging from the constant stream of customers of all ages, there are many more people who can also make this claim. Pie and mash remains the comfort food of the London blue-collar worker, and Manze's on Tower Bridge Road has been feeding them since the 1890s and is recognized as the oldest pie and mash shop still standing in London. It was founded by

TELEPHONE
020-7407-2985

TUBE
London Bridge, then bus 1, 42, or 188

OPEN
Mon–Sat lunch only

CLOSED
Sun, holidays

HOURS
Mon 11 A.M.–2 P.M., Tues–Thur 10:30 A.M.–2 P.M., Fri 10 A.M.–2:15 P.M., Sat 10 A.M.–2:45 P.M.

RESERVATIONS
Not accepted

Robert Cooke in 1892, bought by his son-in-law, M. Manze in 1902, and is now owned and run by M. Manze's grandsons Graham, Geoffrey, and Richard Poole. What is pie and mash? It consists of individual ground beef pies, mash (mashed potatoes), liquor (parsley-based sauce) with a squirt or two of chili vinegar added at the table, and eels—stewed or jellied. It's an experience, all right.

You order and collect your food from the counter to take away or to eat here (it's open for lunch only). If you take your pie and mash with you, you can BYO thermos or have it poured into a Styrofoam carton with a lid. But half the fun of Manze's is the people and the surroundings. When you eat here, you sit at marble-slab tables in the original green, white, and brown tile interior, see the boiling pots in the window, and watch the matronly, rosy-cheeked ladies ladling up the orders as fast as they can. Statistic junkies take note: twenty-five hundred pounds of potatoes, fifty to sixty pounds of eel, and between four and five thousand pies are sold here per week. Now that adds up to success.

Pubs

THE ANCHOR (2)
34 Park Street (at Clink Street), Southwark, SE1

The Anchor is an eighteenth-century pub with a maze of rambling corridors joining dark, low-ceilinged rooms with open fires and wooden benches. At the Anchor, you can wine and dine or just eat. In all, there are five small bars, three restaurants, and an outdoor terrace with a spectacular view across the Thames to St. Paul's Cathedral. The formal upstairs restaurant serves large doses of English food at prices most Cheap Eaters will find over budget. That is not to say that enjoying a rack of lamb or a grilled fish while sitting at tables 6 or 7 with their inspiring views is an experience you should miss. The pub used to play host to William Shakespeare, whose Globe Theatre is close by, and later on, Dr. Samuel Johnson had a special room in which he wrote his famous dictionary. I think this is one of the more interesting pubs in London, so be sure and stop by, if just for a beer and a look around.

GEORGE INN AT SOUTHWARK (3)
77 Borough High Street, Southwark, SE1

The George Inn is a taste of London as it was fifty years after Columbus discovered America, when Henry VIII reigned and Sir Francis Drake was sailing around the world. The inn has stood on this spot since Elizabethan times and is the last galleried coaching inn from that period still standing in London. The current inn is only one quarter of its original size and dates from 1542. It was rebuilt in 1676, following the Great Fire of Southwark. Its purpose then was to provide food, drink, and lodging for travelers en route to Kent and the port of Dover. Inside the walled yard, tradesmen had offices, plays were performed, and musicians entertained, while lords and ladies relaxed in front of roaring fires after their strenuous journeys. Later on, Charles Dickens ate and drank here, but he only became a patron after he had become rich and famous. As a child, visiting his father in the Marshalsea prison just down the road, he would have been too poor to enter. In *Little Dorritt,* Pip goes into the George to write begging letters. Today, the inn is part of the National Trust for the Preservation of Historic Sites and still provides food and drink to its many customers every day.

The ground-floor bars are small, with bare wooden floors and benches. In the back bar is a parliamentary clock, from the time when Parliament imposed a tax on all timepieces. The bar front in the half-timbered wine bar is from a French church. Some of the old coaching bedrooms that overlook the cobblestoned courtyard are now part of the Coaching Rooms Restaurant. More bedrooms make up the George Room function area, where you can spot a photo of Franklin Roosevelt to the right of the brick fireplace. The Talbot Room is reported to be haunted by a ghost who appears when the pub installs any new equipment to make sure that new installations never work on the first try. The large courtyard has picnic tables and benches, and in summer it's full of people eating and drinking. The menus in the various eating areas of the inn highlight all the English favorites: roast meats, grills, hot and cold pub food, meaty sandwiches, and fattening desserts.

TELEPHONE
020-7407-2056

TUBE
London Bridge

OPEN
Daily

CLOSED
Never

HOURS
Pub: 11 A.M.–10 P.M., hot food noon–3 P.M.; restaurant: lunch Mon–Fri noon–2:30 P.M., dinner Mon–Sat 6–9:30 P.M.

RESERVATIONS
Not necessary

CREDIT CARDS
AE, DC, MC, V

PRICES
À la carte, pub £5–9, restaurant £16–22; set-price, Sun roast lunch £7

SERVICE
No service charged or expected in pub, service discretionary in restaurant

Glossary of English Food Terms

The English have really everything in common with the Americans, except of course language.
—*Oscar Wilde*

The English speak English, we speak American. It doesn't matter that we share the same language; London is still a foreign capital and you are a foreigner in it. Sure, you won't have the serious communication problems you would have in Moscow or Tokyo, but you will have to deal with some different meanings and terms. To *queue* is to line up (and you will find yourself doing this often). A *subway* is an underground walkway, but the actual underground transportation system is referred to as *the underground* or *the tube*. If you are going to see a stage play, you are going to *the theatre,* and for a film, you head for *the cinema*. You *ring* the restaurant to make a reservation, but you *call* your dog. The following list of food terms and related words should help you sort out any dining dilemmas.

A

aubergine	eggplant

B

banger	sausage
bangers and mash	sausage and mashed potatoes
bank holiday	legal holiday, many restaurants and pubs closed
bap	soft bun, like a hamburger bun
bill	check (restaurant)
biscuit	cookie or cracker
black or white?	black or milk/cream in your coffee?
broad bean	lima bean
bubble and squeak	mashed potatoes mixed with cabbage and fried (sometimes leftover meat is added)

C

caff	inexpensive café; rhymes with "half"
chicory	endive
chips	french-fried potatoes
cooker	stove
Cornish pasties	meat, onion, and veggies wrapped in pastries
cottage pie	similar to shepherd's pie, but the meat is ground
courgettes	zucchini
crisps	potato chips
crumpet	like an English muffin, but with bigger holes and more of them
cuppa	cup of tea or coffee (slang)

D

doorstops	type of pub sandwich

F

fish-and-chips	cod, plaice, skate, or other whitefish dipped in batter and deep-fried
fool	fresh whipped cream mixed with seasonal fruit
French beans	green beans
fry-up	fried breakfast of eggs, sausage and/or bacon, baked beans, toast or fried bread, with additions of mushrooms and tomatoes depending on the poshness of where you are eating

G

grease-out	see fry-up

J

jacketed potato	baked potato, usually served with a variety of toppings
jam	jelly
jelly	Jell-O
joint (meat)	roasted meat on the bone (leg of lamb would be a joint of lamb)

L

Lancashire hot pot	mutton and vegetables in a rich sauce, cooked in a pastry crust

M

mains	main courses (slang)
mange tout	snow peas
Marmite	savory yeast spread that can be found in hot drinks, soups, and stews
marrow	squash
martini	straight vermouth (to get a real martini, ask for a double gin or vodka with ice)
mince	ground meat, usually beef

O

off-license	retail liquor store
other half	either another half-pint of beer or your spouse, depending on your location

P

peckish	a little bit hungry
pickled wally	pickled dill cucumber
ploughman's lunch	pub lunch consisting of cheese or pâté with crusty bread, a pickle, and sometimes chutney or an onion
plum pudding	served at Christmas, made from suet and dried fruit, steamed and then soaked in brandy or other similar liquor

pub grub	pub food
publican	manager of a pub
pudding	dessert
puds	desserts
R	
rasher (bacon)	slice of bacon
ring	to call on the telephone for a reservation, as in "to ring for a booking"
rocket, roquette	arugula
S	
salt beef	corned beef
sausage and mash	sausage and mashed potatoes
Scotch egg	hard-cooked egg encased in ground sausage and bread crumbs, which is then fried
shepherd's pie	diced meat and vegetables covered with gravy, topped with mashed potatoes, and baked in a casserole
spirits (drink)	liquor
spotted dick	steamed sponge cake with diced fruit and raisins, served warm with soft custard sauce
steak and kidney pie	mixture of pieces of steak, kidneys, and mushrooms in gravy, cooked in its own deep-dish pastry crust
sticky, toffee pudding	similar to spotted dick, but without the fruit, served with a warm butterscotch sauce
sultana	raisin
sweet	dessert
sweets	candy
Swiss roll	jelly roll
T	
tatties	potatoes
toad-in-the-hole	sausage baked in batter, served plain or with ale gravy
toasties	type of pub sandwich
top-up	refill
treacle	molasses
trifle or tipsy cake	sherry-soaked sponge cake, layered with raspberry preserves and topped with cold custard sauce and whipped cream
W	
Welsh rarebit	melted cheddar cheese and mustard or Worcestershire sauce served on toast
whitebait	tiny whole fish, deep-fried

Index

250

Readers' Comments

The listings in *Cheap Eats in London* are described as they were when the book went to press, and as I hope they will stay, but as seasoned travelers know, there are no guarantees. This is especially true when it comes to prices; in fact, there is usually a 10 to 20 percent price increase between editions of this guide. Inflation, fluctuating exchange rates, wage increases, new ownership or staff, revised holiday periods, and the whims of managers can all result in changes, and often higher prices—sometimes overnight. While every effort has been made to ensure the accuracy of the information presented, the author and publisher cannot accept responsibility for any changes that occur that may result in loss or inconvenience to anyone. The publisher and author also cannot be held responsible for the experiences of readers while traveling.

Cheap Eats in London is revised on a regular basis, but there are some places I have no doubt missed, and maybe you have some new Cheap Eat discoveries you would like to pass along to me for the next edition. Your comments are extremely important to me, and I read and follow through on every letter I receive. Because of this, I do not provide an email address, since the volume of mail it would generate would make it impossible to personally reply to each message. I hope you will understand and please take a few minutes to send me an old-fashioned letter with your comments, tips, new finds, or suggestions for *Cheap Eats in London*. In your letter, be sure to state the name and address of the restaurant, the date of your visit, a description of your findings, and any other information you think is necessary.

Please send your letters to Sandra A. Gustafson, *Cheap Eats in London,* c/o Chronicle Books, 85 Second Street, Sixth Floor, San Francisco, CA 94105.